Living with My
HIMALAYAN MASTER

SRI SRI BHAJAN BRAHMACHARI—
A BIOGRAPHY

Living with My HIMALAYAN MASTER

Sri Sri Bhajan Brahmachari—A Biography

Shuddhaanandaa Brahmachari (Bodhi)
(Author of The Incredible Life of a Himalayan Yogi)

LOKENATH DIVINE LIFE MISSION

KOLKATA

LIVING WITH MY HIMALAYAN MASTER

Sri Sri Bhajan Brahmachari—A Biography

Edited by: Ann Shannon

Cover Design by: Sumon Mondal & Bodhi Youth Sangha
Paperback Interior Formatting by: TeaBerryCreative.com
Kindle Formatting by: Anirban Banerjee and Sue Berg

ISBN 978-81-87207-17-7

Please send your personal experiences and comments in reading this book to susan@feelinghearts.org and we will personally answer your mail.

DEDICATION

This Book is my worship of Holy Ganges
with the water of the Ganges.
Oh My Beloved Master! Yours I offer unto you.
May you be pleased to accept this
humble offering of your child.

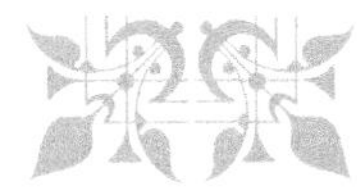

CONTENTS

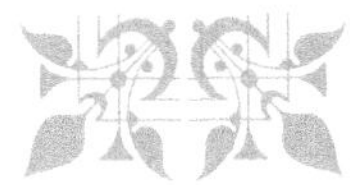

ACKNOWLEDGMENTS

Nothing would be possible for any human being—no work of art or literature, not a single accomplishment—without Mother Nature. I offer my deepest gratitude to Her for the precious elements of earth, air, fire and water upon which all life, all human existence, creativity, and potential rely. *Living with My Himalayan Master Sri Sri Bhajan Brahmachari—A Biography* celebrates all of that infinite potential realized in Her enlightened child, my Beloved Master, who came to take me and countless others to the shore of perennial love and light.

Prabhat Kumar Ray, your commitment to Master, along with the commitment of your family, was invaluable. You did the critical groundwork of preserving the written materials I would need. It would have been impossible to piece the episodes of Thakur's life together in one place without you. Prabhat, I bow to your *Guru-bhakti*, to your longing to see the biography of Thakur published. You made it possible for the Master to flow through me to create this humble shared offering of our *Guru Puja.*

Ann Shannon from Portland, Oregon, you edited *The Incredible Life of a Himalayan Yogi,* which has lit the hearts of thousands of seekers all over the world. This *seva* (service) in editing *Living with My Himalayan Master Sri Sri Bhajan Brahmachari—A Biography* is your love offering to your own Grand Master. I can't thank you enough for your efforts at polishing the manuscript as an instrument of the pure love that Master embodied. Gurudev used to tell me, "Shuddha, when you write about your Guru, you are in meditation."

Thank you sweet kitties from Chicago, Norman and Adari, for sitting on Sue Berg's computer keyboard and helping with proofreading with the pitter-patter of your paws. I know Sue Berg could not have contributed half as much to proofreading *Living with My Himalayan Master Sri Sri Bhajan Brahmachari—A Biography* had it not been your presence on her lap or on the keyboard. Thank you Anirban Banerjee, from Australia, for constantly being in touch with kitties Norman and Adari and making time for boring proofreading even while making interesting pop music on your synthesizer.

Debdutta Ray, you are indeed blessed to have received your name from Thakur, and true to your name, you are a divine gift, who has always been reminding me of Thakur's infinite love for animals which must find its place in the book.

Lastly my endless gratitude to the Bodhi Youth Sangha members, Sumon, Navoneel, Asmita, Rana, Debdutta and Matt for bringing the Master alive on the Book cover designed by you.

PREFACE

It is with incomprehensible joy that I share the life and teachings of my dear Master and Gurudev with you in *Living with My Himalayan Master Sri Sri Bhajan Brahmachari—A Biography.*

When the great Himalayan Master Mahayogi Baba Lokenath Brahmachari appeared to me at my Gurudev Thakur Bhajan Brahmachari's ashram, he commanded me to "*Write and spread out.*" That ultimately gave birth to *The Incredible Life of a Himalayan Yogi: The Times, Teachings and Life of Living Shiva, Baba Lokenath Brahmachari.* Over the years, though, deep within, I have carried the silent pain of having yet to offer my love, in the form of my Gurudev's biography, at his lotus feet. An unseen force had plunged me into spreading the message of Baba Lokenath all over the world. I had no time to focus on writing the biography of my dear Master.

Then in 2015, the call came from within. It was as if my Master was whispering, *"The task I gave you in 1982 is almost complete. Now you can come back to me and spread the message I seeded in you. The world is ready to hear my message of Pure Love. Love is the sole need at this critical juncture of human history."* Meditation alone is not enough. First the heart center needs to be opened. We have to realize that love alone can connect us to the plane of consciousness founded in our relationship with our eternal Beloved based on our personal faith and beliefs.

My spiritual brother Prabhat Kumar Ray, another close disciple of my Master, had preserved every published article about Thakur and collected many other written materials on Thakur. After researching contact information for most of Thakur's close devotees, disciples, and family members, Prabhat obtained notes and interviews from them. He cross-referenced books from the library to confirm the authenticity of those resources and to validate their chronology. It was as if Thakur had inspired him to do all of the spadework necessary to help me. Prabhat's dedicated work allowed me to put it all together and reaffirm how this land has always attracted the holiest of holy souls from the higher astral planes to become beacons for humanity and its seekers of light and ultimate reality.

Dr. Banerjee, an early devotee of Thakur, recorded his own experiences and those of other devotees in a notebook that he entitled, *"The Guru as I See Him."* One day, my Master handed that notebook to me and said, *'Keep this. Someday it could be of some use to you"*. Indeed, that proved to be invaluable when I was contemplating how to approach writing Thakur's biography. Many of the episodes contained here on Thakur's life have been taken from Dr. Banerjee's notebook. I am privileged to share them with you as a reader. Though Dr. Banerjee has left this world, his efforts remain as the authentic account of a Divine Life. For simplicity and clarity, all material from Dr. Banerjee is shown as quotes, which are indented and italicized.

The golden phase of my life came as I had all the materials I needed. I was finally ready to meditate on my Master, the simple and humble being of light he was, and paint the canvas of his life and teachings. In my initial days as a devotee, it had been Thakur who had possessed me. Then in 1982, Thakur offered me as his *Guru dakshina* (offering to one's own Guru) into the service of his Grand Master, Baba Lokenath. He shifted the task of spreading the message of Baba Lokenath, which had been his, to me. From 1990 on, I was single-pointedly immersed in the life and teachings of the Himalayan Master and spreading Baba Lokenath's message around the world. For me, Thakur had merged into Baba Lokenath. I saw him in Baba Lokenath and Baba Lokenath in him. Then in 2015, my Master re-emerged. Thakur possessed me again. The irrepressible longing to spread Thakur's message, as I had done all these years for Baba Lokenath, took fresh hold of me. The incubation of Thakur's biography had begun.

Obstacles persisted, however. An undercurrent of regret would rise up from time to time. I would find myself asking, "*How is it that I have authored so many books, yet have not been able to write about my own Guru?"* None of us, though, can accomplish anything until the time ripens and it is ordained by the divine. Grace comes with its own, perfect timing, in its own way, according to its higher wisdom. That grace has come. The lengthy gestation of *Living with My Himalayan Master Sri Sri Bhajan Brahmachari—A Biography* is now complete.

Please understand that there are too many miracles in the life of my Master to include them all here. A truly enlightened Master never does anything to show his or her power. Though they manifest supranatural powers, they only do so to reveal and call us to the path of love by living and acting with compassion through their own mundane life. From the heights of egoless, pure divinity, the love of the Great Masters always flows with the singular purpose of awakening sleeping souls to their own, infinite possibilities and joy.

For almost twelve years (1970-1982) I had lived close to Thakur. Between 1976-1982 I was at his ashram as a monk, always at his feet, attentively witnessing how God walks on earth. I saw Thakur's moments of human despair and laughter, his physical illnesses, his total indifference to his physical body, all while living in his body like a bird lives in a cage. I saw him experience every shade of emotion that is at play in every human life. I was touched by his states of trance and ecstasy when he sang *bhajans* and chants and went into *samadhi*. I have seen him as the Omniscient One and also as one who knows nothing. I have seen him as God incarnate and as the most ordinary human being. At times, it was difficult to fathom his infinite attributes, the multidimensional divinity he embodied. He never allowed us to remain in awe for long. He instantly came down to our level, mingling with us to help us realize that Godliness is not something other worldly; it is something that is down-to-earth, utterly natural. He was here. He was there. He was everywhere.

My prayer is that *Living with My Himalayan Master Sri Sri Bhajan Brahmachari—A Biography* will give you a glimpse not just of someone "up there," but of someone who is as close to your heart as your own loved ones, someone with whom you can talk, someone in whom you can trust and confide. My prayer is that you will invite him in, push him to play with you and reveal not only his divinity, but also the divinity in your own heart.

In searching for one word to describe Thakur, what kept flooding my being was "Pure Love". Thakur was the epitome of pure, unconditional love for one and all. His message to the world was his life, which was an outpouring of pure love. Only pure love can save this planet and bring balance to every walk of life, so that we can all live here as beings of light and love, creating heaven on earth.

Humanity is in agony today. We are all desperately looking for ways to overcome an overwhelming array of crises unfolding all around us. We are all walking through fires of one sort or another: internal, external, and societal. Yet we can always rely on the inner path, the path of the spirit, the path of love, to light our way. The imperative is to dive deep within, to find the true purpose of our human existence, to live from our soul in the face of every obstacle.

The lives of great Yogis and Seers inspire us. They offer us clarity. They illuminate our understanding of the path and inspire us to practice ever more earnestly. Ultimately, and more importantly, the biographies and teachings of the Great Ones offer us personal access to their eternally living spirit. They serve as a conduit of presence that carries the seed of a more personal connection, an ongoing relationship. They open our hearts to draw on the currents of eternal grace that a given Master still seeks to bestow. I have said many times: the grace of the Masters is eternally available to everyone everywhere. It is available all the time. We have only to turn to them. They will hear us. They will lift us up and guide us through every storm.

Living with My Himalayan Master Sri Sri Bhajan Brahmachari—A Biography is a love offering. I lay it tenderly down at the feet of my Master. It is also my heart offering to you. I hope it helps you to connect to Thakur, to the fountain of divinity that eternally flows through him, and that it quenches your thirst for happiness, peace, and true oneness.

My obeisance to my Master as I offer this handful of flowers at His feet.

Shuddhaanandaa Brahmachari (Bodhi)
6 July 2020

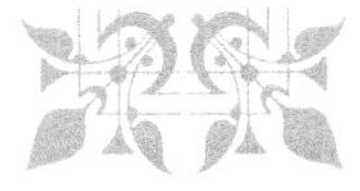

INTRODUCTION

"Living with My Himalayan Master" is the first ever biography of the great Himalayan Master Sri Sri Bhajan Brahmachari, one of the very few disciples of the renowned Himalayan Yogi, Sri Divyananda Saraswati (popularly known as Devgiri Maharaj) — the living Shiva who was at the same time the grand Master of all saints and monks who wandered in the Himalayan Tehri region. Sri Divyananda was also known and deeply revered as 'Mother' by all the Himalayan sages for his motherly nature. Everyday he used to sit on the road before the Uttarkashi Ganges and serve food to every monk who happened to pass by. Sri Divyananda Saraswati was in turn the disciple of Sri Vijnanananda Saraswati, the Raj Guru or Royal Spiritual Master of the Tehri Naresh, the King of Tehri Himalayas.

This Biography of Sri Sri Bhajan Brahmachari is the first one of this living saint who belongs to this rare Himalayan lineage of high order. It is priceless in terms of its first-hand authenticity, extensive research from old documents and direct experience of the wisdom and living Presence of the Master himself. It is interesting that during all the years that the Master lived, many attempts were made to write his biography. As is documented in an old journal, "Some mysterious force stopped the publications. Either they were lost at the printing house or at home. Or, when the manuscripts were shown to Master, he declined acknowledgment. Moreover, Master's life was a mystery and the Master rarely spoke about it, and when he did it was only in front of a chosen few."

This Biography comes from the heart of the author, who unlike many other disciples of the Master, saw his Guru not in vague terms of 'God' or 'Incarnation', but as a man — a simple, humble man who was not God because of his boundless mystical powers of healing but because of his extraordinary capacity to live and teach the greatest lessons of love, laughter, joy and sorrows through his inimitable humility. This book explores the Himalayan Master in the light of not his Himalayan descendance but the Himalayan magnanimity of his living presence.

A cult is a narrow minded following of a great Master by those blind to the Master's simplest and purely human essence. A cult is the result of followers engaging their own tiny ego-self to the Master's vast egoless entity of indiscriminate expansion. Those whose emphasis is solely on their Master's greatness in his or her Godhood and their Master being the one and only surpassing all other Masters only unconsciously try to assert their own ego. A true disciple is one who takes to heart at least one of the Master's 'human' qualities of selfless love, compassion, purity, and simplicity, and thus becomes a true human being. Those who forgo the master's simple human qualities but only stress his miracles or extraordinary capacities fail to attain even the basic spiritual stature of a good human.

Rising above this fallacy of ego-entangled worshipfulness towards the Master, the author has presented his Master as one who, in his own words, is the definition of "pure love, pure joy."

Once, two men came to see the author on the same day. The first man who came was an 'ardent' disciple of the Master and had served the Master at his ashram for a very long time. He praised Master Sri Sri Bhajan Brahmachari in very highflying words. The author asked him the reason and asked him to tell in one word what his Master meant for him. The man said, *"He is God incarnate!"* The author just smiled. Sometime later another man came to him. He had never seen the author's Master but had only imagined him in his own way through the author's words. The author, inquisitively, asked him, *"Do tell me, in one word, what my Master symbolizes to you. Remember, one word that most appropriately described him."* The man just looked into the author's eyes, smiled peacefully, and whispered, "Joy". The author's eyes glistened with a tear even as a gentle smile appeared on his face. Shallow eulogizing the Master as 'greatest of all' can attract a cult, but not make a good human. But acknowledging the simplest of the Master's human qualities can move the heart and transform consciousness.

This book is one of the many true gems of narration about the life and teachings of a true Master, a *Sadguru*, by a person who understands the true essence of his Master, carries it in his own heart everywhere he goes, and from there, has shown to many others, this Light.

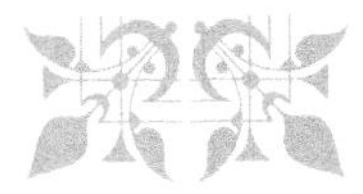

CHAPTER ONE

MY FIRST ENCOUNTER WITH A LIVING MASTER

After returning home from college one day in the 1960s, my mother greeted me with joy in her heart and said, "*A saint is visiting our town (Vijayawada, Andhra Pradesh). Why don't you go and meet him? I have heard he sings very well. Go meet him. This is a great opportunity for you.*"

Reverence for those dedicating their lives to the divine is central to Hindu tradition. The mere sight of a holy person (*darshan* in Sanskrit) is considered a paramount blessing. Religious ascetics dedicating their lives to God are called *sadhus* and *Mahapurushas* (Holy Ones) and are venerated. This was part of me and my upbringing. Besides, I have always loved music. Devotional chants steal my heart and fill me with indescribable joy. I couldn't wait to go.

That evening, I made my way to the bungalow of Dr. Mukherjee in the Rail Quarter, where the saint was staying. Lots of devotees had already gathered there. I was only one of many who had come that night to listen to the *sadhu's* words and hear him sing *bhajans* (devotional songs).

I was young and new to this kind of gathering, so I stood at the doors behind all the other devotees, who sat closer to him. My first sight of the unassuming holy man was purely one of curiosity, anticipating his singing. But Thakur Bhajan Brahmachari had an extraordinary energy all his own. Though he was clad in simple white clothes, his eyes belonged to another world. I was transfixed at seeing an aura of light around him. His presence was so powerful; it was as if it was only him in the room. His presence was palpably everywhere. Sitting on a simple cot covered with a white bed sheet, he played a harmonium and was singing. His eyes were half-closed; his face radiated a divine light. As he swayed from side to side with the music, I was amazed at the ease with which he was playing the harmonium. And though I had grown up around harmoniums, the sound of it was different from any I had heard before. His voice did not belong to this world either. He was pouring his heart into every word of the devotional chant as he sang to Lord Krishna. His eyes were moist, lost in sheer ecstasy and pure love. His singing was transporting everyone there to realms beyond themselves and their mundane miseries. We were all mesmerized.

Standing at the doors, my heart melted. Spontaneously, I started singing with him. I had loved music from childhood and often sang *bhajans* on my own, but never had I experienced such ecstatic feelings overwhelming me. It was as if I was not in me. The words of his songs, his voice, his devotion, his presence all mingled to evoke divine love that had always been waiting for expression.

Though I had visited my grandmother in Varanasi regularly while on vacation and had seen many *sadhus* over the years, I had never seen such palpable divinity or light in any of them. As he continued singing, the assembled devotees joined in. Then he began singing the ancient *Vaishnava* chant *Hari Bol*. Divine energies were flowing with abandon through every molecule of the room and everyone present. Here was a man in the world but beyond it, his body glowing with light, his voice melting in the ecstasy of divine communion. I could not take my eyes off of him. My heart was like an iron filing drawn to a magnet, falling at his feet.

I Witnessed Super Conscious State for the First Time

Lost in rapture, he suddenly stopped singing and collapsed over the harmonium. A devotee standing behind him laid him on the cot. For some time, his body went through a series of yogic *mudras* (symbolic gestures of hands and fingers). With everyone enveloped in the energy and mysteries of the transformation taking place before us, the *kirtan* (a gathering of devotional singing) continued.

Gradually coming back to this mundane plane, he looked around the room in lingering ecstasy. When his gaze met mine for a few seconds, my heart stopped. I felt I had known him for ages. I knew I could surrender to him without a hint of doubt or reservation. Something at my deepest core, beyond any capacity to comprehend, was happening. The evening closed with him calling one person after the other forward. He mumbled privately into each person's ear in a tenuous, hushed voice. Then they offered their obeisance, received his blessings, and left.

I waited among a handful of remaining devotees for one-on-one time with him. Approaching slowly, I whispered into his ear, "*Would you please give me deeksha* (initiation)?" He whispered back, *"First finish your education. Then I will initiate you."* I was crestfallen and felt very deprived, but something had changed. A deep inner call had claimed me. I belonged only to him, to that world where he went through his music. Only he could take me there. No one else. Despite never wanting to leave, I bowed, took his blessings, and headed home.

The next day, I again went to him. The house was already full of devotees from every corner of town when I reached Dr. Mukherjee's. "Thakur," (as he was called by his devotees, which means Divine Being) had gone into the *puja* room (*puja* is an act or ritual of worship) to offer Lord Jagannath, the Lord of the Universe, the evening food offering. The doors of the small temple-room were closed. The devotees waiting outside were all quiet, silently doing their *mantra japa* (repetitions of the Holy Name). When the doors opened, Thakur came out holding a huge wooden plate full of *khicheri* (a dish of rice and lentils) on his head with both hands. His body was still trembling with ecstasy from the ritual. Walking slowly to the center of the hall, he placed the plate of *Jagannath*

Prasad (food that had been ritually offered to God and which is therefore blessed) on the floor and sat down. Asking for the *Prasad* to be put into his mouth, he opened his mouth.

Several devotees took the first turns at putting the food into his mouth with their own hands. Now there was a scramble. Everyone present wanted to feed him all at once. I was in shock. Standing at a distance away from the crowd rushing to feed him, I was awestruck. Everyone was putting the food into his mouth; yet without his chewing even once, the food was instantly passing to his stomach. How could anyone take in so much food, offered by so many people at once, without chewing it? As they finished, I took my turn and came up to put the food into his mouth. The huge wooden plate full of *khicheri* was almost finished. To my surprise, he took a little from it and put it into my mouth. It was like nectar. The few remaining devotees came one after the other, fed him, and the plate was empty. Thakur was in *samadhi*, total absorption into the divine. He left Vijayawada the next day, but he had taken his seat permanently in the shrine of my heart.

Of course, I became intrigued about this rare person. In the crowd of humanity running after the gross, materialistic things of life, how could he attain such a state? He was so simple, so humble, so utterly at ease with himself. How could he radiate such peace and impart it the way he did to me and others? How could he appear so ordinary, yet have the magnetic power to bring so many thirsty souls to his holy company? He had extraordinary energy in and around him. Everyone listening to him speak felt his wisdom. They were bathed in the depth of his intense love for the divine.

Gradually getting acquainted with devotees of Thakur, (we all addressed him as Thakur which means 'Divine Being' 'man of God'; even Sri Ramakrishna Paramahansa was addressed by most of his followers as Thakur) I started gathering stories of his intriguing life. The more I heard, the more I wanted to hear. Each anecdote conveyed an intense manifestation of love for anyone who trusted him, loved him, or who sought his help and protection.

Today, I feel compelled to share the details of what I learned about the life of this extraordinary human being. He was like any one of us. Yet, through complete surrender to the divine, he became a manifestation of the divine. He became a bridge to transport many from this world of bondage to the world of freedom.

Like many other great saints of India, Thakur Bhajan Brahmachari had some unusual circumstances in his early childhood. When Thakur would, from time to time, speak about his Brahmin parentage, many followers became confused. They only knew about the parents who had raised Thakur, and they were not Brahmins by caste. For some unknown reason, he never publicly narrated the story of his birth in a Brahmin family. He did, however, tell a very few close associates like Prabhat Kumar Ray that he was born to Brahmin parents who were living in a village in a part of the then undivided Bengal, India, which is now Bangladesh. He also instructed that the story should not be revealed during his lifetime.

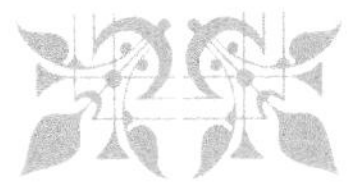

CHAPTER TWO

BIRTH AND EARLY CHILDHOOD

Thakur was born on 9 September, Wednesday, 1925 around 7:27 a.m. in a village called Rarikhal in the district of Dhaka, Bikrompur (presently in Bangladesh). When he was a baby, an epidemic broke out in the village where his family lived and hundreds died. When his parents became ill and were at the brink of death, a very close friend of his father's, Sachinath Bose, approached them and promised to care for their son with all his love and affection. Thakur was handed over to the Sachinath Bose family by his dying parents.

Though Sachinath Bose did not share in the religious beliefs of those around him, he was deeply duty bound and honest to the core. He always lived according to the highest values, with a commitment to truth and equality. His wife, Ma Priyabala, was soft-spoken and an embodiment of pure motherly love. Her heart was totally given to God. Sachinath and Ma Priyabala had eleven children, six daughters and four sons, in addition to Thakur, who was the fourth in age. Most of the daughters were his younger sisters. Both Sachinath and Ma Priyabala showered Thakur with loving attention; he was the apple of their eyes.

Thakur often told me that Ma Priyabala was so spiritually evolved that even when the children played together and created intolerable noise, she would look through the windows to the sky utterly unperturbed. When Thakur would ask how she could stand the noise and disturbance and whether it caused her any irritation, she replied with absolute serenity, *"Children love to play! They are enjoying each other. Why should I stop them?"* Then she added, *"Every householder should learn how to detach oneself from the things that go on in every family, so that you are in the family, but not pulled into every little distortion."* Thakur told me often how much he adored his mother for her spiritual state and her sense of detachment. Ma Priyabala was a devout worshiper of the infant Lord Krishna, Gopala. After attending to all the daily household chores for their huge family, she always made time to go to the altar and worship Gopala. Whenever she felt down or physically stressed, she would sit with her Gopala and talk to Him. In minutes she would come back to the light of her higher nature, restored and renewed, ready to begin again with all the chores involved in caring for the children and family. Through simple devotion and surrender to Gopala, she grew in her spiritual self.

SACHINATH BOSE (FATHER) AND MA PRIYABALA (MOTHER)

After spending some time in Rarikhal, Sachinath moved to Calcutta in a rental premise at Ishwar Ganguly Lane, Kalighat, along with the newborn child. He worked in a Government Office in the Settlement department at a transferable job. But once they moved to Calcutta, Thakur fell very sick. Most of the time the child would be lying on the bed without any sign of life. Ma Priyabala was always worried and spent most of the time taking care of the child that she thought of as her own little living Gopala. Three of Thakur's great grandparents had left their family life to become wandering mendicants and had reached a high state of yoga. They had predicted that in later years a holy child would come in their family who would be an incarnation of divine love offering shelter to many seekers in the path of love.

As the child Thakur grew in the lap of this loving, devout mother, his own eyes were always wide open, looking for something beyond. Neighbors were often drawn to the home, fascinated by the child's magnetic presence and huge eyes. He was a source of delight to everyone. Visitors would often remark, *"What a divine child! Look at his eyes, his smile! And he never cries!"*

As a baby of hardly one year, Thakur was afflicted with an unknown disease and confined to bed. The entire family was distraught when all efforts to medically treat and cure him failed. Ma Priyabala and Sachinath were in great pain. Despite doing everything they could, the child's condition continued to deteriorate day by day. Even the best physicians could not find a clue to the cause of the disease. Most of them gave up all hope. Their consensus was that the child would not recover. Ma Priyabala spent night after night nursing the child, in constant prayer for mercy and for the child to regain his lost health.

Bhairavi Ma Saves Thakur's Life

After all hope had been given up, Thakur was sinking close to death. One morning, a woman *sannyasin* (one who has renounced all material possession in pursuit of the spirit) whom Thakur learned years later was named Bhairavi Ma, appeared at dawn, knocking at the door of their home. When Ma Priyabala answered, the *yogini* asked for permission to come in. Ma Priyabala was hesitant to allow this stranger—with matted hair, wearing a red-bordered saree and a big bindi on her forehead—inside. With determination in her voice, the woman insisted, *"Take me in. I know the little one is sick. He is in very critical condition. He is passing through a dire threat to his life. This is very urgent."* Ma Priyabala could not stop her. Without any prompting from Ma Priyabala, the woman walked directly to the room where the child was lying. Standing at his bedside, she looked at the child with deep attention and compassion, as if she was bathing the child with the power of her extraordinarily bright eyes.

Suddenly a smile flickered across her face. With her voice filled with loving command, she told Ma Priyabala, *"Bring me a little Ganges water in a bowl."* Ma Priyabala ran and got a bowl of water without any questioning. The *yogini* took the bowl in her hands and drew it close to her mouth while softly chanting a *mantra* of deep, incoherent sounds. Then, smiling with assurance, she handed the bowl back to Ma Priyabala and said, *"Keep it safe. Take a little water every day and make him drink it. Very soon the child will be cured and healthy."*

Bhairavi Ma then told Ma Priyabala to call the child *Hari Bhajan* from now on:

> *"I am naming him Hari Bhajan (divine chant). In the future, this child's voice will inspire many people to the path of devotion and the love of God. His voice will always be filled with divine chants that will attract one and all to him. When the time ripens, he will leave home to serve the large family of the Lord. Don't hold him back then."*

She looked back at the child again, held him in her lap, and blessed him with the infinite love of the Divine Mother. Then she gave him back into his mother's arms.

She left the home as quietly as she came, from nowhere, without giving Ma Priyabala a chance to ask who she was. Ma Priyabala's heart was surging with gratitude and hope that her child at last would be healthy and happy. She stood there in the early hours of the morning, with her eyes riveted on the road, as the woman slowly disappeared from her view. Many searches were made to find some trace about this saintly woman who came to save the life of this child and name him as he would later be known to the world. It was as if she had materialized out of air and again melted into air. Nobody could find a trace of her.

Ma Priyabala had always trusted the divine as the ultimate reality. She knew that when everything fails, the supreme intelligence comes with its mystic solutions. She had the holy water in the bowl in her hands and longed with all her heart to give it to her child, but it was the norm of the day to ask the permission of her husband before she could do that. She had deep faith and reverence for her husband. She would not do anything without first seeking his permission and approval.

Ma Priyabala approached Sachinath and narrated the whole story of the mystic *yogini* who had come early that morning, blessed the child with her incantations and holy water, and predicted that the child would soon come around. Though Sachinath was not as religious and god-fearing as his wife, the story instilled the sense that there was something at work beyond the rational mind. After all, the doctors had given up hope for the child from the medical point of view. This mysterious woman and her *mantra*-soaked water was the only thing that he had with which he could try to breathe life back into the dying child. He readily agreed to the mother's wish and said, *"Let us see what happens. Do as she has instructed."*

A miracle became evident after feeding the child this holy water. Signs of improvement began from day one. Within a few days the whole family was celebrating his recovery. He had been healed.

In later years, Thakur's disciple Kalyan Bose, asked Thakur, while writing a short biography of him, if he had ever met the woman who saved his life, Bhairavi Ma, again. Thakur replied with a sublime smile, *"Oh yes, not once, but many times."* When Kalyan remarked, *"Bhairavi Ma must have grown pretty old,"* Thakur replied,

"These great sages don't grow old. They are in the physical world, but their bodies are so divinized that they live long periods of time. They visit wherever they need to be in their subtle body, manifesting in a physical form. Whenever there was need, she just manifested her physical form and helped me."

An Early Blessing by a Master

When Bhajan was three, one of Ma Priyabala's friends came and told her that she was going to have the *darshan* of her Gurudev, a great saint from Haridwar, Sri Sri Bhola Giri. He was camping at the Bholagiri Ashram near Bhawanipur, South of Calcutta. She even asked Bhajan, who was very dear to her, whether he would go and have *darshan* of the renowned saint. Bhajan's eyes sparkled in joyful anticipation of seeing the sage. Accompanying her friend, Ma Priyabala took the child to see Bhola Giri, and prostrated to the Master when they reached the ashram. Despite the huge gathering of devotees and followers present, when Bhola Giri's eyes fell on the child Bhajan, his attention instantly withdrew from the rest of the crowd. As if in a state of trance, he deeply looked into the very core of the child, as if he had known him for a long time. He took Bhajan in his own lap and started caressing him. Looking into Bhajan's eyes, he said again and again, *"How come you are here, Shiva's son?"*

Ma Priyabala was deeply reassured that the great Master was blessing her child. Still, to make sure that the child's health would improve, she asked him, *"Would you give him some amulet so that he can regain his health? He has never been in good health. We are always concerned about his health."* Bhola Giri looked at the worried mother with a smile in his face and said, *"None of you need to worry about this holy child. He will be all right. He will be healthy; but he is not born to live a life like anyone of you. Don't ever try to bind him with marriage and family life; set him free when time ripens."* As he spoke these words, he stroked the head of Bhajan with intense love, blessing the child.

Early Traits

Sachinath would often go to Rarikhal, the village in East Bengal, and stay there, leaving the home in Calcutta. This gave the scope to Bhajan to leave the din and bustle of the city life and live in the countryside, which he always longed with all his heart. There were orchards and rivers, temples and simple life of humble villagers. One day Ma Priyabala went to the nearby temple of Laxmi-Narayana along with her child Bhajan. She went inside the temple asking Bhajan to wait for her to return after her worship from the sanctum sanctorum. After a while she came out and looked for her child, but he was not there. Ma Priyabala went around worried looking for her dear Bhajan and lo! Bhajan was sitting under a banyan tree and singing devotional chants dedicated to Mother Kali. Ma Priyabala was amazed to hear her son singing so well, with such intense devotion and spontaneity. Bhajan had never learned any bhajans, but here he was singing so effortlessly and with such love and devotion for the Mother Divine. As such, during his stay in Calcutta, whenever he used to visit the temple of Mother Kali at the Kalighat close to their home along with his mother, he would sit and listen to every *sadhu* who sang bhajans to Mother Kali. He joined them on his own. Back home, he would keep humming those songs and, on his notebooks, he would fill the pages drawing pictures of Mother Kali.

Bhajan's mother had a shock of her life when one day in Rarikhal village, Bhajan went out and climbed a tree. Sitting on one of the branches, he started singing bhajans. Gradually, his consciousness shifted to higher realms of spiritual bliss. Going into a trance like state, he forgot that he was up in the tree, sitting on a thin branch and fell from the tree. His mother came searching for her child and was shocked to see him in pain lying on the ground under the big tree.

This is how the days of his adolescence passed. In Calcutta, there was not much formal education. The children were more schooled at home by their mother. At Rarikhal, however, Bhajan started to go to the local school along with two of his elder brothers.

As Bhajan grew up, his tendency was to keep to himself, away from others. He would find some isolated corner where he could be alone with his eyes glued to the infinite sky. At times, he fell into mysterious sobbing for no reason. It was as if he was searching for someone close whom he had lost. Withdrawing into wild bushes and trees, his heart found the space he craved.

His family began to worry that he was not a normal child! '*What is wrong with him? Everyone loves him. He is given more love and care than any of his sisters or brothers! Every tiny desire of his is instantly taken care of. What makes him so cut off from the others, as if he does not belong to this world or to this family?*' His parents' primary concern became what would happen to him in the future, since he had no interest in any formal education. '*With books in hand, he drifts away into unknown worlds. Nothing registers in his brain. He is too unmindful. He is not fit to be a serious student.*'

The only thing that captured his full attention and deep interest was music. He loved to sing. He loved anyone who sang. He was most strongly attracted to those who sang *bhajans*. Listening to songs dedicated to God, he slipped easily into ecstasy. No one taught him how to sing; songs came to him naturally. He sang with pure devotion, with the words pouring out of his heart to the Divine Mother. His songs were a natural gift, divine renderings that endeared him to one and all. Those listening to his songs were effortlessly transported to a deep connection to the divine.

Sachinath worked in a transferable government service job. At one point, he suddenly received an order of transfer to eastern Bengal, in the smaller town of Rangpur. Once he secured a place to stay, he moved the family there. Bhajan was around 8 or 9 years old at the time and was admitted to Kailash Ranjan High School in the primary sections. His name as recorded at the school was Amal Kumar Bose. Though his mother Ma Priyabala named him as 'Ranu' from his birth till Bhairavi Ma came and instructed her to name him as Bhajan, and from then on he was known as Bhajan to one and all.

Bhajan walked to school with his elder brother. He was strongly drawn to nature: the trees, the ponds, the ducks, grazing goats and cows. He would get lost gazing at the open sky. With his whole being soaking in the abundance of nature, he would often simply miss the road to the school, drift along toward the river, and sit by the bank absorbed in inner contemplation. He would take soft mud from the riverbank and make beautiful idols of divine Mother Kali or other forms of gods and goddesses. This was his favorite play. He would first make them, then collect flowers from the surrounding area, offer them at the feet of the deities, and then sit silently, lost in inner contemplation. This was worship which came naturally to him, nobody ever asked him or taught him how to make idols or how to worship the deities.

Rangpur was a small town, with a small population and a simple life that included all kinds of religious ceremonies throughout the year. Theaters and other cultural programs were staged during those festivals. Devotional songs rendered by the young Bhajan came to be among their most loved events. Devotees flocked in large numbers to hear the outpourings of the young boy singing with all of his heart. He was already stirring everyone's heart toward love and devotion.

Bhajan was equally gifted at theatrical performance. In village religious festivals like Janmashtami, the anniversary of the Birth of Lord, he would play Lord Krishna in the staged drama. Dressed like the adolescent, playful Lord Krishna, he would sing heartrending songs.

An Early Prophesy by a Great Saint

Bhajan's life continued with very little interest in studies, ever more interest in the life of silence, and delight in singing devotional songs. When he was 15 years old, Ma Priyabala learned the great saint of Bengal, Sri Sri Ram Thakur, was visiting close to her home in Rangpur. She did not want to lose this opportunity to have his *darshan* and to seek blessings for the health of the beloved child whom he used to lovingly call Ranu. When she arrived, despite the big crowd, she was blessed to get a seat close to the saint. As Ma Priyabala prostrated to Ram Thakur, his eyes fell on Bhajan. He quickly picked the child up and sat him by his side. He caressed the child saying, "*Why are you here? You are supposed to be in the Himalayas.*" Then looking at Ma Priyabala, he said, "*Why do you worry about his health? He is no ordinary child. He is here to be the beloved of many, many devotees of the Lord. Don't hold him to yourself. Let him free when the time ripens.*"

Then he blessed the child with indescribably tender love and compassion.

Ma Priyabala was a bit taken aback at hearing the words of the great saint, realizing that her precious son would be leaving home in the future. She had a fearful doubt: Does that mean that this child will grow up to be a *sannyasin* and leave home for good?

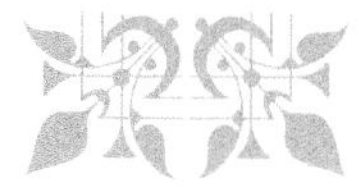

CHAPTER THREE

SETTLING IN CALCUTTA: A LIFE OF QUIET SADHANA

The words of the great sages never fail because they can see through time, into the timeless. Through their third eye, they penetrate the past and future to the infinite. Sri Sri Ram Thakur saw in the child the future saint who would be the refuge of thousands of seekers from around the world.

As Bhajan grew older, his heart continually longed to be alone, immersed in his deepest yearnings. The words of Ram Thakur had stirred his innate call for ultimate reality. The Himalayas and the life of a wandering monk were beckoning. Though he was loved by his family, nothing touched him like the silence of his own heart. It was there that he heard the whisperings of divine song. There, he sang to his heart's content and could cry freely. Yearning for the divine was maddening him more and more as the days rolled by.

Bhajan stayed with his parents and siblings in Rangpur from 1933 to 1946. In August 1946, the gruesome riot between Hindus and Muslims broke out in Noakhali and Calcutta in then British ruled India. It was one of the most horrifying religious riots that took place over several days. (It does not seem out of the place to mention here that the number of people killed in the name of religion through the centuries surely rivals the toll of all the "political" wars put together.)

In 1947, India attained independence from British colonial rule. Eastern Bengal was separated from western Bengal. The eastern portion, with its predominantly Muslim population, went to East Pakistan after the country was partitioned into India and Pakistan. The western part of Bengal became Indian territory, as it had a greater Hindu population. The partition was among the most painful experiences in Indian history. Millions lost their homes and lives, not only in Bengal but also in other parts of India. Millions moved as refugees to new places, forced to start their lives over with nothing.

Though Bhajan was very young at the time, the massacre of the Hindu Muslim riot of 1946, the partition of the country into India and Pakistan, and the partition of Bengal left a deep imprint on him concerning the hollowness of fundamentalist attitudes in religious communities. His own family was part of that great migration, since his father Sachinath was forced to move the family back to Calcutta during the partition to start afresh in the newly independent India.

When the family came to Calcutta, they initially stayed in the Park Circus area where one of Sachinath's uncles lived. Then they exchanged properties with a Muslim family. Park

Circus had more Muslim residents. The Muslim family gave his uncle their house located at Cornfield Road in South Calcutta, close to Gariahat Center.

Sachinath was a man of high ideals, honesty and truthfulness. In Calcutta's Government Settlement Office where he was employed, corruption was rampant. If he continued to serve there, he knew he had to compromise his own life-long principles. He resigned his job and started a small business running an electrical store by the name of Boseac & Co., near Gariahat Junction, at 2, Hindusthan Road.

In the meantime, Bhajan completed his matriculation examination and came to Calcutta to fulfill his parents' wish that he finish his college education, as two of his elder brothers had been doing. But his heart was not in books or formal education. All he could think about was leaving home to seek the divine.

Returning to the huge city of Calcutta, Bhajan felt utterly out of place. The din and bustle of the materially bound life of most people around him left him ill at ease. Everyone was running around chasing after something without knowing what it was. Still, he found a few places and people that gave him some peace. The temples and ashrams offered the fresh air that he craved. But his heart was longing to move where he could just be with himself, in inner silence. Spells of silence came to him naturally. His parents' hope that he would complete his studies and one day assume his own responsibilities persisted in vain. He was simply not born to live the life of the masses, enmeshed in physical and mundane, everyday existence.

Gradually his mind eased. He found he could have a quiet mind in the midst of all the clamor going on around him. He continued a deep meditation practice. The great Himalayan Master Baba Lokenath Brahmachari (1730-1890) regularly appeared in physical form to young Bhajan and guided him in *sadhana* (spiritual practice). As Thakur once told me,

"Baba Lokenath used to come to me from time to time in his physical body (Baba Lokenath had left his mortal cage in 1890) and gave me simple instructions with much love and compassion about what I needed to do in the path of my inner journey. I was almost 7 years old when Baba started materializing in his body to give me darshan and instructions."

While attending college in Calcutta, studies held no interest for Bhajan. What he found compelling was contemplating the indwelling truth beyond the apparent dualism of the manifested universe. He often went missing from home, would come back after a few days, and remained silent about his disappearance and return. None of his relatives, even his parents and siblings, ever knew where he went. He was escaping to places of quiet, retreating into his inner cave to meditate and pray. He would go to some cremation ground and sit in silence while the dead bodies were being consumed in the pyre, which instilled deep realizations of the transient nature of human life in a physical body.

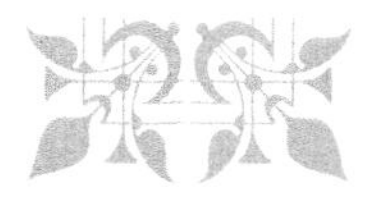

CHAPTER FOUR

DIVINE MOTHER OF SHIMURALI AND HIS PATH OF DISPASSION

One of the cremation grounds that Bhajan often visited during this time, when he was supposed to look after his father's electrical store, was in Shimurali, a small village on the Sealdah Ranaghat railway lines. Escaping the drudgery of business and studies, he answered the call of his indwelling *Atman* (the Eternal, indwelling, divine Self). He frequently would take his friend, Atin Ghosh, who lived in the Cornfield Road neighborhood, with him.

On one such visit, Bhajan and Atin had a fearful experience. When they reached the small rail station at Shimurali, it was already dusk. The place was isolated; nobody was around. The sun had already set behind the distant horizon bordering the paddy fields and the forests. As they walked silently through the narrow soil trail amid the lonely paddy fields, they felt like they were the only souls on earth. Atin became fearful and anxious, plagued with apprehensions. The surroundings felt frightening and uncanny to him. The eeriness haunted him so much that he wanted to go back. But how could he? He saw that Bhajan was not only unperturbed but was walking through the fields in inner ecstasy.

As they walked down the long distance through the village road and through the center of the paddy fields, a black cat suddenly appeared out of nowhere, and began following them. To their utter surprise, the cat vanished and a black dog mysteriously appeared in its place.

To test what was happening, they stopped walking. The dog stopped. When they resumed walking, the dog started walking, too. Atin was struck with fear. There was no light. Atin suggested to Bhajan that they get back home, as it was not safe to continue. Bhajan showed no sign of fear. He was calm and indifferent to any danger. He assured his friend that all was well, that there was no way they could get back home now; they could only move forward to their destination.

Finally, they reached the cremation ground and the small temple dedicated to Mother Kali. In the temple lived a monk who preferred total isolation and was in deep practice of *Shakti*-worship. He was already an adept who had reached a high state of spiritual light. To him, the temple deity Mother Kali was as alive as anyone else and he would often talk to Her as his own loving Mother. The *sannyasin* came out of his small hut and welcomed the two as if he knew they were on the way, saying, *"Did you get frightened by the cat and the dog? What was there to be afraid of? They wouldn't have done any wrong to you."* Atin was curious. How could the *sannyasin* know that they were coming and that they were intercepted by the black cat and a dog?

Bhajan and Atin opened their hearts in conversation with the *sadhu* wanting to learn about his spiritual journey and whether he could give Bhajan guidance for Mother worship. The renounced monk was patient and loving. He talked with the young seekers sharing his own life's journey in that isolated cremation ground for many years, sharing what he felt was the simplest path to God realization. He knew that the two young boys had come a long way and it was time they had some food. He offered both a lot of food and asked them to go and rest for the night.

Atin was very tired and in no time went into deep sleep. But Bhajan did not sleep. He wanted to see and understand more about what the *sadhu* did at night, and whether he might also experience deeper visions in his own meditation. He stayed awake and sat in meditation, aware of the surroundings. By midnight he suddenly heard a divine sound of anklets, as if someone with anklets was walking around the space where the *sadhu* was meditating. Whoever it was that came sat before the *sadhu*, stayed there for some time, then left. When She came and when She left, the space was lit with a divine radiance and filled with an enchanting aroma. Then Bhajan fell asleep.

The morning broke with the music of birds in the branches of the few trees that surrounded the cremation ground. The *sadhu* came to Bhajan and said, *"Now go and have darshan of Ma Kali in the temple."*

Both friends had their morning ablution and bath, then walked into the temple of the Divine Mother and prostrated before the idol of the Mother. When Bhajan looked into the radiant face of the Mother, he noticed that the nose-stud that Mother wore was not there.

At this time the *sadhu* came and instructed Bhajan to go and return their beds where they had been stored. To Bhajan's utter surprise, while cleaning the bed, he found the missing nose-stud of Mother Kali was lying right in his bed!! Picking it up, he took it to the *sadhu* to give it to him. The *sadhu* said, *"You got Mother's nose-stud. Good. Do you know that when Mother came last night, She laid down on your bed beside you for a while? Do you know how much She loves you? Mother loves you and you must come again to have darshan of the Mother."* Bhajan was overwhelmed, remembering that before he fell asleep, he could hear the sound of Mother's moving where the *sadhu* was sitting in meditation and he could distinctly hear the musical sound of the anklets of Mother's lotus feet.

The *sadhu* was a highly evolved *sannyasin*. He had dedicated his life in the worship of the Mother and lived in the secluded cremation ground so that he would not be disturbed by inquisitive villagers. He also was waiting for someone to come take charge of that temple ashram. He now had reason to believe that Bhajan was the holy child of the Mother and that if Bhajan came and stayed there, then he could leave. He said to Bhajan, *"Keep coming here. Why not come and stay here permanently, so that I can leave this place and go away."*

Bhajan was a free soul from his earliest childhood. He never wanted to be bound to any one place. So, he readily replied with all respect and humility, *"No, Baba, you please stay here. I will come to you whenever you and Mother call me."*

Bhajan would take every opportunity to escape the din and bustle of the city of Calcutta and run away to the quiet solitude of the Shimurali cremation ground and Mother Kali. The *sadhu* eventually left the place. No one ever knew anything about him and his whereabouts again.

DIVINE MOTHER OF SHIMURALI

CHAPTER FIVE

BHAJAN MEETS MA ANANDAMAYEE

This was also the time when the much loved, living incarnation of the Divine Feminine, Ma Anandamayee, came to Calcutta from the then East Bengal. As the divine willed, her ashram on Ekdalia Road was close to Bhajan's family home on Cornfield Road. When Ma often came to this ashram, hundreds of devotees would throng her ashram to have *darshan*.

Bhajan was deeply attracted to Ma Anandamayee. He visited the ashram often and, in the evening, he started singing his heart-stirring *bhajans* there. His singing enchanted Ma and she encouraged him to lead the *bhajans* as the assembly continued to increase in number. Around this time in 1947-1948, Ma Priyabala and Sachinath (Bhajan's parents) came in touch with Ma. Ma later initiated Ma Priyabala through her mother, as she avoided initiating anyone directly.

Bhajan had the privilege of accompanying his mother

to have the *darshan* of Ma Anandamayee at her ashram in Varanasi whenever possible. She came to play an immensely important role in his spiritual development.

During this period, Bhajan was also very active with a completely different aspect of culture. Having a natural talent for theatrical performance and dancing, he often visited one of his favorite families in Calcutta. Paresh Das Gupta was a staunch devotee of Baba Lokenath. Bhajan was like an elder brother to all the sons and daughters of Paresh. They affectionately called him Bhajan *da* (*Da* being the short form of *Dada*, which means the elder brother). Bhajan composed his own melodious *bhajans* and sang to his own tunes.

Dipu Roy, the youngest daughter of the Das Gupta family, tearfully reminisced recently about those golden days, when their loving Bhajan *da* would visit their home and then teach them to sing, perform drama, and dance. He was so unassuming and mingled with the children and elders with such natural ease that they never could have guessed that their Bhajan *da* would be a man of God.

He joined the family to visit Champa in Madhya Pradesh (in the Central region of India) where Paresh was working and the family got together to celebrate *Durga puja* (the festival of worship of Mother Durga, one of the forms of Divine Mother Shakti). Bhajan planned and scripted a drama, then directed and staged it at their wonderful home celebration. He stunned the audience who had assembled there by dancing in the role of Urvashi, the great nymph of Hindu mythology, whose beauty surpassed all.

MA ANANDAMAYEE

This enlightened Master came into this world with diverse gifts and brought excellence to every field of culture. He was ordinary, so utterly natural and unaffected in his demeanor and relationships. Still, Paresh whom Bhajan called "Mama" (maternal uncle) knew what an exalted state Bhajan belonged to. He would often remind his children that they should not take Bhajan *da* for granted by saying, *"He is no ordinary person. Did you not watch how, when he sings and chants, he goes into the deepest trance, which is the natural state of samadhi?"* Dipu Roy admitted that, *"I could never believe that Bhajan da would be someone who is God-like. To us, he was our elder brother, most loving, most affectionate and most compassionate. He was closer to our heart than any of our blood relations."*

When Paresh celebrated the anniversary celebration of the great Himalayan sage Baba Lokenath's *Mahasamadhi*, it was Bhajan who initiated the ritual of singing *bhajans* and congregational chanting in this yearly ceremony, which attracted large numbers of devotees of the great Yogi.

Inspired by the great Master Baba Lokenath, Bhajan would often leave for some unknown holy place to spend days in meditation. When asked by his devotees for details of his experiences in these places, he avoided speaking about them. He was not interested in talking about his own spiritual journey. He would often say to me, *"To whom should I say? Who would understand it all?"*

He did often advise devotees of the benefits to a spiritual seeker of spending time in the crematorium where bodies are burned to ashes. It awakens thc latent dispassion in the heart of a true seeker. One sees the near and dear ones mourning as dead bodies are brought in. The body that was so important, that was everything when alive, then becomes a log to be burned. It has no value. Seeing the whole drama of life end in a handful of ash again and again, one naturally begins to feel more spontaneously detached and called forward to the Eternal. Those who seek the Truth need to develop this deep sense of dispassion, in Sanskrit called *vairagya*, as well as detachment from all relations, so the mind can flow, unobstructed and unrestricted, toward the divine.

With the grace of Baba Lokenath, this early practice in secret silence nurtured the innate divine qualities that Bhajan was born to manifest without great effort or austerities. Still, his heart longed for the life of a wandering monk and to reach the tranquil heights of the Himalayas.

Both his presence and his ecstatic voice were so compelling that he was frequently invited to houses for religious gatherings to sing *bhajans*. Wherever he went, people continued to be enchanted by his music. They thronged to hear him. Devotees felt an instant connection with this young, pure devotee, and to the wisdom which flowed so naturally from him whenever he spoke.

CHAPTER SIX

FINDING GURU, THE HIMALAYAN MASTER

After renouncing my worldly life and becoming a monk in 1976 when I started living with my Master (Thakur Bhajan) at his ashram, he told me how he had found his Guru and how his initiation came about through Ma Anandamayee. This is exactly what he shared:

On the night of his 24th birthday in 1949, Bhajan went to bed and soon fell asleep, as he did every night. Suddenly the doors of intuition opened. He could see vividly, though it was a dream, that he was in the ashram of his beloved Ma Anandamayee. Seated there, he found a Himalayan sage with large, matted hair and a Shiva-like appearance. This great sage called Bhajan. Just as the sage was preparing to whisper the *Guru Mantra* in Bhajan's ears, Ma Anandamayee opened the doors of the Shiva temple, came in, and stood behind them. The entire temple was alight with the light of a million suns. The great Himalayan sage initiated Bhajan with a Shiva *mantra*. The entire vision was as vivid as if it happened in a wakeful state.

It was only much later that Bhajan learned the great sage of his dream was the famous Himalayan Yogi popularly known as Sri Sri Devgiri Maharaj, although his *sannyas* name was Sri Sri Divyananda Saraswati Maharaj. Devgiri Maharaj was born on 1st May 1864 and lived till 20th September 1952, a period of 88 years. He spent nearly 60 years at Uttarkashi, a small holy pilgrim center in the Himalayas, and 12 years with his Gurudev Vijnanananda Ji Maharaj in lofty Himalayan heights in caves, and the remaining 16 years were spent as wandering monk in pilgrimages around the country. His Ashram, called Sri Devgiri Ashram, at Ujeli, Uttarkashi still stands at the bank of the Mother Ganges. Today it is headed by his disciple, Swami Sachidananda Ji Maharaj, more popularly known as Gita Swami Maharaj's disciple Swami Kamaleshananda.

Waking from the dream, Bhajan was still in deep trance. Thinking about it, he realized this was no dream. He could see the Himalayan sage Devgiri Maharaj and Ma Anandamayee clearly in his mental eye. How he longed to see them again, to be immersed in the bliss he felt when he was initiated! Intense, overwhelming love for the Guru enveloped him. He could not think of anyone or anything else but his Guru, the sage from the Himalayas. Now he was haunted with questions. How can I find him? How can I go to him? How can I experience initiation in real life?

He knew that the Guru is a must in the life of the spirit. The dream had intensified his belief in the age-old Indian philosophy of the need of the Guru to be enlightened. Bhajan's only thought was to reach him, but he did not know how. It was a dream. He did not even know the name of his Master. All he had was the vivid remembrance of his Shiva-like appearance, the innocence and divinity that was written large on his child-like face.

After the vision, Bhajan lost all interest in everything else. All his family ties, all attachments had been let loose by unseen hands. The feelings were palpable. A new wave had come into his life, sweeping everything else away, leaving only a deep meditative silence and uninterrupted remembrance of the Divine Name in his heart. He was being pulled more and more toward that infinite expansion of consciousness and joy of the spirit. At the heart of it all was the effulgent light beaming from the vivid face of his Master. The fragrance of pure love was all around this holy Master. His heart sang only with the thought, *"All Glory to the Guru. Jai Guru!"*

He remembered the *mantra* that the Guru whispered in his ears in the dream. Repeating it incessantly in his heart became his sole refuge. He could feel his Guru's divine presence in the *mantra*. Guru and *mantra* are inseparable. *Brahmavidya*, the science of Consciousness, revolves around the Guru and the path the Guru shows to reach total awakened consciousness of the divine presence within and without. Bhajan knew from his association with the great Master Baba Lokenath that only by chanting the divine *mantra* given by the Guru could one reach that final state of Self-Realization.

But Bhajan had yet to meet the Guru of his life in his physical presence, take the *mantra*, and walk the path shown by him. All he could do was to cry for that dream to materialize. And cry he did, constantly.

Bhajan yearned for his Guru's physical presence so intensely that being separated from him was unbearable. Mercifully, Baba Lokenath and Vijaya Krishna Goswami appeared to him to reassure him that he would reach his Guru and receive *Mantra Deeksha*. (consecrated *mantra* initiation). They also talked to him about his previous birth and his mission ahead.

With this glimpse of his future life mission, Bhajan's abject pain subsided, though his eagerness to fall at his Guru's feet asking for the seed to fertilize his *sadhana* remained as strong as ever.

When a message came from the ashram of Ma Anandamayee in December 1949 summoning Bhajan to Varanasi to attend the *Savitri Maha Yajna*, which was performed for a long period of three years, the moment arrived. Ma Anandamayee promised Bhajan he would be initiated by the Himalayan Master who had appeared and initiated him in his dream.

Bhajan wasted no time taking the train to Varanasi, along with his father, who was still uninitiated. Bhajan knew there would be no better opportunity to beg the sage for the *mantra* for the redemption of his own father. Reaching Varanasi, Bhajan met Ma Anandamayee and offered his *pranam* (reverential prostration). Ma instructed him to go to Varanasi rail station along with other senior *brahmacharins* (celibate student of the Vedas) monks and devotees to receive the great Master Devgiri Maharaj. Though it was early dawn when they arrived, a huge crowd was already waiting for him. Word had spread that a great Himalayan *Siddha* (one who has attained spiritual perfection) was coming for the first time in his life to the mainland and to Ma's ashram. Even a glimpse of such a man of God was considered an inordinate blessing in any life.

Bhajan hid in the crowd, with his mind and heart singing inwardly to his Master. Communing with the Master in silence, he ached to touch his feet. When the train arrived, a very graceful, middle-aged *sannyasin* named Swami Nityananda Saraswati, who was an ardent disciple and personal assistant to Devgiri Maharaj, came and stood at the compartment doors. The monk stepped down and walked through the crowd of people and saffron robed monks searching for someone. When he reached Bhajan, he lovingly asked, *"Are you coming from Calcutta?" "Yes, Baba,"* young Bhajan answered. *"Guruji wants to see you,"* the monk said. Taking Bhajan's hand, he hurriedly pulled Bhajan through the waiting crowd.

DEVGIRI MAHARAJ

Having instantly recognized the sage in his dreams when they approached him, Bhajan was speechless. The sage was lying on the lower berth of the train compartment wrapped in a blanket. This is the moment that Bhajan had craved. He fell at the feet of his Gurudev to take the dust of his feet on his head. The sage quickly held him by the hand, pulled him closer, and asked in a whisper, "*You know why you came here?*" Bhajan could only nod his head in reply.

• • •

Little detail is known about this great Himalayan Master Devgiri Maharaj Even at a ripened age, whenever anyone expressed the wish to write his biography, he instantly rejected and discouraged the idea.

While recently visiting Devgiri Maharaj's Ashram in Uttarkashi to learn as much about him as possible, I asked, "*Why doesn't the ashram have any publication on the life and teachings of this great sage?*" The in-charge, Swami Kamaleshananda, a *Vedic* scholar and a saint himself, could only say,

> *"We tried. We tried every means, but one simply could never materialize. It was his wish that nothing remain on paper. He was totally against any kind of propaganda. So, all my attempts and those of my Gurudev Gita Swami Maharaj's (Devgiri Maharaj's main monastic disciple and successor) could never bear fruit. We cannot do anything against the wishes of these great sages."*

A brief sketch of his life was told by Sri Shaswat Chaitanya, who was later given *sannyas* by Devgiri Maharaj, and who became famous as Gita Swami, an authentic scholar of the *Bhagavad Gita*. At one point, he had asked Devgiri Maharaj, *"Maharaj, why do you have two names, one Devgiri and the other Swami Divyananda Saraswati Maharaj?"*

Devgiri Maharaj answered,

> *"Both my parents died soon after my birth. It was the good karma and samskar (the root impressions of all thoughts, actions, and intentions accumulated through various lifetimes that are the seed of one's current life experience) of my previous birth that I developed a deep dispassion to all worldly attraction. I just left home without anyone's knowledge in search of God. While wandering, I fell into the hands of a group of sannyasis, called Naga sannyasis, who took me into their group at that early age, shaved my head, gave me ochre clothes, and named me Devgiri without the formal ceremony that traditionally initiates one to the Order of Sannyas.*
>
> *"I lived and wandered with them, but did not appreciate their way of living, particularly the way they smoked opium and marijuana. I left the group to start my own journey traveling all over the country, visiting holy centers, and meeting sadhus, mahatmas (great souls), and saints in different parts of India as I moved towards the Himalayas. Though I had left the group, the name they had given continued to be part of me. Wherever I went, I was known as Devgiri.*

"Coming to the Himalayan kingdom of Tehri Garwal, I had the greatest fortune to meet the Raj Guru (the King's Guru), Swami Vijnanananda Saraswati Maharaj. He was a great sage from South India, a great scholar of all the four Vedas and of the scriptures of Sanatana Dharma (the eternal Teachings that transcend history and individual religion). He was an enlightened Master who taught Vedic knowledge to those who aspired to scriptural knowledge of Vedic literature. Seeing him, I knew that I had waited all these years only to come to the feet of this holy Master.

"Offering myself at the Master's feet, I prayed for his mercy, that he accept me as his disciple if he thought fit, and teach me the deep knowledge of the scriptures that leads to the realization of God. He accepted me and allowed me to be at his service while he taught me the Vedic knowledge. One day I told him, 'As I was not formally initiated into sannyas, I pray to you, please formally initiate me.' This was a very humble surrender to the feet of the Master. He was kind. He looked into me with deep, penetrating eyes, as if he saw through me, and then on an auspicious day he granted me sannyas deeksha initiation. He then named me Divyananda Saraswati, my formal sannyas name. Though I was formally named into the order of sannyas as Divyananda Saraswati, my old name had been with me for so long that it continued. People still called me Devgiri more often than my sannyas name."

Devgiri Maharaj often said that all names belong to God, and that he belonged to Saraswati Sampradya of the Dasnami sects propounded by Adi Shankara of 8th Century. When Gita Swami heard this from his Guru, his confusion about the name of his Gurudev was removed forever.

After the death of Swami Rama Tirth, the great Master, Swami Vijnanananda, who was the Raj Guru or the Guru to the King of Tehri, left the palace of the king and went back into unknown Himalayan regions. He relinquished the status of Raj Guru, royal preceptor for good. As a result, his disciple Devgiri Maharaj succeeded his place, but when the king offered him the status of Raj Guru, he dispassionately denied it. But continued to live in the Himalayan kingdom and due to his high scholastic attainment, became the Vedic teacher and taught all the eminent priests of the famous ancient temples of Kedarnath, Badrinath in the science of ritualistic worship of the Lord. The present Sankaracharya of Dwarka and Badrinath Maths, Swami Swarupananda Saraswati was student of Devgiri Maharaj in earlier days.

Devgiri Maharaj's kindness was renowned. He was a constant figure sitting at the gate of his hermitage so that he could personally feed all the wandering monks and others who would pass by.

Despite being in a man's body, everyone called him "Mother" because his love for all was so tender and motherly. As a mother takes care of her children and feeds them with love, so did he, all the time. When children would come to the ashram, he would ask them if they knew how to climb up the mango tree to pluck mangoes. If they were afraid and said, '*No*,' even at a very old age and ignoring the risks, he would climb the tree himself, pluck the ripe mangoes, and feed them. That was the extent of his love and generosity. Just as his own Gurudev had been, he was considered one of the greatest scholars of *Vedic* tradition.

This was the great sage who had come to the Varanasi Railway Station on his way to Ma Anandamayee's ashram to do the *Purnahuti*, the final oblation to the *Savitri Maha Yajna* ceremony.

One day, my Gurudev, Thakur Bhajan, reminisced about his initiation from Devgiri Maharaj. On the auspicious day, Ma arranged for the initiation ceremony in the Shiva temple in the ashram premises. Bhajan came to the temple and prostrated to the Master. The Master had Bhajan sit beside him. Just as he was about to whisper the *mantra* to Bhajan, the thought rose in Bhajan's mind that Ma Anandamayee had been present in the dream just behind the sage, standing and blessing the whole event, but now Ma was missing! Ma instantly entered the room, came to stand exactly where Bhajan had seen her in the dream, and said, "*You are being initiated by Shiva himself.*" Bhajan saw Shiva and Ma Shakti, side by side, in Devgiri Maharaj and Ma Anandamayee. At that moment the Master Devgiri Maharaj initiated Bhajan while he was in a state of trance. He then took Bhajan's head in his hands and placed it on the Shiva Lingam, hitting his forehead thrice, as if he was offering the child of Shiva to Shiva himself. He later initiated Bhajan's father.

THAKUR'S GURUDEV'S GURUDEV HIMALAYAN GRAND MASTER SWAMI VIJNANANANDA SARASWATI MAHARAJ

Thakur's face always lit up with the light of his divine spirit when he talked about his Guru for his love for his Guru was boundless. Whenever he would mention to me about his Guru or even at times during *satsang* when he talked about his Guru, his body spoke with such ecstasy. He told me that he himself was awed when the moment of holy ceremony of initiation arrived, because from that moment on he was seeing literally every minute detail of what he had seen in the dream vision of his *Mantra Deeksha* enacted in the earthly plane. It was as if the dream was the script and initiation ceremony was a pure dramatization!

I could realize when I heard this from my Gurudev Thakur that at the causal plane of existence it is all done, what we see in this earthly plane is only the manifestation of what is already scripted in the causal plane of every soul in the process of evolution for ultimate perfection and freedom.

Soon after the great *Savitri Maha Yajna* fire sacrifice ritual in the Varanasi Ananadamayee Ashram, Devgiri Maharaj left for Mirzapur. From there, he returned to his Uttarkashi ashram, where he left his mortal body.

In later years my Gurudev Thakur said to me,

"You are all so fortunate. You have been able to enjoy the physical presence of your Guru. You are able to serve him. I was not so fortunate. Soon after my initiation, Devgiri Maharaj told me, 'We will meet again;' but once he left Varanasi, he went back to the Himalayas and left his body. I could not see him again. I so wished and wanted to serve him. To me, he appeared as Shiva himself."

In the tradition of Himalayan Masters, Devgiri Maharaj left his mortal body with inimitable grace. As always, he went to the small Shiva temple that he had erected and named *Jnaneshwar Shiva* in his Uttarkashi ashram. All through his life, he had worshipped Shiva so deeply that he had become Shiva himself. He had a humble and tender gesture of worship of Lord Shiva. Putting his head on the Shiva Lingam, embracing it with both hands, he would lose himself in ecstasy. Sitting in meditation that day, too, he put his head on the Shiva Lingam. After he had been there for an unusually long time, the devotees came in. Finding him in prolonged, immobile embrace of the *Shiva Lingam Jnaneshwar*, they eventually reached out to his body, which then fell. He had left his body in a state of *samadhi*, a natural *Mahasamadhi*, by his own divine will. *Mahasamadhi,* the great *samadhi,* is the conscious, intentional exiting of the body by a master while in *samadhi*. Years after Devgiri Maharaj's *Mahasamadhi*, his disciple Gita Swami built a beautiful Shiva temple and moved the Shiva Lingam there. Adding *Atma*, the Spirit eternal of his own Gurudev who merged in it, he renamed it *Atma Jnaneshwar Shiva*.

During my recent visit in June 2016, I had the immense fortune of worshipping this living Shiva Lingam, *Atma Jnaneshwar*, in the Devgiri Ashram on the bank of the Ganges at Ujeli, Uttarkashi. It is a small temple, but the inner sanctum is filled with powerful vibrations of Shiva and Devgiri's statue. The Shiva Lingam is small and smeared with sandal paste and covered with bilwa leaves. I gathered some bilwa leaves from the adjacent garden and some flowers and there was the water from the Ganges with which I did my worship of Lord *Atma Jnaneshwar.* I chanted the hymns to Shiva and to our Gurus, offering flowers and leaves to please the Lord and shower his blessings to one and all. The granite statue of my Param Gurudev was so alive as I offered flowers and leaves at his holy feet. I could feel the presence of Thakur and Devgiri Maharaj. I had cherished in my heart for a long time to visit this holy place and offer my obeisance to the Master of my master and worship the Lingam worshipped by Devgiri Maharaj and in his *Mahasamadhi* at that place.

In the presence of this living Lingam, worshipped by my Param Gurudev, there are two living statues, one of Swami Devgiri Maharaj, and one of Gita Swami Maharaj. Sitting in meditation before the white granite marble statue, the form of my Param Gurudev came alive, smiling and blessing me. Touching the feet of the *murthy*, it was indeed the living idol of my Param Gurudev, the Living Shiva.

CHAPTER SEVEN

CALL FROM THE HIMALAYAS

Bhajan returned from Varanasi with his love for God reaching a new peak. Though he returned to his home in Calcutta after initiation, his heart was no longer there. The call of the Himalayas was too strong. He knew he could no longer stay. The time to leave for the mountains as a wandering mendicant had arrived.

One morning he woke up with the firm conviction that the time had come. He had to leave for the quietness of the Himalayas. He needed the company of the holy ones who had been in prayer and penance for centuries in those holy and spiritually vibrant mountains.

There may be many awe-inspiring mountains with snow-capped peaks in the world. But none have been inhabited as these have, from time immemorial, by so many yogis and renounced monks steeped in meditation. Therein lies the eternal mystery of the Himalayas. No other mountains can match their beauty, the height of their spiritual vibrations, or the intensity of their call to the journey beyond the physical to non-physical reality.

Bhajan told his parents, siblings, and all his kith and kin of his decision to leave. They had all seen his inner renunciation, his god-intoxication, the way he lived in and for the divine presence. They had known from his early childhood that he was never like others, that he lived only for God, that his life was dedicated from birth to love and devotion to the Beloved of his heart.

That did not mean his father and mother were ready for his decision now that it was at hand. They could not comprehend why he had to leave home and retire to caves in the mountains, throwing himself into a life of such uncertainty. Why couldn't God be sought where he was, in the midst of family and friends? After all, God is everywhere. However they tried to convince him, Bhajan remained unmoved. Taking a couple of pieces of clothing, one blanket, and one bowl, he left home.

Ma Priyabala, his mother, remembered the prophetic prediction of Bhairavi Ma, the ascetic mother who had come to their home when Bhajan was dying. She had given him life and health; but she had also cautioned, *"When the time ripens, do let him go. Don't stop him."*

Ma Priyabala finally surrendered, along with the rest of the family. In tears and gripped with loss, she watched her son leave home with almost nothing and walk farther and farther away down the street. She called to one of her other sons, pressed money into his hands for Bhajan, and told him to run, catch Bhajan and accompany him until he bought his train ticket. Wasting no time, his brother rushed off and caught up to Bhajan just as he was about to board a tramcar. Bhajan refused to take anything. Feeling his mother's deep love and concern, Bhajan did agree to his brother traveling with him to Howrah rail station. Asked where he wished to go, Bhajan replied, *"To Haridwar."* (Haridwar is the gateway to the Himalayas, where the mountains reach the plains. It is one of the ancient and holy pilgrim centers in India).

His brother ran ahead to the ticket counter, returned with a third-class ticket to Haridwar, and handed it to Bhajan. He tried again to give Bhajan some money for his immediate needs. Bhajan took the ticket but refused the money. *"I don't need any money. Reassure Mother that her son will never go unfed or hungry and will not meet with any dangers. I am now completely surrendered to the One who is the sole reality. I know He will take care of me, as I am His."*

Boarding the train from Calcutta, Bhajan took his seat in front of a middle-aged couple from Rajasthan who were also bound for Haridwar on pilgrimage. As the train pulled out of the station, he looked rather lost to them as he sat staring out of the window. They whispered to each other. Thinking the young man must be running away from home, they were deeply concerned about him.

As the journey continued, the man asked Bhajan, *"Where are you bound?"* Bhajan kept silent, still looking through the open windows, staring into the distant horizon where the land and the sky blend into each other. Gradually coming back to this world, he replied, *"I am going to the Himalayas. The Lord is calling me. I know by His grace I will see Him there."*

The voice of a mystic is often permeated with deep vibrations of love and silence, as it flows from a different world altogether. The mystic has been blessed to lift the veil and see the face of the Beloved. One who hears such a voice senses that world beyond the physical if he or she is attuned to that frequency. Most people are caught in this materialistic realm. They cannot see beyond the veil. That mystical essence permeated Bhajan's voice. The couple was captivated by both his words and the depth of his passion for the life of the unknowable that he was seeking.

As Gurudev Thakur later told me,

> *"Throughout the journey, they were both so loving toward me. They kept pestering me to eat all that they had with them and bought anything they thought I might like to have. We talked about God, about devotion, about the path that leads to God vision. I had only one blanket. Unhappy that I had no bed with me to spread on the wooden berth, they took out their own blanket and helped me spread it on my berth. Then they used my blanket to cover my body. At first, I resisted, but their love and affection won out. I surrendered to their generosity, feeling it was my Divine Mother taking care of me."*

In the early hours of that first dawn as they traveled, Bhajan awakened with his heart surging with joy. His dreams were finally taking shape. He had broken the chains that bound him to his family, his parents and siblings. The confines of his small home, with all the entanglements it involved, were behind him. He had always longed for a world without borders or boundaries, a world free from all fetters, where he could live with only God in his heart and in the lap of nature at its purest. To him, the Himalayas personified his dream of pristine nature. He was too excited, too delighted to be going to the Himalayas, to sleep. Finally, the chains of attachments were broken; he could live in his own freedom. Overtaken with inner joy, he started humming devotional chants. Soon, he was singing them with all his heart, pouring his soul into each song.

Drawn from their sleep by the bliss permeating Bhajan's indescribably melodious and soulful voice, the Rajastani couple was transported by the power of his devotion as he sang to God with all his heart.

To hear Bhajan singing was to be uplifted to that space where only the divine matters. Tears rolled down his cheeks. He was oblivious to those around him, to the time of day or place, when pouring his heart and devotion out to the Divine Mother. His co-passengers felt as if they were being bathed in the holy waters of Mother Ganges in those early hours of dawn.

Haridwar literally means "Gateway to Lord Hari's Abode." It sits at the foothills of the Himalayas of the Garwal region. The entire region has two major sections, Garwal and Kumawoon. The gateway to Kumawoon is Haldwani.

Reaching Haridwar station, all the passengers got down from the train and started bidding goodbye to the acquaintances with whom they shared the journey. When Bhajan got down with his small packet of belongings, the Rajasthani couple was in tears at leaving their son-like co-passenger. Without the painful attachment of *maya* (the illusion or appearance of the phenomenal world), Bhajan could only feel and express his deep gratitude to them for taking care of him like his own parents. *"God willing, we will meet again,"* he said as they parted.

Walking out of the station, Bhajan eagerly asked for directions to the bank of the Ganges, the ancient, sacred river that flows eastward from the Himalayas to the Indian Ocean. Bhajan had always lived in Calcutta, near the eastern end of the river, about 90 miles from Ganga Sagar, where Mother Ganges finally meets the ocean. Every year there is a huge festival there. Millions of pilgrims come from every corner of the country to take a dip in that holy confluence. Here in Haridwar, one of the most auspicious Hindu pilgrimage sites, he could bathe in the Mother Ganges where, after dancing her way down from the peaks of the Himalayas, she first touches the plains.

As the Ganges descends from the heights to the plains, the current is fast and includes a strong undercurrent. Devotees must be very cautious. Bhajan came to Har Ki Pawri, the *ghat* built where it is the safest for pilgrims to bathe. Chains were provided to hold onto while in the river. Unlike today, in the early 1950s, the waters at Haridwar were still pristine, as clean and clear as crystal.

Bathing in the Ganges with folded hands, Bhajan prayed to Divine Mother, to all the greatest sages and saints of the Himalayan regions and to his ancestors, asking for their blessings, that they inspire him as he walked the path of eternal light and left mundane reality and attachments behind.

Coming out of Mother Ganges, he placed the cloth that was wet on the branch of a tree and sat with only a loincloth around his waist to meditate. Suddenly a monkey came out of nowhere, took the cloth from the tree branch, and ran off to a higher branch of another tree, out of his reach. Though Bhajan's immediate impulse was to run and catch the monkey to get back his cloth, he heard the still, small voice of his conscience, '*If you are a sadhu, a monk, a wandering mendicant, why are you so attached to a piece of cloth that covers your body?*'

He thought to himself: Wasn't the One who gave that cloth through someone's hands the same one taking it away now through the hands of the monkey? Whatever the form, human or animal, the life principle is the same. He concluded that his instinct had revealed a lack of faith and trust in the divine. After all, he had come to this land to realize that the Beloved of his heart lives in all forms and in all names. '*Sarvabhut antaratman*', the One is in all, down to the finest atom.

He took out his small bag and the second cloth he had brought from home. Tearing what was now his only cloth in half, he used one half as a towel to rinse his body and the other half to barely cover his body.

Going to a nearby tree, Bhajan sat down again, closed his eyes and went within to do his *japa mantra sadhana,* and repetition of the *Guru Mantra*. After some time being lost in *japa*, his inner silence was suddenly broken by the sound of a woman who had approached him with a plate full of food, saying, *"I don't eat until I have fed a sadhu."* With all humility, he replied, *"Mother, I am neither a sadhu nor a sannyasin. I have just started to walk the path of total renunciation."* Having none of that, the woman adamantly persisted, *"I live here in this region and I have the eyes to see who is a true sadhu, so I know I have come to the right person. I will not take this food to anyone else, so you have to accept it."*

Realizing this, too, was the love of the Divine Mother being expressed, Bhajan extended his hands to respectfully receive the food from the woman. She waited like a loving mother, with joy and satisfaction, for Bhajan to finish the food.

The next morning, Bhajan left Haridwar and all of its pilgrims, heading toward Rishikesh, about 23 kilometers away, which in those days was inhabited more by *sannyasins* and monks than householders.

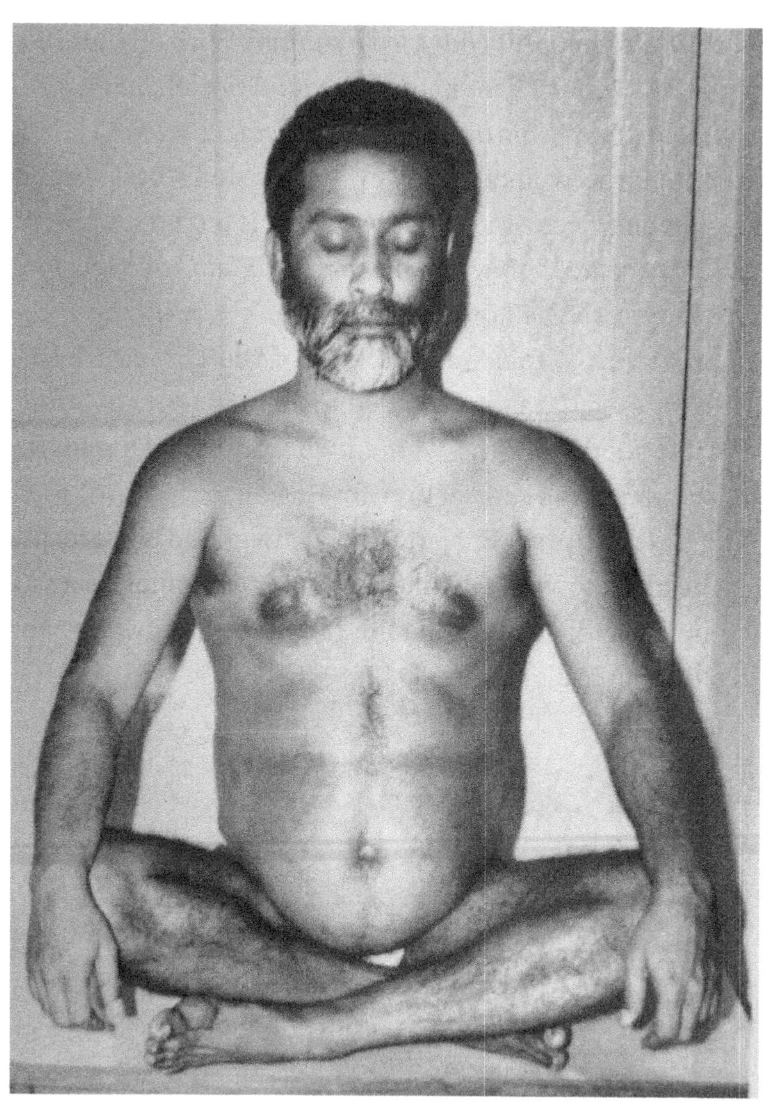

A RARE PICTURE OF THAKUR IN MEDITATION

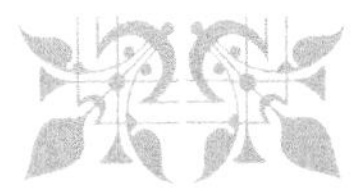

CHAPTER EIGHT

AUSTERE PENANCE IN THE HIMALAYAS

Bhajan's real life as an ascetic began on the walk from Haridwar to Rishikesh along with many other wandering mendicants. Unlike the external outfits of the other *sadhus*, Bhajan wore nothing but a simple white cloth and had only his blanket and mug in his hands. He did not look like the typical monk clad in saffron. He sang throughout the walk alongside the flowing Ganges.

In Rishikesh, Bhajan's goal was to find a place where he could totally give himself over to the life of the soul and the austerities that would help him rise above the body's needs. He needed a place where he could spend hours doing *japa*, reciting the *mantra* his Guru Devgiri Maharaj had given him.

As the scripture says, "*Japat siddhi, Japat siddhi, Japat siddir na samshayah*": the path of repetition of the Holy *Mantra* given at initiation by the *Sadguru* (true Guru) is the surest path to *siddhi* or enlightenment. *Na samshayah* means with no tint of doubt. Having left home with all its assured comforts and conveniences, Bhajan was beside himself with eagerness to dedicate his whole focus to *mantra-yoga* and meditation.

Achieving the ultimate state of *nirvana* or self-realization is always first motivated from within, by feeling the transitory state and superficiality of materialistic life. Until that dispassion comes, passion for the ultimate reality cannot make its way to the inner shrine of the heart of a seeker. After all, Truth can only be attained by truth and nothing less than truth. The Beloved can be beheld only through the eyes of a passionate lover!

When Bhajan reached Rishikesh, he met a senior *sadhu*, whom he felt might guide him to the next step. He asked, "*Where can I go to find a small space to live and do my austere practice of japa-yoga?*" The monk told him of a place in the mountains where many *sadhus* lived in small caves. Perhaps some benevolent donor had paid to build those small cottages for wandering mendicants to come and stay to do their *tapas* (genuine practice) for self-realization.

On the way there he met another *sadhu*. This one suspected that Bhajan was one of the many who come in a sudden urge to leave home and find God in the Himalayas, but who are incapable of withstanding the hardships and return to their comfortable homes after only a few days. With that doubt in his eyes, he questioned Bhajan,

> *"In the life of a practitioner of true yoga, on the path of the Spirit there is a lot of ecstasy and joy. But at the same time, it is most arduous, often painful, uncertain and trying. Are you sure you can withstand all the trials and tribulations of this painful path?"*

Bhajan did not say a word to defend or justify himself. He just smiled and went on. He finally found a very tiny cottage, just large enough for one person, which was sufficient to protect his body from the cold and rain. After all, he had to keep his body healthy since a healthy body is needed for any practice of divine contemplation.

Going to the nearest source to fetch water, he found other local *sadhus* who were very helpful and cooperative. The cottage felt like just the space that he had always longed for and dreamed of finding for his life of penance in the Himalayan mountains to realize his own Self. He spread his only blanket and lay down on the floor. After his long journey, his body was tired. He needed rest. Lying there, his mind went back to the past, its ups and downs, its turns and twists that led him here. He remembered his parents, his mother Priyabala's loving face. Then his mind stretched to the future, to all that lay ahead on the path of self-realization.

That is the spirit of a true seeker. The mind will have a tendency to live in the past, but the seeker has to move forward, leaving the past behind. As the *Vedas* say, "*Charaiveti!*" Move forward. Look forward. Keep moving until you reach your Beloved in the sanctum of your heart.

Meeting other *sadhus*, Bhajan learned about their daily routines. The *sadhus* got up at early dawn, bathed in Mother Ganges, and set out to the nearest village, sometimes to a distant village, to beg for food. Returning from the long trek to nearby villages for alms, the *sadhus* went to their own cottage to cook food for themselves. They focused on their practice for the rest of the day, keeping company with holy ones.

The next morning Bhajan's real life of a mendicant began. Waking early, he joined the band of other *sadhus* going to the Ganges, took a dip, and then walked for a long time with them to a remote, hilly village to beg for alms. The householders of these villages were religious people. They understood providing food for the *sadhus* of the Himalayas to be one of their duties, one that brought abundant blessings and grace to their own lives. They kept some rice and lentils aside to give to the monks. Bhajan reached the village and stood before the door of a hut. Following the example of the other *sadhus,* he begged with the customary, "*Narayana Hari.*" A woman with her face covered with her saree came to the door and handed him some rice, lentils, and salt that were sufficient for the day.

To cook the food, however, he would need a fire. He asked the woman for a matchbox with a few matchsticks. She directed him to a nearby shop and told him to ask there. Bhajan moved on to the shopkeeper and begged for a few matchsticks. The shopkeeper returned with the matches and a few beedies, (country cigarettes, rolled by hand). Explaining to the shopkeeper that he did not smoke, Bhajan returned the beedies to the shopkeeper.

With the day's alms collected, he returned to his cottage, collected some wood from the forest, lit the fire, and cooked his meal. Without any plates, he found a leaf big enough to use as a plate. Filled with joy and gratitude for this new life of renunciation, he ate his first meal in the true spirit of *sadhu* life.

Being in the mountains near the sacred river of Ma Ganges and the company of the *sadhus* had created a wonderful feeling in his heart. He sat for meditation. His Guru Devgiri Maharaj had instructed him to do the *japa* of the *Guru Mantra* as much as possible. Here he could practice and translate his Guru's instruction into reality. He practiced his *japa* for hours, until his heart was brimming with ecstasy. As the night deepened, so did his meditation, until he was startled by roaring animals and was brought abruptly back to physical reality. Realizing the cottage hardly had a door worthy of the name and that any wild animal could crash in, he felt vulnerable, unprotected, and gripped with fear. Then he heard an inner voice, "*Why fear? I am here! You have to give up your sense of fear and all negative emotions.*"

He went outside and sat for a while. Coming inside the cottage, he spread his blanket out on the floor. It was late night, time for a little rest before beginning fresh the next day. He lay down. His talks with other *sadhus* came floating into his mind, as he recalled, "*In this path you have to be following the way of the birds. They don't save; they live for the day. Never hoard.*"

In the path of the Spirit, *Shraddha* (trust in the words of the Master) and *Nistha* (regularity and commitment of practice) are of paramount importance. The seeker is put to a continual test to have a steadfast devotion and single pointed commitment to Truth. It is the trust and faith in Guru and one's own self that takes the practitioner forward in the midst of endless obstacles and difficulties. Bhajan's mind was calm, his devotion to Guru was pure and his commitment to a life of penance was set. So, there was no wavering of his mind about his path and the goal of God realization. When the heart is open to the universal grace, it descends. After all, just as the devotee yearns for divine union so also the Lord longs to manifest His infinite grace and love to His devotee.

Early the next morning and every morning thereafter, he got up, joined the group of *sadhus* going for alms, returned, cooked, ate, then meditated and did his *Guru Mantra japa* late into the night. In the steady rhythm of that routine, his inner world deepened with each passing day. He was becoming absorbed in the richness of the path of silence.

Days passed, one morning, after receiving an abundance of rice and lentils, Bhajan thought, *"This is good. If one day I do not feel like going out for alms, I can cook what is left."* Suddenly, he heard a heavy voice warning him, *"Here too, you are saving for tomorrow?"* It was the voice of Baba Lokenath, who always followed him wherever he was, guiding him as the Guru, on the path to the ultimate realization. Bhajan threw the excess into Mother Ganges and returned to his cottage with the lesson sitting in his mind and heart. This is a path where the seeker should not save for tomorrow. There is no tomorrow. There is only today. Tomorrow is also today. Without saving, there is a possibility for total surrender. If

He feeds me, I eat; if not, I don't. I will live each day by the wish of the Master.

The seeker of Truth goes through many tests to hone and strengthen his or her resolve to pursue Truth and nothing less than Truth. On yet another day, divine grace descends!

Years later, Bhajan told his disciples and devotees at the ashram another story of his time in the Himalayas. One day after returning from begging for food, he returned to his cottage and finished cooking. He then went to fetch some drinking water. As he returned with water, he found a dog eating the food that he had left on a leaf plate. The rice was steaming hot. Since dogs cannot normally eat such hot food, he was awed to see the dog eating the hot food without any discomfort or pain. Bhajan realized that this was no ordinary dog. He folded his hands and prayed to the Lord, "*Thy will be done.*" The dog left after eating his fill.

Bhajan concluded that it must be the wish of the Lord that he fast that day. He went inside the cottage, pulled his blanket out and lay down for a while, then got up to do his *mantra japa* and meditation.

Suddenly there was a knocking at his cottage door, followed by a stranger's voice asking, "*Is there anyone inside?*" Bhajan replied, "*Yes, I am here.*" The voice said, "*Today is the birth anniversary of Maharaja of Burdwan estate. I have come to give food and clothes to all the sadhus.*" He handed Bhajan freshly cooked food and a new cloth.

Bhajan had had no complaint at the thought of needing to fast. By this time, he saw even the most minor happening in daily life as a manifestation of divine will, the same will that runs the myriad universes. His heart swelled with love at the Lord's compassion in sending food, knowing that Bhajan would go without, since *sadhus* did not cook twice on the same day. His only cloth was by then torn in many places. With no money of his own and never even touching money, he had no means to replace the cloth. He was overwhelmed with gratitude for such tender and personal divine attendance to his needs.

This episode highlights how true surrender and devotion work. When directed to the all-compassionate Master, they are met with constant miracles. Most people in the world, driven by the dictates of the illusioned mind, believe that by working hard and earning money, they take care of themselves. But Bhajan surrendered to the divine will, accepting that his only food had been eaten by a dog. And even though he had been ready to go without, his Divine Mother was not ready for that. She sent someone to the doorstep of Her beloved child not only with food, but also with a much-needed new cloth.

The seeker here was not even praying for food or clothing. The Mother was granting a deeper prayer to one who is surrendered to Her. Her responsibility is to provide food or anything else that is needed for one who is totally dependent on the divine. This dependence of surrender is the deepest transformation that has to happen in this path. When the individual self is surrendered at the altar of the divine will, then nothing remains as individual will or effort for anything. It is not just an intellectual understanding about the glory of surrender. An aspirant of the path of Truth has to prove that his or her faith in the benevolence of the Lord is never shaken when he or she is thrown into situations which pose a difficult challenge.

In spiritual practice, one aligns oneself with the universal will and tries to see its unseen hand in every little thing that happens, however unpredictable, in this transitory world. The goal of spiritual practice is to awaken to the reality of the higher world both within and without, and to realize that true security and love can come only from the One who is Love Herself.

• • •

Bhajan brings us a model of a true saint in the making. He reveals the mindset needed in a true devotee, a true seeker. There are many who renounce the world and run off to the Himalayas to become a *sadhu* or wandering mendicant after experiencing a great loss or failure. They are driven by ego, running from one way of life to another as an escape rather than from a deep yearning for the divine light, for God vision. Ego is very deceptive. Many of the seekers escape to a life of monastery or mountains and put the garb of a renunciate monk and get trapped by unconscious surrender to their subconscious programs of repressed desires. Very few who renounce the worldly life and go into seclusion are driven by an intense passion to experience the truth beyond all the superficialities of life. They are the ones who overcome the urges of the physical body through their constant contemplation of the higher light and the joy of inner silence attained through hours of meditation.

A true seeker has single pointed devotion towards the path and the goal. The true seeker never compromises with the truth. Truth has only one price and that is Truth.

Not many people can manage to stay on this arduous path for long. The hardships are too great, too exacting. They return to the security and self-effort of the material world. For those who are ready, who come due to the *karma* of previous births, their *sadhana* and practice will sustain them through the difficulties and trials of the path. They never give up. They know that the path demands selflessness. This path demands total self-effacement, self-giving. It is a path of sacrifice. It is not a path of attainment and acquiring gifts. They have nothing to gain, nothing to lose. They are on the path to reach the point where ultimate reality reveals itself in the depth of one's own consciousness.

Over a short time, Bhajan gradually reached that dimension of utter surrender to the Mother Divine.

The most difficult part of the journey is to surrender the ego at the altar of the divine, to the Guru, to God. Bhajan came to the world prepared for that leap of consciousness. It happened naturally, spontaneously. He went through the process of inner transformation quickly because his soul had traveled through all of these paths in previous incarnations. He came to this world as a prepared soul, ready for ultimate realization. The fact remains, however, even when a soul comes prepared for the ultimate realization, it must pass through every stage, all the phases, to ripen. Here in the Himalayas, on the bank of the Holy Ganges, Bhajan moved through all those layers and levels quite naturally, traversing the most arduous, diverse streams of practices in the shortest possible time.

What is critical is pure devotional surrender and deep commitment to daily, consistent practice without setting the mind on any results. As Lord Krishna says in *Bhagavad Gita*, "*You have the right to the action, but not to the results thereof.*" A true seeker of God follows this instruction, doing all the penance and practices according to the instruction of the Master or Guru without clinging to any result along the way.

As the days rolled by in Bhajan's isolated little nest in the mountains, he went deeper and deeper in the realms of meditative silence. Going once a day to beg for food, he came back, cooked it, offered it to his Beloved before eating it. Other than this little chore of maintaining his physical body, he spent all day and night meditating, remaining in a state of deep inner communion, taking only a few hours of sleep. Even his nights were spent in a state of self-absorption, in *samadhi*, blissful union with the divine.

• • •

One day Bhajan returned with his alms of rice, lentils and vegetables to find his matchbox empty when he was getting ready to cook. He had forgotten to ask for more, which the shopkeeper readily gave whenever he needed them. The wood and everything else were ready. Right then a young girl appeared at the doors of his small hut with a matchbox in hand. She smiled. There was something intensely divine in her smile. Her dark complexion was so full of light that she glowed. This was not an earthly mortal. "*Take this,*" she said, tossing the matchbox to Bhajan. Bhajan picked it up and lit the fire. He then started talking to her as she stood at the doorway of the cottage. Bhajan asked her where she lived, what her name was, who her parents were, etc. She smiled, avoiding all of his questions and continued talking to him. Suddenly one of the bamboo sticks in the fire burst loudly. Turning instinctively toward the fire, Bhajan then turned back to the doorway. She was no longer there! He could only hear the sound of laughter off in the distance that came floating as if it was from another world.

Bhajan realized that the girl was none other than the Divine Mother Kali, his *Ishta* (the chosen form of God for a disciple), whom he saw as his Beloved Mother. In deep ecstasy, he cried out, *"Oh my Mother, Mother!"* and offered his obeisance to the Mother of the Universe, who made sure that Her blessed child had his evening meal. In a state of rapture, he sang to the Mother and merged into *Bhav-Samadhi*, the deepest meditative absorption in the Mother.

This drew Bhajan closer than ever to his Beloved Mother. From then on, he spent most of his time drowned in deep meditative silence. Bhajan was coming closer to the ultimate realization of the Self in the all-pervasive oneness of Self-realization.

When he personally told me about this episode of the Divine Mother's appearance as a teenage girl, he said, "*When you give your heart to the divine, in whatever form, the divine comes to you. But you have to be alert all the time, for She/He can come to you in any form. She is formless, but She assumes form for Her devotees.*"

CHAPTER NINE

DIVINE ROMANCE WITH KRISHNA

After Bhajan had spent all that night in deep absorption and divine intoxication, he slowly came out of deep meditation in the early hours of dawn to find the small cottage suddenly flooded with luminous effulgence. A heavy, commanding voice spoke out, *"Go to Vrindavan!"* The divine voice resonated and gradually faded away. The same voice that had commanded him to go to the Himalayas was now telling him to move on to the next stage of his *sadhana*.

Coming out of the cottage, looking for the source of the sound, he saw none, though he felt the divine presence of the Himalayan Master, Baba Lokenath. His days of *sadhana* in the Rishikesh Mountains were over. Following the instruction, he left immediately for the holy pilgrim center of Vrindavan, the playground of Lord Krishna in His earthly incarnation.

Bhajan had no belongings when he came to this place. Now he had no belongings other than the old torn blanket and a small wooden bowl as he set out to leave. He did not say anything to the other *sadhus*. He simply started walking down the mountains toward Haridwar, the foothill of the Himalayas where the Ganges reaches the plains. Reaching Haridwar, he took a prayerful dip in the holy Ganges, and sat in a quiet place along her bank to meditate, drowning in deep absorption. He had forgotten to go begging for food for the day. Coming out of his meditative state, though, a woman was there, waiting for him to finish meditating. With love and deep respect, she invited Bhajan to her home for food. Feeling it was the Divine Mother's will, Bhajan accepted her invitation to come to her home, but he explained that he needed to leave for Vrindavan immediately afterward.

Her home was close to the Ganges. It had been a long time since he had food with ghee (clarified butter), curd, and rice and lentils. After eating, he blessed the home and family and moved on to the railway station.

Having no money, he could not buy a ticket, but he had to go to Mathura to get to Vrindavan. According to the directions, he could go via Delhi. So, he took a train to Mathura via Delhi.

The journey began quietly. When the train reached Modinagar, however, a ticket examiner came to his compartment and demanded that Bhajan show his ticket. Bhajan explained that he had no money and, therefore, no ticket, but that he had to go to Mathura.

In his austere physical state and long hair, Bhajan was obviously a wandering mendicant. Nevertheless, the examiner insisted on his ticket and became extremely agitated, *"If you do not have money and a ticket, why did you get on the train?"* In a fit of rage, the ticket examiner insisted that Bhajan must get off the moving train. In complete humility, Bhajan folded his hands and pleaded that he would get down from the train if that were what the examiner wished, but the train needed to stop or come to a station. The examiner threatened to throw Bhajan off the train himself. Feeling the examiner was none other than the Lord himself and that he must obey, Bhajan opened the door of the train and was preparing to jump, regardless of the danger, when the examiner suddenly pulled him back inside.

"Who else is with you?" the ticket examiner asked.

"It is just me and my God," Bhajan answered with calm certainty.

"Does your God look like a tall thin man with matted hair and a long beard? He chastised me and wants me to take you wherever you wish to go?" the ticket examiner asked.

Bhajan broke into tears, realizing that the tall thin man with matted hair was none other than the incarnation of Lord Shiva himself, Sri Sri Baba Lokenath Brahmachari. (The biography of this Himalayan Master, *The Incredible Life of a Himalayan Yogi, The Times, Teachings and Life of Living Shiva Baba Lokenath Brahmachari*, is available at Amazon.com/Amazon.in.)

The ticket examiner was in a state of awe that he had had a vision of the great sage of the Himalayas. He could not believe his eyes and ears when he saw this human form, with unimaginable power in his non-blinking eyes and penetrating gaze. Baba Lokenath's presence had overwhelmed him as the sage appeared at the doorway of the train compartment.

The ticket examiner had encountered many non-paying, wandering *sadhus* on the train over the years, but he had never before experienced such a life-altering vision. No other *sadhu* had ever followed his command literally by attempting to jump from the moving train. This was a *sadhu* whose God literally followed and protected him. He had heard all of his life that God protects His devotees, that God takes care of all obstacles and pains for one who totally trusts and places all faith in Him. This *sadhu* had come to his train, lifted his ever-doubtful mind, and opened the doors of his heart to the world of the spirit.

At the next station, the examiner rushed from the train to a fruit vendor to quickly buy some fresh fruit. After getting back on the train, he brought the fruit and offered it to Bhajan with devotion and love.

When the train finally reached Mathura, the ticket examiner personally escorted Bhajan out of the compartment and reverently touched his feet. Because of this young man, he had had his first glimpse of a Himalayan ascended master. Earthly mortals hardly ever see such a master! Feeling a deep connection to this young *sadhu*, he took money from his pocket and tried to press it into Bhajan's hands. Bhajan refused it, asking, *"Why should I need money when all that is needed in my life is continually being taken care by the Divine Lord?"* Touched by Bhajan's detachment from everything worldly and by how utterly his heart was set only on the divine, the examiner made one last request, *"Can I have an address for you in Calcutta so that when you finally return there, I can find you some day?"*

Bhajan gave his sister's address. Before returning to the train, the ticket examiner called a cab and paid the fare to Vrindavan, instructing the driver to drop Bhajan wherever he wished to go.

After I joined his ashram as a monk, Thakur told me, *"This ticket examiner later came in search of me. He was my first initiated disciple."* Inscrutable are the ways of the divine! The man who was intent on throwing Bhajan out of a moving train ultimately took shelter under Bhajan to guide the life of his spirit.

The taxi ran through the dusty, uneven road towards Vrindavan. The driver asked him, *"Where do you want me to drop you?"* Knowing nothing of the city, Bhajan replied, *"You can leave me wherever there is a marketplace where there are people. I will find my way."*

As the taxi moved along, many horse and cattle carts were passing as well. Suddenly, out of nowhere, a young boy of around ten or twelve appeared, running alongside the taxi. When he came closer to the open window of the car, Bhajan's attention was drawn to the boy's charming face and eyes. This was no ordinary human. He had an otherworldly charisma and obviously belonged to the world of light. At the window, the boy looked into Bhajan's eyes and said with a naughty smile, *"Come to Banke Bihari Temple."* (Banke Bihari is one of the names of Lord Krishna and one of the temples dedicated to Lord Krishna in Vrindavan is known as Banke Bihari Temple. This temple is the most popular among Krishna devotees who visit Vrindavan.) The boy slowed down and then suddenly disappeared into thin air before Bhajan's eyes! Bhajan intuitively felt that this boy was no other than the playful Krishna.

The driver asked, *"How far do you want me to take you?"* Realizing that the driver could not hear the celestial boy, Bhajan told him, *"Take me to Banke Bihari Temple."*

Vrindavan is the land of the divine play of Lord Krishna, the human manifestation of ultimate divinity. Located in North India, close to Delhi, it is the holiest of the holy pilgrim centers in India. Sri Chaitanya Mahprabhu (1486-1534), a Vaishnava saint and founder of Gaudiya Vaishnava Sampradaya, identified each holy center associated with the divine play of Krishna and Radha, his consort, in Vrindavan during their lifetimes more than 5000 years ago. His work restored the lost glory of this sacred place, which is now the heart center of the *bhakti* movement.

Bhajan was being sent to Vrindavan after his deep *sadhana* in the Himalayas to experience the immensity of the divine intoxication of the supreme path of *bhakti* (devotional worship). Only those who are pure at heart and who are totally surrendered to Krishna and Radha can attain to this state of maddening love for Krishna. Great Vaishnava saints followed this path of unconditional surrender and love and reached a state of ultimate union with the divine. Those who tread this path of *bhakti* see Krishna or Radha in every manifestation of the creations.

The taxi approached the temple on a side lane and the driver bid farewell as Bhajan got down. Bhajan then moved through the road asking passersby about the location of Banke Bihari Temple. It was evening. The *aarati* (the ritual offering of a lighted lamp to a deity) to the Lord Bihari was over. Devotees had all left and the temple premises looked empty. The main doors of the temple were closed.

Bhajan found a small place to spend the night under the steps to the temple. He spread half of his blanket out and covered his body with the other half. It had been a long, eventful day. He was tired and fell asleep in just a few moments.

As always, he woke up in the early hours before dawn. He did not move from under the steps, for the sun had yet to rise and light the premises of the darkened temple. He sat there meditating. After a short while, he heard someone on the stairs approaching where he was hidden, who then inquired, *"Is anyone there?"*

Bhajan replied in Hindi, *"Yes I am here."*

"Come out," the stranger coaxed in a loving tone. Bhajan crawled out of his space under the stairs.

"From where are you coming?" the stranger asked.

"From Rishikesh," replied Bhajan.

The stranger introduced himself. He was the chief priest of the Banke Bihari Temple. With a voice filled with humility he said to Bhajan, *"Come along with me."* Lord Krishna had appeared to him in a vivid dream and instructed him to immediately go find Bhajan from under the stairs, put him in a proper room, and take care of him.

The priest led Bhajan inside to one side of the temple where there were a series of rooms. Showing Bhajan to one, he said, *"I give you this room. Now you can stay here. The minimal facilities are all available. During the day, you can take food when it is served free for the sadhus right outside the temple."*

Bhajan went into the temple. Banke Bihari Temple is unique in all of India. Here, the deity of Krishna can be seen only in glimpses. The priests pull the curtain before the doorway to the main shrine back and forth, guarding devotees from continually seeing the mesmerizing form of the deity.

As Bhajan stood there with other devotees, catching a glimpse of the Lord, the stone image came alive and smiled at him. His whole being was flooded with unspeakable joy and tears rolled down his cheeks. Every cell of his body was singing the name of Krishna.

Returning to his room, Bhajan lay on the ground face down, prostrating to the Lord, and remained in a state of surrendered rapture. Someone eventually came to remind him that he should go to the place beside the temple gate where free food was being served for the *sadhus*. Bhajan went to stand in the queue with his small bowl. Feeling no need for food, his only craving was for more time at the feet of the Lord, for pure, devotional surrender and contemplation of the Divine Name. He returned to his room, where he drank a little water, then spent the rest of the day taking the Holy Name of the Lord, doing *japa*, and meditating. Being on the same holy ground as the temple of the Lord intensified the natural, deep connection he felt. Hadn't the Lord called him to stay close? Wasn't the Lord taking care of him?

He did not go for food that night either, since he only took one meal and fasted for the rest of the day and night.

THE MOST ATTRACTIVE IDOL OF BANKE BIHARI (LORD KRISHNA)

The next morning, the chief priest appeared at his door in the early morning. The priest had had a vision of Banke Bihari, who had come in a dream, instructing him to provide Bhajan with the food that had been offered to the Lord in the temple each day. Fifty-six courses of very special food, called *bhog* (*Chappanbhog*), are offered to Bihari every day. The priest told Bhajan that, at the instruction of Banke Bihari, Bhajan henceforth would never have to beg for food, or go to the places where free food was served to all *sadhus*. Bhajan would be given the same food that the Lord took as *Prasad*.

Bhajan smiled. When the priest asked why, Bhajan said, "*I am smiling at the inscrutable ways of the Lord! How He takes care of His devotee who totally depends upon His divine grace.*" From the moment he came to Bihari's temple, Bhajan had been showered with grace and loving care. He no longer had to go out. He could focus all of his energy and attention to his practice and be utterly absorbed in his Beloved. The Lord's *Prasad* would be served to him in his own living space! How could he not smile at his Beloved's tender care?

Years later, reminiscing with me one-on-one about his days in Vrindavan's Banke Bihari Temple and his austere practices there, Thakur said, "*During the days I spent in the Banke Bihari Temple, I did sadhana of Gopi and Radha bhav. This sadhana in its truest sense is very difficult, for even males have to deeply feel like a woman in love with the Lord.*"

Bhav is a profoundly emotional state of absorption, of immersion in the divine. In the highest state of *bhakti sadhana,* one of the ways to connect to the Lord is *kanta-bhav*, to become immersed in identifying with the Lord as Beloved of the heart and husband. *Purusha,* the immutable Cosmic Spirit or Universal Principle, the One Without the Second, is seen as male, while all that is manifest and changing is the female aspect or *Prakriti*. Krishna alone is *Purusha*. Other than Lord

Krishna, all are in essence part of *Prakriti*, the female aspect of cosmic manifestation. In *Radha-bhav* or *Gopi-bhav*, the devotee realizes that there is only one *Purusha*, Lord Krishna, a male. Absorbed deeply in the love of Krishna, even males feel like a woman in love with a man and come to feel themselves to be Radha or a *gopi*. My Gurudev told me that he had even undergone a physical transformation during this period of *sadhana*.

With our analytical mindset, it is difficult to comprehend what Thakur is sharing with us. Here the concept is more like Shiva and Shakti, where you see Shiva as a male and Shakti as female. These are two aspects of the infinite energy related to manifestation. Try to understand Shiva as the male is Pure Consciousness and Pure Witness and is in a state of *Samadhi* or is unmanifest. Whereas, Shakti the Mother creates infinite creations, Shiva (Pure Consciousness) does not create. But Shakti cannot create without the power from Shiva. (As with a man and woman, if the male does not give the seed, a female cannot have a child. She is the one in whom the whole process of fertilization of the seed (unmanifest but with pure potential) takes place. Thus comes the birthing process. So, for those who are Shaivaite or Shiva followers, Shiva is male, and Parvathi or Shakti is the female aspect of Infinite Reality. So also, those who are Vaishnavites, for followers of Lord Vishnu or Krishna, Krishna is the only male and Radha, the *gopis*, and the rest of creation are all the female aspect.

Gopis were the simplest cowherd women of Vrindavan. They loved Krishna as their own husband. The love the *gopis* had for Krishna had nothing to do with physical pleasures or lust. Krishna was an adolescent boy at the time of His Vrindavan *lila* (divine play). Theirs was the purest, sacred love. It was "Love for Love's sake." *Gopis* worked with their hands, but their heart was ever absorbed in Krishna consciousness. They had no other thoughts, no attraction to other males. Krishna had stolen their hearts permanently. They breathed every breath in remembrance of Krishna. Theirs was spontaneous remembrance, a state of natural, spontaneous *samadhi*, conscious union with their Beloved.

As Bhajan's prolonged period of ecstatic union with Lord Krishna continued, the priests took care of his body, whether he was in his room or in the temple having the *darshan* of Banke Bihari. Bhajan was oblivious to the physical senses. He would lie there for hours on end. When he came out of this state, the priests would feed him some *prasad*, but the call from the inner world was so deep that he did not move even then. Most often the milk or any liquid food that was put in his mouth by the priests would fall away from his mouth, as he would have no physical sensation other than being in deep *samadhi*.

Thakur talked little about this time and *sadhana* other than to speak of the sublime ecstasy of being a *gopi* and experiencing the ultimate elixir of divine love.

BANKE BARI TEMPLE VRINDANVAN

One morning in the early hours of dawn, as he was sitting quietly singing to the glory of the Lord and His all-enveloping love, he heard that familiar heavy voice of Baba Lokenath again:

> *"Go back to the Himalayas. Keep this divine intoxication in your heart. Now you have to touch the highest peak of yoga to be a siddha yogi. You also have to do tantra sadhana so that you taste the same divine principle through all paths. You have to attain Nirvikalpa Samadhi."*

Nirvikalpa Samadhi is the highest state of *samadhi*, where the faintest trace of individuality, separate existence, is also effaced. It is a state where the seeker is merged totally into the sought. The spark merges into the fire to become the fire. The drop merges into the ocean to become the ocean. The seeker goes beyond all dualism to the ultimate state of non-dual unity consciousness. This is the ultimate state, which Baba Lokenath, Bhajan's eternal guide, wanted him to reach by traversing every path of Yoga to the state beyond all definitions. Bhajan was now directed to move to Rishikesh, to live in the mountains again to continue the journey to the Beyond.

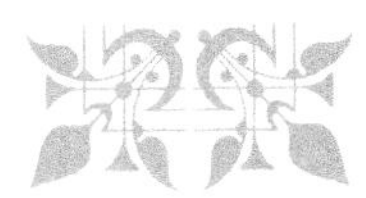

CHAPTER TEN

RETURN TO THE HIMALAYAS

Through the months of intense devotion to Lord Krishna, Bhajan had entered that state of divine love that surpasses all physicality. This path in yogic *sadhana* is called *prema-bhakti*, (love and devotion) or *raga-anuraga* (intense absorption in one's beloved) *bhakti*. *Prem* is love. This love is not the love that we all understand. It is love of the spiritual world, possible only for those who have transcended beyond egocentric infatuation and lust; beyond the polarity of love-hate, attraction-aversion, and all dualism arising from the illusive state of mind in ignorance. Bhajan's *sadhana* at the Banke Bihari temple with the playful Lord was pure, beyond human understanding.

Even yogis of ultimate perfection rarely qualify for this *raga-anuraga-bhakti*. It demands the complete annihilation of all physical identification and the experience of loving in its purest form. Being mostly in the state of highest *bhav-samadhi* (ecstatic consciousness) and having merged into Krishna, every cell of Bhajan's body had transformed into purest love and had been divinized in its essence. Descending to the plane of physical consciousness, the whole universe became an eternal, living manifestation of that One consciousness. His inner and outer dissolved into the life of that love flowing through him as naturally as his own breath.

This transformation happened at the deepest ground of quantum reality. Continual thoughts and rapturous love for the Lord gradually transformed every molecule of the atomic structure of his gross physical body. Every cell is holographic in nature. With the intensity of the energy of his or her cosmic love, a yogi can transmute the molecular or atomic structure of a gross particle. Then it vibrates at the macro level of existence. Bhajan's transformation during his *sadhana* as a female (though he was a male) was again not to be misunderstood as something of a male-female love. We see him as a lover offering himself utterly to the Beloved, akin to Rumi or the Sufi mystics who were consumed in mystic love. Here, female is the symbolic representation of the feminine aspect of the manifested cosmos, not an individual in love with another individual of the opposite sex.

Bhajan had to go beyond sex, gender, and all that separated him from ultimate divinity. His *samadhi sadhana* of divine love transmuted his individuality so completely that he literally became the universal feminine in cosmic union with Existence. He became the personally embodied form of the impersonal Self. The impersonal Self became personalized for the purposes of the divine play of Lord Krishna.

Bhajan realized love beyond human comprehension. Who can understand the love that Radha or the gopis of Vrindavan had for Krishna unless one was transformed into being a gopi or Radha? By becoming a gopi, by total identification with Radha (the divine consort of Lord Krishna), Bhajan's love of Krishna became Love itself. No longer was there any need for him to love anything or anyone. He *was* love.

The Essence of Love

Love is the pure energy holding everything in the universe together. Every atom, every cell, everything in the universe is enveloped with its purest essence, its sublime energy. It is love energy that sustains the creative process. It is love that unites all apparent fragmentation into a cohesive unity that maintains harmony and peace. All efforts of humanity find their ultimate fulfillment in love. At the societal level, love brings about a sense of security that assures self-preservation. When we are loved, we feel secure at the physical and emotional level.

When we love animals and plants, they flourish and grow. Experiments have proved that everything in the universe responds at a higher vibratory level when exposed to even the sound or written form of the word 'love'. Love is the language of nature, of the universe, of the Divine. In the absence of love energy, everything gets corrupted into disharmony and discord and is ultimately destroyed if love is not recovered. At the physical level, it helps in the very process of self-preservation and sustenance of an individual, a family, or society at large.

When love is directed towards the light of our soul, our soul-consciousness is preserved. The seeker experiences a sense of security not just at a gross physical level, but also at the quantum level of consciousness. Security reaches the point where an individual goes beyond the fear of death and annihilation to a state of deathless immortality. It is love that dispels the darkness of the fear of death and destruction by giving the intuitive experience of soul consciousness, which is deathless. The great saints and sages rise above the societal need of love for self-preservation at gross physical level. They go through the arduous spiritual journey to transcend all limitations of the physical to enter that boundless space of love that pervades and preserves both individual and universal existence. That is the reason all disciplines of Yoga philosophy culminate in unity, in integral synthesis, in the ultimate symphony of Love divine.

The question then arises: Is 'love' a verb or a noun? Is love something doable? Is it a subjective abstraction or a pure experience? We have always understood that we need to love others; we need to show our love; we need to express our love. All of this has gone into our individual and collective psyche: that love is something that we need to do. If we see the harsh reality of the history of humankind and the present state of the human mind, love has remained more at the physical level, as something that can be demanded and controlled, even as something to be owned. All frictions, all falling out of love, are due to fallacies of perception. Love is a soul reality that has been distorted by perception and reduced to the physical level.

Love is the essential state of our unified being. All sense of separation is created by the false perceptions inherent in our dualistic view of life. We are attracted to things that we love. We want to possess what we love. But can we ever get love by force? What science tears apart by force, splitting and dividing to explore reality, is that reality? What is lost in the process?

What is the difference between a scientist and a mystic lover? Both want to know the secrets of the Universe. Both want to unveil the mask that covers the face of reality. A scientist splits and divides to reach an answer, while the mystic as lover surrenders the false sense of ego that separates the lover from the loved. Through intense love, the mystic reaches the point where reality stands unveiled, in its true nature. The scientist forces nature. The mystic surrenders and merges into nature, allowing nature to reveal its secret out of love. This is pure love, our innermost true nature. When our false identity with physicality drops, our spiritual beingness manifests the magnificence of love that is transcendental, eternal and abiding.

Love in its essence is never physical, though at the gross level it is perceived in this manner. As humans evolve through love of the physical world, which is essentially rooted in attachment, we gradually experience its limitations and pain. Then the search outside for love turns inward. Through continual contemplation of the Beloved and through meditation on Light, the mind is purified. Pure mind is identical to our soul, our spirit. Love that begins as an external search is then internalized as an experience of the innermost state of soul consciousness. Love changes from verb to noun. No effort is needed any more. It is as spontaneous as fragrance to a fresh, blossoming flower. The eternal lovers, the mystics and saints of every faith tradition of the world, have always said that Love is God. Only in a godly state of soul consciousness can we experience the grandeur of Pure Love that Bhajan experienced.

• • •

Perhaps Baba Lokenath wanted Bhajan to leave the mountain caves and austerities and go to Vrindavan because he knew Bhajan had the *samskaras* (inherent potentiality) of the ultimate *bhakti*. Few on the path of yoga qualify for that. Bhajan not only qualified for this *bhakti-sadhana*, he excelled at it. He reached the highest peak of *prema-bhakti* in the shortest possible time.

Absorbed in *raga-anuraga bhakti*, the ultimate self-giving in divine love with Lord Krishna, Bhajan was directed to leave Vrindavan and go back to Himalayas to reach the final milestone and ultimate flowering. He went to the chief priest and other priests who had taken care of his body when he was immersed in *samadhi*. They had all provided him food and shelter. They provided him with the care of a loving mother during these months of deepest absorption in spiritual union with Krishna, the Supreme Lord. He told the priests that by divine direction he was now returning to the Himalayas. The priests were pained to see him leave, as they had witnessed many of the divine manifestations of a true saint and pure devotee of Krishna (Banke Bihari). They too had the unique privilege of having dreams and receiving instructions from Banke Bihari (Krishna) about ways he wanted them to serve Bhajan. They had seen many devotees of Krishna, but Bhajan was the most outstanding of them all as he was immersed in *samadhi* most of the time and hardly had anything to do with his body in terms of food or other care.

Bhajan stood at the doors of the temple looking at Banke Bihari for a long time. Then he took his leave and walked out of the temple on to the road to Mathura to catch the train to Haridwar, retracing how he had come only a few months earlier. When he moved out of Vrindavan and reached Haridwar, his heart was still full of longing to remain at Vrindavan, immersed in the divine intoxication of love for Krishna.

Thakur used to talk to me from time to time about his days of Himalayan *sadhana* but he was always very brief. For some reason, like all the great sages of India, he was not vocal about his arduous and austere practices in the mountains.

From Haridwar he walked with other *sadhus* up into the mountains. The little that is known about the next phase of his spiritual practice is that he moved to the Kedarnath and Badrinath areas of the Garhwal Mountains of the Himalayas. There he performed intense practice of advanced yoga. He lived frugally in terms of food, being immersed in *samadhi* most of the time. Yogis who reach this high state of union master the art of certain *mudras*, which bring the nectar from the glands to keep the yogi without hunger for days, even months at a time, while maintaining the body's health.

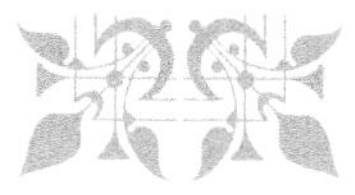

CHAPTER ELEVEN

BHAIRAVI MA REAPPEARS—THE FINAL JOURNEY IN TANTRA

It was my Gurudev Thakur himself who told me that after this period of *sadhana*, Bhairavi Ma came to him again. She had come when he was a child and saved him from death. Now she reappeared in his life to take him through the most advanced practices of *Tantra* (the ultimate science of exploring the reality through worship and meditation on the primordial Shakti or energy essence). What we see in the life of my Gurudev Thakur is that he traversed through all the paths of yoga to reach the final state of non-dual self-realization.

Tantra is profoundly misunderstood. It is extremely subtle and the most difficult path; it can only be practiced under the guidance of a realized Guru. In this path, through specific and secret techniques known only to the adepts, the yogi reaches the state of mind which is no longer enamored by the beauty, physicality and pleasures of the objective world. Only then can one experience the unity of subjective and objective aspects of the pure consciousness that is *Shiva* and *Shakti* in cosmic union.

The yogi is not biased with any kind of conditional perceptions of the physical world of enjoyment or sex. Any seed of desire that lies at the subconscious layers of mind can surface to be transformed in the light of vigilant awareness. Instead of suppressing the subtlest desires lying dormant in the bed of the unconscious mind, the yogi is brave enough to face them. Through meditation and *mantra sadhana* any lower energies are transmuted in the pure flame of awakened consciousness. There is no place for negation. There is no space for suppression or the eventual perversion that happens with many aspirants in the path of *yoga sadhana*. *Tantra* is pure science. It accepts everything as the manifestation of Mother Divine, the Feminine divinity. Hence, why should the Mother be negated in whatever form she manifests, inside or outside? Obstacles are considered as the steps to higher realization. *Tantra* is pro-life in totality. Accepting life in its totality, *Tantra* leads to total transformation of the aspirant into illumined consciousness of *Kaul* (realization).

Bhairavi Ma, the ageless yogini, had come to Thakur's life to give him the ultimate realization of union of Shiva and Shakti. She personally guided him through this *sadhana*. Since Thakur had gone through the path of *prema-bhakti* and the paths of yoga, he was ready for this most difficult *sadhana*. He reached the state of *Kaul*, the ultimate perfection in the path of *Tantra* in a very short time.

After attaining the state of *Kaul* when his consciousness descended from the non-dual state, he had the *darshan* (direct vision) of Mother Divine. The Mother appeared in her cosmic form of infinite light before Her loving child and instructed him, *"Now go back and finish up your unfinished work."*

Receiving the Word from the Mother Divine, Bhajan felt the deep call from the hearts of many suffering souls and from many seekers of Truth and divine love. He was ready to descend from the Himalayan heights to the plains to relieve the suffering of humanity with the light of his awakened consciousness.

Bhajan had become a sage, a seer, a realized Master. He had traversed all the paths of yogic *sadhana* to reach the ultimate state of supreme enlightenment in an exceptionally short time. The total divinization of the mind-body-spirit and the speed with which Bhajan attained this state is impossible for us to understand as everyday human beings, enmeshed as we are in our everyday lives. But Bhajan was a highly evolved soul when he came into the world. That allowed him to give everything he was, and all his heart, to rigorous *sadhana*. He now had all the *siddhis* (supranatural abilities derived from advanced spiritual practice) of the eightfold yogic power called *ashta-siddhi*, and was now available to serve others on their own unique path.

All of this happened in an unusually short period and it was no miracle. Only those who have performed intense spiritual practice in previous incarnations attain that highest state of integral yoga in the brief time that Bhajan did. From earliest childhood, he was completely disinterested in worldliness. While his other siblings lived an ordinary life, his love for God was evident even at play. He made beautiful idols of the different gods and goddesses with his own hands, offered them flowers and bathed them. Unlike other children, he could be found sitting alone as if lost or playing with things that had to do with the divine. He manifested his innate call to divinity from birth. His occasional trance-like state from early life was a sign of the *samadhi* that he would attain effortlessly, without entering any formal training from any adept. For the whole course of his *sadhana* in the Himalayas and in Vrindavan, he only had to touch the heights in this birth for them to come to bloom.

At this point, he could see through his third eye and know anyone's previous births, their past and future, transcending the time-space dimension. He had become the pure instrument of total divinity, an enlightened Master. It was time to return to the world to touch the hearts of the souls who were waiting for him to raise them from ignorance and unconsciousness. He and his Beloved had merged in each other, dissolving all mind-made barriers and borders. He had become the compassionate Buddha.

CHAPTER TWELVE

THE MASTER DESCENDS TO THE PLAINS

From here onward, we will call this incarnation of love "Thakur," as his devotees, disciples and I always called him. Thakur means Divine Self or Living Divinity.

A living Master is like a lit candle capable of lighting a million other candles. The Universal Mother wanted Her ordained child to get back to Her children who were waiting to be shown the path of Light through a realized Master. Now a perfected instrument, Thakur was one with the whole of the cosmic manifestation. The self-limiting perceptions of bonded souls had disappeared in his highly evolved spiritual state. The inner and outer, the Spirit within, and all external manifestation had merged to create a symphony of life in its totality. As a natural mystic who could fathom beyond all superficial names and forms of material nature, he now was an embodiment of love who could touch and open the hearts of those groping in the darkness, pain and miseries of the sense-bound world, with all its fleeting changes.

Thakur Comes to the Plains as an Enlightened Master

The core tradition of India is the *Sanatana Dharma,* the timeless principle or doctrine that came to us from the seers and sages but not from any one prophet or man of God. Structurally, it revolves around kindling and perfecting the light in one soul and taking that light to kindle the light in many other souls to dispel the darkness that prevails in earthly life.

The Mother now sent Her perfected child to offer divine guidance to those seeking freedom from the fetters of *karma,* the law of cause and effect that operates through the cycles of birth and death. Throughout Thakur's *sadhana*, he could often see millions of souls suffering in the quagmires of the world. He always felt a deep calling to wipe away their pain.

When Thakur reached Calcutta, the differences between the quiet, tranquil heights of the Himalayas and the din and bustle of the city were striking. Nevertheless, with his enlightened consciousness, he could only see the One manifested as many. To him, the outer was merely the divine play of the infinitely creative universal Mother, the creator, sustainer and annihilator of the universal process. Thakur knew that many, many souls were thirsting for inner happiness and that this was where he had to begin his work helping to heal the suffering of humanity.

However spiritually realized he now was when Thakur arrived back in the world, he looked like a madman. With unkempt long hair and nails, and wearing only a single, extremely tattered and discolored cloth, those who saw him walking through the roads of Calcutta only had pity for his poverty and mad-like appearance.

Thakur Returns to Calcutta and His Family

Thakur knew that he was going to the house of his second sister, Laxmi, who was married and lived with her in-laws. Around midday, he reached the home from the Howrah rail station and stood at the threshold to ask for alms. It was an odd time for any beggar to come for alms or food. He heard his sister's voice inside saying, *"This is not the time when beggars come. Who has come now?"* Thakur instantly recognized that it was his sister, Laxmi. Her mother-in-law responded, *"Whoever it is, just see and give him some food. This is food time."* Thakur stood waiting at the door for his sister to open it.

Laxmi came, offered some food, and felt sorry at the plight of this young man in pathetic clothes, with such an uncared-for body. She was surprised and felt uneasy when the beggar stood still and kept looking at her! Suddenly, the silence was broken when the man spoke up, *"Is your name Laxmi?"* (Lakkhi in Bengali). *"Yes, but how do you know my name?"* Laxmi asked with wide, surprised eyes.

Thakur walked through the doors and stood in the middle of the drawing room. Though Laxmi was surprised, somewhere in her heart she had the feeling that the man's voice was very familiar and that he was known to her. Still, she wasn't sure. The man looked like a total stranger. In the meantime, Laxmi's mother-in-law walked in. She asked the man a few very common questions, which he answered with a naughty smile on his face.

Suddenly, Laxmi asked, *"Ma, don't you think his voice is a lot like that of our Sejda* (third brother in Bengali)*?"* The mother-in-law knew that her daughter-in-law's third brother had left home as a wandering mendicant in search of the divine, but no one knew where he went, where he lived, or what he did. Nothing was known about him by anyone in the family. Somehow Laxmi was becoming more convinced that this stranger was no stranger at all, that he was her beloved *sadhu* brother, *Sejda.*

Now he was ready to reveal the truth. With a smile, he confirmed that he was her *Sejda.*

Laxmi broke into tears. She could not believe her eyes. She went on sobbing and asking, *"What plight have you created for yourself, Sejda?"* The few years of separation from her brother felt like ages. Now her heart was dancing with joy that he was back, that he was back at her home!

Indeed, she was blessed. But she was only happy that her brother was back. What she did not know, due to the veil of *maya* (illusion), was that he was no longer the brother who had left home in search of Truth and God. Now he was a living Buddha, an enlightened sage from the Himalayas, the eternal lover of Lord Krishna. She could only rejoice because her brother was back, that her brother was no longer lost to her and their family.

She did not want to waste any more time. Taking him by the hand, she made him sit down on the couch. Then she ran to make sure that the bathroom was ready so he could have a good bath. She also took the liberty to quickly cut off his long hair with all the dust in it, so that he could look gentle (according to her). Lovingly, she pushed her brother toward the bathroom, assuring him he would have a refreshing bath with new soap. Suddenly, she was filled with a deep ecstasy that she could not express. The whole world seemed to be dancing with joy. All the happiness in the world was wrapped around her. Her inner being was flooded with unspeakable joy. From the moment he identified himself as her brother and started addressing her as Lakkhi, the sound of his voice and every word he spoke were magical. She was beginning to sense this was no longer that brother who left home. There was something about him, something she could not understand, that was filling her soul with pure delight.

She could tell that Thakur was very hungry. She rushed to the kitchen to see what was there and started cooking some fresh rice and vegetables while he was in the bath. When she finally served him food, she followed the practice of the past and brought him fish curry, served on a plate. With loving appreciation, Thakur explained that he was a strict vegetarian now and that he would not take any non-vegetarian food. Laxmi, understanding, went back to the kitchen, prepared a vegetarian meal, and served him.

Once Thakur had eaten, he went to have a midday rest. Laxmi instantly got very busy sending messages to all her siblings, other relatives and friends that her long-lost brother was back in Calcutta and was staying with her.

By evening, all the relatives and other acquaintances poured into Laxmi's small house. It was a big celebration for the whole family. They had missed their loving brother for so long. Thakur's parents, Ma Priyabala and Sachinath, rushed to see their beloved child. Ma Priyabala kept looking at him, with memories flashing through her mind. She remembered how he left home and how she missed him every day. How she thought about his whereabouts and most importantly worried about what he ate. This is the love of a mother. She had done that every day since Thakur first came to her as a child. She was only happy to see her child healthy and happy, well fed and well taken care of.

Thakur began spending the days at his parent's home and going to his sister's home at night to sleep. In those days, his parents stayed in a house with tin shed but with four spacious rooms, of course, with a large family. Occasionally, Thakur visited the houses of many devotees of Baba Lokenath and participated in evening *satsangs* and *bhajans*.

Thakur Leaves Home and Goes to Ranchi to Ma Anandamayee's Ashram

Very close to the Cornfield Road house was a small ashram of his mother's Guru, Ma Anandamayee. In the late 1950s, Thakur frequently visited that ashram. From time to time, Ma Anandamayee came there. Large numbers of devotees and followers would come to have *darshan* of Ma and also to participate in *satsangs* and *kirtans*. Ma herself used to sing *kirtans* and Thakur would join in the singing. Thakur's mother, Ma Priyabala, was an ardent devotee of Ma Anandamayee. She was always overcome with the sense of fulfillment when Ma would praise her son Bhajan.

On one such occasion in 1959, Ma Anandamayee called Thakur and said, *"Could you go to our Ashram at Ranchi? It needs someone like you to build it and spread the glory of the Lord."* Thakur was looking for an opportunity to stay away from home and this call to go to Ranchi was just what he needed. So, he left Calcutta for the Ranchi Ashram of Ma Anandamayee and took charge there.

The ashram residents saw him as a devotee like themselves, never guessing that he was an enlightened Master. He safely hid his infinite spiritual powers and worked as a *brahmachari sadhu* most of the day. He wanted to repay his rich debt of gratitude to Ma Anandamayee, who had showered so much grace on him throughout his life and had gifted him his Guru, Sri Sri Devgiri Maharaj. Accepting Ma Anandamayee's wish to go to Ranchi was Thakur's *Guru dakshina*, an offering to his Guru, since it was at the Anandamayee Ashram in Varanasi that Thakur met his beloved Master and was initiated in the divine presence of Shakti-personified, Ma Anandamayee. Thakur stayed in the Ranchi ashram of Ma Anandamayee for almost four years. During this time, his mission was to rebuild the whole ashram, to expand and popularize it among the people of Ranchi.

Throughout the day, he worked in the ashram and in the evening he conducted *Naam Gaan*, (musical rendering of congregational chanting of the Holy Name of the Lord).

That was his simple way of inspiring people to connect with the divine. Gradually, these evening *Satsangs*, with his *kirtans* and talks, began drawing many devotees, not only from around the ashram, but from distant places in and around the city of Ranchi. As the number of devotees grew, so did his popularity as the loving *sadhu* whose divine voice enchanted whoever heard it.

Thakur stayed in the Ranchi Ashram of Ma Anandamayee between December 1958 and February 1963. Ma Ananadamayee gave him the responsibility of establishing the Kali Temple, installation of Mother Kali *murthy* (idol) and also to reorganize and popularize the ashram to inspire people to a life of a true spiritual journey.

The most important thing to note about enlightened masters is that they live life as it comes. Thakur could have remained happy only to conduct chants and *bhajans* and to teach people the path of devotion and *mantra* yoga. From early dawn, he would do every job at the ashram, cleaning and mopping the floors, at times doing the dishes, cooking for large numbers of ashram residents, and visiting devotees of Ma Anandamayee.

THAKUR (RIGHT) AT ANANDAMAYEE ASHRAM IN EARLY 1950'S ALONG WITH ASHRAM BRAHMACHARI

In my own initial days at Gurudev's ashram as a monk, he would teach me and other monks the essence of *karma yoga*. The key is to consider every task an opportunity to serve God rather than thinking of any work as small or big, significant or unimportant and menial. Work is *Seva*, an offering of selfless service to the divine. As a tool, an instrument, work cleanses the dross of the mind, which is the primary function and goal of all spiritual practice.

Thakur gave us the example of his own life. Although he was a *mukta-purusha*, a liberated sage, at the ashram of Ranchi he moved about just like any other practicing monk. He never even hinted to anyone there that he was a great Himalayan Master, or that any odd job was beneath him in any way.

He often said to us, "*Apani achari dharma opore shikhai,*" "*First I practice and then alone I teach you all about the path of true dharma.*" That is the essence of teaching by a Master. His life and living itself are the teaching, from moment to moment. Those who live with him see what happens when one realizes God. Does he become something different from others? Thakur proved the only difference is while others worked from the plane of the unconscious mind, the enlightened one does the same things, living like others, but his actions are all in a state of heightened awareness. His presence is alive, exuding pure love all the time, in whatever he says or does. The play of ego that is common to everyday individuals cannot be seen in a man or woman of wisdom. Thakur did every menial job that others would shun and did it with delight because, to him, no work was big or small. It was all manifesting the divine wish in material form. It was translating his mission on earth.

This is a lesson to all seekers of Truth. There is a mad rush in today's world to become a guru, a master, to immediately create a package, to trademark a technique, sell it and become an overnight hit. The race is on to develop a marketable product, a brand. This is sadly conspicuous in the multi-billion-dollar spiritual industry of East and West, and in New Age spirituality.

One of the sayings of saints of India is, *'Guru mile lakh lakh chela na mile ek'*: *'You get millions of gurus, but you can hardly find one disciple!'*

Someone once asked me why there are so many false gurus and teachers and priests in all religions? I humbly replied, *"When there is demand for anything, supply comes automatically to cater to the need. That is the way nature works. As long as there are superficial seekers looking for an instant spiritual utopia, for shortcuts and flash programs for kundalini* (Awakening), *false gurus will flood the marketplace!!"*

When there is such a huge demand from seekers of superficial happiness, how can nature keep quiet? You are only hearing about the gurus and babas that are on the supply side of the equation.

Thakur embodies the Truth. He is not teaching from books or scriptures. He is living Truth and sharing it. He is not a preacher who has gone through a course on theology, like a college professor teaching a class that requires no inner transformation. Book knowledge is enough for that. Most spiritual teachers in the marketplace have bookish, limited knowledge which is sufficient for those who are content with the periphery.

The question arises about those sincere teachers of spirituality from all cultures around the world that are contributing towards an awakening of consciousness. They may not be Enlightened Masters, but as long as they are sincere practitioners and teachers who make every effort to be keenly aware of the play of their own ego, they do have a role in the world of spiritual transformation. When the seeker and the teacher are both committed to Truth and God, they are the torchbearers of the holy tradition of inner transformation leading to peace at both the individual and planetary level.

Those who are Enlightened Masters, however, have undergone the rigorous practice required to complete the process of transformation. They have been guided and are made to function as Gurus by the great grand Masters who have ascended.

Those who seek genuine Truth are few. They always find the right teacher: one who lives the teachings, who has become walking divinity because he or she has gone through every step of inner transformation to divinize the ego.

I was incomprehensibly blessed that one such living divinity reached out to me and lifted me out of the dust. Breathing the life of Truth and God love, he made it possible for me to leave my job and the world behind, and finally to enter his ashram as a monk.

Date: 15 March 1959, from 1pm to 4 pm.

On one hot summer afternoon after a hectic morning, followed by cooking and feeding devotees, Thakur was very tired. He went to his little room and lay down on the floor. In a few seconds he was in deep sleep. The following account is quoted directly from Thakur's personal diary.

> *"I was fast asleep during the afternoon. On waking, I felt someone was sitting on the side of my head and fanning me with a hand fan. I opened my eyes to see and found Baba (Lokenath) sitting with a hand fan. I hurriedly sat up and said, 'Baba what is this Lila (divine play) of yours?' I started crying profusely and told him, 'Baba, you have been fanning me for so long; it must have been so painful for you.' Baba replied, 'It is too hot here. It is so uncomfortable for you to sleep here; I have been fanning you for the last three hours. Whom do you think I was fanning? In you, I am manifest. In you, I see myself.' With tears of gratitude I offered my pranam (obeisance) and he melted away".*

The most important thing to note here is that this was not a dream or a vision on the part of Thakur while in a sleep state. Baba Lokenath, the ascended Master who had always helped him, who was with him guiding his *sadhana* from early childhood, had always appeared before him in actual physical form. Baba Lokenath, like *Maha-Avatar* Babaji of the Himalayas mentioned in Paramahansa Yogananda's *Autobiography of a Yogi*, could materialize his own body at will for the sake of advanced yogis and *sadhaks* (true spiritual practitioners) to lead them in the path of divine realization. This type of appearance by a great Master highlights the infinite compassion and love these great Yogis and ascended

Masters have for those who are highly evolved. Baba sat beside the head of my Gurudev for three hours, fanning, simply because Thakur was tired, and it was hot. What motherly love! What infinite compassion Baba Lokenath embodied!

Baba Lokenath asked my Gurudev. "*Whom do you think I have been fanning for the last three hours? It was myself.*" Enlightened Yogis like Baba Lokenath always see their own self in everything that is manifested. In the mirror of their pure consciousness, they see the reflection of their own inner image in every sentient being.

Thakur during his long stay in Ranchi virtually rebuilt the whole ashram and expanded every activity of the center attracting a large following for it. The time for his own divine play as the Master was almost ready, and now the call came for him to return back to Calcutta, and start his own work of manifesting his divine state of Universal Teacher.

CHAPTER THIRTEEN

THE MASTER BEGINS HIS DIVINE PLAY

The Ticket Examiner Becomes His First Disciple

The divine plays at the mystery of life and its movement toward the ultimate goal in inscrutable ways. None of us knows how some simple, routine task of our daily life could turn into a life-changing event that takes us to higher realms of the subtle world of the Spirit.

One day, Thakur was on his way to a devotee's home. Coming to Howrah Railway station to catch the train, while walking through the crowded platform, he suddenly saw a man following him, looking at him intently. Looking back, it did not take long for Thakur to recognize the man, who was still searching through his own memory banks. Thakur took the initiative and approached him. Putting his right hand on the man's shoulders he said, *"Do you recognize me?"*

The man was a bit surprised and responded, *"I have seen you somewhere but the person I know had long hair and a long beard. You look so similar, yet so different without such long hair and beard."*

Thakur said,

> *"Yes, you have seen me; you have met me. Try to remember the day when I was traveling from Delhi to Vrindavan. I had no ticket. You wanted me to get out of the running train, but you could not do that and instead you helped me so much that day, taking me to Vrindavan."*

It was like a dream. In a flash, everything came alive in the screen of the man's memory. He could see this man, the wandering monk without a ticket, about to jump from the running train just as he had demanded. And the unusual looking, tall and thin Yogi with matted hair and a long beard, appearing out of thin air, rebuking him with, *"What are you doing? Take him where he wants to go!"* Then he simply disappeared into the air without a trace!

Thakur was in a hurry since his train's departure was imminent. He had to get to his compartment. He quickly wrote his address on a piece of paper, handed it to the man and said, *"Come and meet me soon."*

In later years, the ticket examiner was blessed to become the first person to receive formal initiation from Thakur. The enraged man, who insisted that Thakur jump from a running train, was being saved from the cycles of birth and death as the Guru came to hold his hands and lead him across the ocean of life. We simply never know what life event might become the bridge to perennial peace and bliss.

We are all souls on a journey to the eternal. We come; we go. We change the clothes of our bodies. But we are the same soul, moving through time, through timeless time, toward the one goal of God Realization, the realization of the divinity that lives at our core waiting to be rediscovered and fully claimed. No casual meeting of anyone, even for a short while, should be taken casually. We don't meet anyone unless we have some past connection. That simple ticket examiner had no way of knowing the significance in his life of that stranger in front of him, a penniless, ticketless *sadhu*. He had no inkling that in a few moments, the humble *sadhu* with whom he was so furious would cause the great Yogi, Baba Lokenath, to materialize and appear before him in a physical body and totally change his life. Or that that stranger would one day be his own Guru, the divine fully embodying itself in human form.

• • •

In Calcutta, Thakur had been spending his days in his mother's home. The word had spread that he was no ordinary man, that he could heal suffering simply with a word or touch. People in distress were running to him.

One of those was a battered woman who was being abused by her drunken husband. Thakur reached out to her and her husband with deep compassion. With his loving presence and words, he soothed the drunken husband, gently telling him to calm down and to respect his wife. He explained the bad *karma* that the man was accumulating for himself and that ultimately no one else but he himself would suffer the consequences. No one had ever spoken to him with so much love and wisdom. He had never been touched so deeply. He hadn't been able to understand the consequences of his actions. The drunken, abusive husband became a follower of this man of God and was forever changed.

Another woman came to him crying, *"My mother is extremely sick, I love her with all my heart. Please, come and see her. I am sure if you bless her, she will be healed."* Thakur wasted no time; he accompanied the daughter to see her mother and found her in intense physical pain. Thakur stroked all over her ailing body with his hand, then reassured her that she would be all right soon. The old lady calmed down. The agonizing pain and burning sensation that had plagued her throughout her body subsided. She felt as if she was being bathed from within with divine healing. With utmost gratitude, the daughter bowed at the feet of this compassionate master, washing his feet with her tears. Imagine the overwhelming awe both this woman and her mother felt at being so personally attended to by the divine as Thakur left.

Thakur gradually revealed the infinite wealth of the divine that he brought with him from birth and his arduous *sadhana* in the Himalayas to the many who had been waiting for him to come into their lives.

It is important to understand that the Guru is none other than the embodiment of divinity. Divinity, ultimately, is beyond human comprehension. It is beyond the realms of mind. But we humans can experience it. The Guru has wholly merged with divinity, has utterly surrendered the ego, the body, mind and soul to the divine. As the living embodiment of the divine, the Guru comes to those souls who are ready to reach out to the next levels of mystical experience.

Beyond the peripheral, the external reality we perceive through our human eyes and the filter of our mind is the unified field of being from which all of Creation arises. Its subtle vibration, its infinite grace surrounds and abides within each soul. That is who we are. But human beings are blind. We see ourselves and the world through the ego-centric lens of the illusion of separation. We believe, think and respond to others, to the world, and to the divine as separate. No one can fully pierce those veils of illusion until the Guru comes. Until wisdom dawns from the inside, we cannot see through the haze to realize the unity at the heart of all existence.

When the bud opens and becomes a blossoming flower, the flower does not work or do anything to spread its fragrance. The blossoming itself sends out the sweet aroma. This is nature. This is the law of the universe. When the flower blossoms, the fragrance spreads. The fragrance is the invitation to the bees, who come to sit on the flowers and drink the nectar. The flower does not give. The nectar is simply there, ready to be taken. The bees know how to take! The flies do not know. The flower never says 'yes' to bees and 'no' to flies.

This is true with the living Buddha as well. Thakur was no longer giving. He was not distributing the nectar or the infinite wealth that he was here to distribute. He was simply available to all who came to drink from the well of his blossomed being. He became the fragrant flower whose bud of divinity had flowered.

That is what Buddhahood is all about. When the seed of divinity flowers in anyone, he or she becomes a living Buddha, the enlightened Master. There is no effort involved. All efforts die with the death of ego. It is the death of the false reality that gives birth to eternal light and eternal love. Thakur had become that light and love which he embodied.

Like honey loving bees, people seeking happiness and higher truth came to him. Like iron filings to a powerful magnet, they came. His love for men, women, and children, his love for all animals, was like the soothing dewdrops of early dawn. The process is silent, yet vast, all-encompassing. Those touched by his quiet spiritual aura were enchanted by the call from that subtle world of the infinite vibrating at the core of each soul. Thakur came like a magician. A mere look or a touch acted like a magic wand, creating incredible miracles. People came and sat near him, feeling something first-hand about which they had read in the scriptures or heard from their ancestors. Thakur talked, smiled, did very simple things, but his every movement, his every word, his every song conveyed unspeakable joy and ecstasy.

As the number of followers increased, the desire to be initiated by him with the *Guru Mantra* increased, along with the number of those accepting him as Guru. At this time, Thakur would visit Patna, the capital city of the state of Bihar. The place is called Bihar because it is where, 2,500 years ago, Buddha walked. On one such visit in the 1960s, Thakur was conducting an evening *satsang* with assembled devotees. One, Gopal Das, who was a photographer, came for *darshan*. Gopal Das had never seen anyone so intoxicated in God love. He was seeing him with the eyes of a photographer. The idea came that if he could take a good picture of Thakur, he could sell that picture among Thakur's growing number of disciples and followers. It was a typical commercial mindset.

Gopal Das approached Thakur and requested that he accompany Gopal to his studio. Initially Thakur resisted, but Gopal was persistent. Finally, he admitted to Thakur that he was looking at it from the standpoint of his business. Thakur was pleased with Gopal's confession. After all, if it helped a family man to earn righteously, why not help him? Thakur accompanied Gopal to his studio. Quite a few photos were taken, but the masterpiece was one of Thakur when in a state of ecstasy, with a beautiful smile. This photograph, which conveys the innocence and purity of Thakur's divine aura, became the signature image of Thakur. The cover image of this book is this photo taken by Gopal Das of Patna, who subsequently became his disciple.

Thakur's Parents Pass Away

As time passed, Thakur would go from time to time to various devotees' homes. His presence would bring many seekers to his *satsangs*. His ecstatic *bhajans* never failed to instill deep devotion and love in the devotees who were present. Invitations also came pouring in from many places outside Calcutta. Then quite suddenly, he stopped going anywhere. He stayed at home. Amitabha Dasgupta, an ardent disciple from Patna, wrote to him time and again asking Thakur to visit Patna during this period, but Thakur stayed in Calcutta. The reason soon came to light when his mother fell seriously ill. Everyone was wondering about the cause of her illness, when Thakur declared it was cancer. She was taken to Chittaranjan Cancer Hospital in Calcutta. All efforts to save her yielded no results. After a few days, she breathed her last on the auspicious occasion of the full moon, the festival of colors on 12 March 1971. That same year toward October, his father fell ill and left the world after only a few days of illness.

Thakur remained unmoved. Though he loved his parents with all his heart, he knew that everyone comes to this world for a certain number of days and breaths. Once that is complete, the return to the astral planes is inevitable. No one can stop the course of destiny.

Thakur took the responsibility of observing all the rituals and ceremonies that are prescribed in the scriptures related to the death of parents. As a renounced monk, that was not traditional or expected. He could have avoided it. Instead, he did everything that a householder would when parents depart. The great sage Adi Guru Shankaracharya had done the same when his mother died, demonstrating that even a *sannyasi* should pay respects and observe the rituals when their parents die. He performed all the rituals according to the scriptural injunctions to emphasize the importance of performing the last rites to those of the Vedic Hindu faith.

Another great sage of Bengal, Bamakhyapa, also performed the last rites just like every householder son does for his father. Bamakhyapa lived in the famous *Shakti-Pitha* (place of worship in honor of *Shakti*) of Tarapith, did intense *Tantra* practice and had reached the highest state of supreme knowledge. The story goes that when the ceremonial rites for his father were about to begin, dark clouds covered the whole area. Everybody was sure that a huge storm was about to break that would spoil the last of the final rites that were to be conducted under the open sky, with no covering. Bamakhyapa, the great *siddha* (adept) looked at the sky, muttered something and then walked around the whole place in a circle, drawing a line on the ground. He then asked everyone to continue with the ceremonial rituals. As expected, a huge thunderstorm hit the area. While it poured torrentially, the power of the great saint over nature was instantly evident. The rain poured everywhere except in the circle that Bamakhyapa had drawn. Not a drop of rain fell where the people were assembled and the ceremonies were being performed. It was as if there was a huge, invisible umbrella protecting them.

These sages of infinite power were beyond all earthly attachment. Yet they performed the last rites for their parents, offering us reminders of the honor we all owe to the souls of our parents. Thakur did this for both his father and mother with total dedication and love for their departed souls, showing his followers that our first gods are our parents. Our parents bring us into this world; they give us life and birth. However fully human any parent may be, they create the opportunity for us to evolve in spirit beyond birth and death and offer us profound lessons for our own life path.

• • •

After his parents left this world, Thakur felt greater freedom for his work. He started visiting various holy pilgrimage sites of India and other cities, wherever devotees arranged for him to visit their homes to have *satsang* for other seekers. Those homes would become a holy temple, with visitors pouring in from all around. Sometimes he talked to them like a child. Sometimes he looked with empty eyes, lost in higher realms. At times he sang, completely absorbed in the divine, utterly intoxicated. At times he would loudly cry, *'Ma, Ma'*, invoking the Divine Mother, as if he could see Her, before going into *samadhi*, the deep absorption and total merger with the divine. Most often he was down-to-earth, laughing, joking, like an ordinary person.

Hindus, Muslims, Christians, people belonging to diverse faith traditions came from all over the world to meet him. He embraced them all, mingling with them in the one religion of universal love. He would say,

> *"Have intense faith in your own dharma or religion and follow the instruction of your scriptures. Sing to the glory of the divine, to the all-merciful, the all-compassionate One, who is right here with outstretched arms of love. Take the leap. Let it take you to the infinite lap of the Eternal. Cry out! Yearn with all your heart for Infinite Grace. That is the only way to be peaceful and fulfilled in life".*

Thakur was dear to people of all ages, from the youngest children to the old and infirm. He always found time for anyone who came to him for help, whether his or her motivation was grossly material or purely spiritual. Many *sadhaks* came in silence or sat to talk with him for a while and then left without anyone knowing. Whoever came, with whatever desire, or wish, it was fulfilled. As a result, word of Thakur quickly spread near and far.

A RARE PICTURE OF THAKUR IN ABHAI MUDRA

CHAPTER FOURTEEN

ACCOUNTS FROM DR. BANERJEE'S DIARY

Thakur shared with me his personal diaries in which he had written journals after his return from the Himalayas. One morning, during early days of my monastic life at the ashram, he called me. He was alone in his room. Handing over a few diaries he said to me, "*Shuddha, these diaries I give to you, keep it safe.*" I was overwhelmed with gratitude for his grace and his love for me. Then another day, Gurudev called me and handed over a manuscript with a title *The Guru as I See Him* written by a senior disciple, Dr. Banerjee, which was given to Thakur as humble offering many years back that had so far remained unpublished. It was yet another moment of feeling overwhelmed with joy and before I could ask him why he was giving that to me, he said, "*Keep this notebook with you safely, one day you will need it.*"

Below are accounts of Dr. Banerjee, who was a railway doctor who resided in the Rail Quarters of Secunderabad's Lallaguda area.

24 April 1970. (The date Thakur came to Secunderabad to Sri Pradyut Ranjan Mukherjee's house. Mukherjee was the Chief Engineer of South-Central Railway.) I received a telephone call from Mr. Mukherjee saying, 'A sadhu has come from Calcutta. He is my Gurudev. He will stay here for a few days. Try to come and see him in the evening.' I told him, 'I am already preoccupied this evening, but I will come tomorrow evening.'

I started having my own apprehensions. I was not very comfortable with sadhus as such, having heard of many fake sadhus and gurus. And this was the Guru of a highly placed officer! I decided to take someone with me. I tried here and there inviting a couple of my friends, but none were interested. The whole day passed with me thinking about this sadhu and whether or not I should go at all, asking myself what was I going to do. It was more an obligation, a call from one of my own senior officers in the Railway. I was in a dilemma.

After dinner, as usual, I read a few books and then went to bed. But sleep was far away from me. Any other day, I would just lie down and instantly go into sleep; but not today. I was tossing from one side to the other. The thought of the sadhu seemed to possess me. The more I wanted to forget all about it and sleep, the more the thoughts related to the sadhu came flooding my head. Questions of what kind of sadhu is he? How does he look? How does he talk? How does he behave with strangers? All these thoughts were overlapping one another.

I do not know at what point I fell asleep, but it was not deep sleep. It was as if I was half awake, half asleep. I started seeing a man clad in white with a short beard moving all over my house, playing around, asking me to rise above my doubting mind. Usually I am not an early riser. But that morning it was early dawn when I was kind of pushed out of my bed. I came out of bed, moved into the garden adjacent to my house, and sat in a chair. It was a beautiful morning; the birds were singing all around. Inside of me, there was a feeling of natural joy, as if I had rested very well. There was such happiness inside of me.

The thoughts came. Well, the sadhu must be clad in saffron, but this man who came to my home was wearing white clothes. He had such a smiling face and was so childlike and playful.

One of my close friends, a doctor himself (also named Mukherjee), working in the Railway Hospital at Vijayawada, was suffering from Pleurisy. He had come to Secunderabad to consult a senior physician. He had come to stay with me. As soon as he woke up, I called him and told him about Mr. Mukherjee's call, about his Gurudev from Calcutta. I would be happy if he would accompany me to see the sadhu this evening. When he immediately agreed, I was relieved. I don't have to go alone!

• • •

25 April 1970, evening 6 p.m.: I got ready to go see the Guru of our Chief Engineer. We both left home to have darshan of the sadhu. The bungalow was not far away. It was a huge one for the Chief Engineer's high position, well decorated. Mr. Mukherjee was waiting for us outside. With initial pleasantries, he escorted us to the room where the sadhu was sitting and introduced us both to his Gurudev.

I was in awe! I could not believe my eyes. This is very clearly the same sadhu, who had come to my house in my dream. He wore the same white clothes, that very same smile, and had that same childlike innocence. I could not take my eyes off him. I kept seeing him with wide-open eyes of exclamation. My whole being was flooded with unspeakable bliss. I was totally overwhelmed!

'Please sit down', he said. The words were so musical. I prostrated to him as if moved by some unknown force and took my seat a little away. Looking at me, he was smiling. Sometimes, I saw him looking at us with deep, x-ray eyes. Again, he talked with a few others. There was such a grace over the whole place. In the middle of the conversations he was going into peals of laughter!! I was transfixed.

After a while, he moved the harmonium onto his couch. At the request of the hostess, Mrs. Mukherjee, he started singing bhajans. I don't think I have ever heard such ecstasy and devotion in a voice. He sang one chant after the other, filling the room with ethereal vibrations of divine melody. It was as if the gods had come down. It was a voice that was not of this world! The whole mind was mesmerized by the sound of that music.

I lost all perception of time. Late into the night, I suddenly came to my senses and knew it was time to go home. Just then, a lot of food was served to us and we ate. Finally, we went to the sadhu to ask for his permission to leave. When Dr. Mukherjee, my friend from Vijayawada, lifted his head after touching his feet, Thakur looked at him intently. Then he said, 'You are not well, but don't worry, you will be all right.' He stood up, left his couch, came up to my friend Dr. Mukherjee, and started stroking his hands on his chest and his back. Then he said 'Go, treat yourself well and come back again.'

I returned home, but it was as if only my body returned. My mind and heart were left with the strange man I had just encountered. What has he got, that he can be so down-to-earth, natural, and yet have a presence that does not belong to this earthly plane of existence? He seemed to epitomize the wisdom, 'Live in this world, but don't be worldly.' He was so much in this world with his occasional peals of laughter and mundane conversation. Yet it was evident that he lost touch with the world often. His eyes lost their normal look and became in-drawn, lost in a world altogether different from the one known to the rest of us.

My world, too, changed. Whether I was awake or sleeping, or in the midst of my daily routine, his thoughts and words chased me. I could see him right in front of me all the time! Nothing was of any meaning. All work became mere mechanical repetition. My whole being was longing for evening, after work, when I could run to Mr. Mukherjee's home and see him again.

I did not miss a day as long as he was with the Mukherjees. I just sat, drinking in his presence, his words, and his melodious bhajans. Thus, a few days passed in divine companionship of my first spiritual Master.

Then one day, at my earnest request, he graced my home with the dust of his holy feet. I prayed to him for Guru Mantra, and he agreed. On an auspicious day, me and my wife Anu both received the Guru Mantra from our Master.

Word started spreading. More and more seekers started coming to his presence. A few came from distant places; many came from nearby. Many came out of sheer curiosity. Some to have the darshan of the visiting sadhu. A few came to learn about their future. Others came to find a way out of painful family situations. In India, whenever the word spreads that a sadhu is around, many people just come to test his holiness or his powers.

That all happened with Thakur as well. But most people came to be in his presence, to be enchanted by the devotional chants that poured from his heart whenever he sang to God. Whatever the reason, whoever came, they felt a deep connection, a deep awe and attachment to this man of God. They would come back again and again.

The visitors were not only Hindus. Muslims and Christians, men and women belonging to all communities of faith came to him. There were seniors, old ones who came with canes. There were young boys and girls, even children. His unconditional love and equal vision attracted all. He responded to each seeker and their questions on the basis of their true need.

That is how his few days at Secunderabad were spent. In true joy of the Spirit. For the first time in my life, my days were spent beyond my material aspirations. It was my same life, but the taste was different. His coming had such a magical impact.

Maybe unknowingly, I had always been waiting to meet this man, who could hold my hands and walk me through those first baby steps toward a new life, into new dimensions of ethereal experience. Most of what happened in his presence and in my daily meetings and interactions were beyond my ability to grasp. Overall, I had a feeling of elation and joy that I had never experienced before, though my life had touched many peaks of so-called success and stability in the financial and social world.

He touched many hungering souls and initiated many. He proved that God is not just an empty word, but something palpable that can be experienced. His presence proved it, as he naturally exhibited the attributes that we usually associate with God.

Then he left Secunderabad, taking our hearts with him. He also left his divine presence etched permanently in our minds and hearts. When his train was about to leave the platform, he quickly passed his eyes over all of us, as if touching each of us with his soul and then said, 'I will come back again.'

There is no way we can understand you.

There is no way we can ever fathom you,

There is no way we can ever recognize you with our material eyes,

Only if you dispel the darkness of our hearts

And give us Your eyes to see You.

Can I ever know who You are

Beyond the veil of my ignorance and ego!

• • •

The lives of the great Masters are beyond that of the everyday human being. The divinity they attain through austere practices and their unimaginably intense yearning for God cannot be perceived by our materially oriented mind and intelligence. Yet, they come as ordinary humans, behaving like an everyday person. The subtle differences are not easy to understand. They belong to realms unknown to us. The heights they reach are beyond our comprehension. Their boundless love and compassion swells. It reaches out to us, drawing our attention to the inner realities of the spirit, helping us to awaken to the abiding and pervasive presence of the divine, to its love for us as children of the divine. This is their *kripa*, their divine grace. They say, *"Come, children of light, listen to me. Walk this path."* They are a treasure house of love and of transcendental powers that we relate to as miracles. They show us that nothing is impossible to the divine.

Dr. Banerjee also writes in his journal about his first experience of seeing a saint (Thakur) in *bhav-samadhi*:

I never knew what samadhi is or what happens to anyone who has reached that state of supreme consciousness and union with the divine. Since I was very fond of reading the lives of saints and sages, I had read about it. But I never had the fortune to see anyone in that state, which is considered the highest in the realm of spiritual attainment.

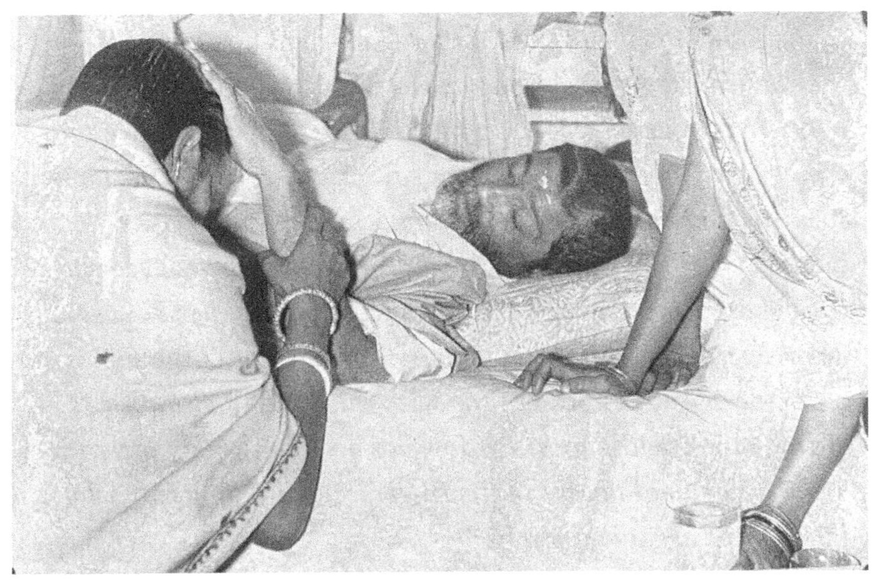

COMING OUT OF DIVINE ECSTASY AND TRANCE (SAMADHI) THE MASTER IS BLESSING A DEVOTEE

One day when Thakur was in Secunderabad, a few devotees received their initiation from him. Thakur wanted to do the ritual of worship of Mother Kali. I had heard that he had gone beyond any ritualistic practice or sadhana. Maybe this was the divine will manifesting itself for the good of the devotees. After doing the worship for a while and offering food to the Mother, he opened the closed doors of the puja room and we could see him crossing the threshold of the room with the big plate, full of the cooked food that had been offered to the Mother. His eyes were half closed, like Shiva's eyes. His body was not in control at all. There was a visibly divine aura and energy emanating from his body. It was taking a lot of effort to keep steady as he was walking. I was in awe. Lest he fall down, I rushed and held him in my hands. Another person took away the big plate full of the food offering to the Mother from Thakur's hands. I felt that he was in a state of unconsciousness. He had hardly any body-consciousness. His clothes also were loose and we put them right. Out of fear (as I never saw anything like this before) I led his body to the nearest cot and made him lie down. His pulse was so feeble. His breaths were almost not there. Even if he took in or released his breath, there was a long gap in between. There were about 30 of us surrounding him in that room. I am a doctor, but was not familiar with this kind of situation, so sitting quietly close to the bed where his divine body lay with some occasional mudra of his fingers; I was wondering what kind of disease this could be.

Dr. Mukherjee broke the silence by saying that no one should think that Thakur is unconscious or that this is any kind of physical ailment. He said, 'This is called samadhi. Thakur will return back to his physical consciousness very soon, once his consciousness, which is now in union with the divine, descends on its own accord.' After a long time, his body showed signs of life. A couple of devotees started pressing his legs and I just started caressing him, stroking my hand on his divine body. After a while he opened his eyes with a look of infinity.

We helped him sit on the cot. After a while he was totally normal again, his usual, talking, smiling self! I have seen Thakur going into this God intoxicated state of samadhi many more times after this. Whenever he sang bhajans, whenever someone sang God's divine name or talked about divine love, his body would suddenly become still, non-moving. He looked almost not there in his body at all. Sometimes this union with the divine would be for a short spell and at others times, it lingered. Again, he would descend from supreme consciousness to the mundane world of the material, from the intuitive world of pure love to the world of physical reality.

Blessed are they who come into contact with such persons in this world of maya (illusion) and miseries. I thanked my parents, my ancestors whose grace must have been the guiding force for me to meet Thakur, the charioteer of my life's journey. I felt infinitely blessed and humbled to think that I did not have to search all over the country for my Guru. The Guru came next door to me. He called me to his presence and impregnated my consciousness with the very essence of bhakti (devotion). He gave birth to the spirit of surrender in me, not an easy thing for a male ego, a man of the scientific world. Thakur became an indivisible part of my very existence. Whatever I did, I felt his presence.

THE MASTER IN DIVINE ECSTASY! BHAV SAMADHI!

• • •

In the year 1970 in the month of December, I had the first opportunity of traveling to Puri Jagannath Dham in the eastern state of Odisa, one of the holiest pilgrim centers in India, to be in the company of my Gurudev. Thakur had already arrived in Puri from Calcutta along with a young man named Sukumar Bhattacharya, who was a bodybuilder. When I met Sukumar, I could feel that he came to Puri more to enjoy the sea and to satisfy lots of curiosity about Thakur.

The next day we were all sitting together beside the sea on the beach. It was a beautiful evening. Thakur was sitting quietly looking at the ocean. Sukumar lived in a place called Dakshineshwar, which is famous for Temple of Ma Bhavatarini, where Sri Ramakrishna Paramahansa lived out his divine play with the Mother. Sukumar was talking about Sri Ramakrishna. In that context, he said, 'My grandfather was Sri Ramakrishna's disciple. He was initiated by Paramahansa. He was a saintly person.' Thakur looked at Sukumar and gave a meaningful smile. Then he told him, 'You do not know that your grandfather was not a disciple of Sri Ramakrishna. He was not initiated by him. Of course, he used to frequently visit the saint and had deep devotion towards him. The rest of all that you said is hearsay.'

Sukumar was adamant and could not agree to what Thakur said. He kept arguing on the basis of all that he heard from early childhood. He lived very close to Mother Kali's temple where Ramakrishna lived. Thakur did not want to argue with him and only lovingly said, 'Don't tell me anything now. When you are back to your home, do ask your parents and the seniors in your family. Then let me know what they say.'

When Sukumar returned to Calcutta and his home in Dakshineshwar, he asked his parents and seniors and learned the truth was exactly what Thakur had said in Puri.

• • •

Thakur stayed on in Puri and we had to go back to Secunderabad. Sukumar remained with him. Nimesh Sanyal, a devotee of Thakur was supposed to come to Puri to be with Thakur for a couple of days. Thakur was waiting for him to come. One morning when Thakur was sitting with Sukumar, he suddenly said, 'Nimesh won't be able to come; he is bitten by a dog.'

Sukumar could not believe this. Nimesh was expected to come at any moment and there was no news about him. But he remained silent. That very day Sukumar received a telegram from Secunderabad addressed to Thakur that Nimesh Sanyal wouldn't be able to come to Puri, since he had been bitten by a dog and was under treatment.

Sukumar was slowly coming to understand this man that he had accompanied was no ordinary human being. He knew everything about everyone and everything happening, though he remained in one place. He could feel that Thakur seemed to know about everybody's life, what was happening and what would happen in the future. He could gradually see that behind the most ordinary things that Thakur was doing like any other man, deep within he was like the omniscient god who knew past, present, and future. This was the first time in his life he had been in the company of anyone who was so ordinary and, at the same time, beyond his mind's capacity to comprehend.

When Thakur said Nimesh was not coming and that subsequently was confirmed by the telegraph, Sukumar proposed to Thakur that it would be better to get back to Calcutta from Puri. Thakur again played the role of the omniscient one! He said, 'How can we go now? In a couple of days Nimesh's wife and children are coming to Puri to meet me. I have to wait for them. You will see that very soon. You will receive another telegram confirming my words.' The next day the telegram came.

Now, Sukumar was convinced beyond any doubt that nothing was unknown to Thakur. He was the all-knowing Self, the antaryamin, as it is called in our scriptures. Sukumar surrendered completely at the feet of Thakur as an ardent devotee and disciple. For the next many years, he followed Thakur wherever he went and took care of Thakur's physical body whenever Thakur would fall during samadhi, whenever his consciousness was withdrawn from the body and united with the higher Self. Sukumar became witness to much of the divine play of an omniscient Master.

• • •

On 12 February 1971, Thakur went to Bombay for the first time. His disciples Sukumar, the Nimesh Sanyal family, and a couple of others accompanied him on the short train journey from Pune to Bombay. The devotees wanted to see Thakur's divine play. They all asked, 'Please tell us who will come to you during your stay in Bombay?'

At first, Thakur tried to avoid the question, but the devotees were persistent. They knew that this was a chance to see the all-knowing Thakur predict something that had yet to happen. While he was laughing and talking, suddenly Thakur became more serious and said, 'A mad man is coming to meet me. He will have long, unkempt hair and tattered clothes. Don't drive him out. Bring him to me. Another young boy is coming. He will talk like a very wise person, asking big questions and seeking solutions to those questions from me. You all will wonder how a young boy can ask such deep questions and you will be surprised. Another young lady is coming who is very good looking. She will come with her husband.' Thakur was speaking as if he was seeing all those people who were going to come while he was in Bombay, though no one else had any clue about it. The devotees now stopped Thakur. They saw that he was talking from a different plane of consciousness. When the train reached Bombay, Thakur was escorted to the host's house.

As he reached the residence of his host, he settled into his room. Within a few minutes a young boy arrived at the house, determined to meet the sadhu who had just come. The moment Sukumar heard the voice of a young boy, he came to the front door and told the host that Thakur has already told them this young boy would be coming. Sukumar quickly escorted the boy to Thakur's room.

As soon as the boy entered Thakur's room, he bowed in reverence and with a voice firm with conviction asked, 'In order to be a true renunciate monk, a true sadhu, what are the qualities that are needed?' His next question followed, 'What is the difference between Savikalpa and Nirvikalpa Samadhi? Give me a reply that I can understand. Give me something so that I can move in the path of God. I am sick of this life in Bombay city.'

Thakur lovingly asked everyone in the room to go out and leave them alone. Then they talked to each other in a low tone for quite some time. Afterward, everyone saw that the boy was no longer restless. He was calm and full of bliss. With loving devotion, he prostrated to Thakur, took his blessings, and then silently left the house.

Thakur was taking rest. After a while, the predicted madman came, shouting near the front doors of the house, asking for permission to be admitted and taken to the sadhu who had just come to the house. Sukumar quickly moved, respectfully escorting the shouting man to Thakur's room. As he took his seat in front of Thakur, all his shouting and agitation vanished. He was silent. Apart from that there was no longer any sign of madness. Thakur gestured to Sukumar to bring prasad. Thakur offered it to the man. As soon as Thakur put the prasad in the man's hands, the man immediately became agitated and shouted, 'Am I a little child that you are giving me candy in my hands? If you have anything that would enrich my spiritual search, then give me that! I know you have that with you.'

Again, Thakur asked everyone else to leave the room. The man became pacified and calm again as Thakur whispered to him and then he fell at Thakur's feet with tears of joy, asking for initiation. Thakur initiated him with Guru Mantra.

Several days later, the lady who was very good looking arrived with her husband, seeking shelter from this man of God. All that Thakur had told the group of devotees on the train had come true. Sukumar again remained a silent witness to this divine play of the great Master. They were all awed.

• • •

It is important to note here that these were not miracles. Thakur was merely revealing a manifestation of higher consciousness. Every human being on this planet is born with this infinite capacity of the mind and heart. It is available to those who, through austere practice, reach a point that is transcendental to earthly, mundane desire-consciousness. Though those who were present saw such manifestations as supra-natural powers, Thakur remained detached and utterly unaffected. It was simply natural to him.

Niranjan Pratap Mathur's Story!

On 22 May 1971, in the city of Hyderabad, Thakur came to visit Mint master D. C. Mukherjee's home for satsang and bhajans. There were many devotees seated in the large sitting room. Thakur was reclining on a couch, talking to a few who were close by. The bhajan started and when Thakur sang in his melodious voice, everyone went into a state of bliss. As the singing ended, he left that hall and took a seat in an adjacent bedroom. Then he instructed his disciples to allow those who were interested in having a one-on-one to come and see him, one after the other.

One gentleman entered the room who, after a few minutes, rushed out intensely agitated in his face, his voice raised. He had come with a few others. He called them all and demanded that they leave with him immediately. The energy of the whole place became charged with a negative atmosphere. No one else dared to enter the room to meet Thakur after that. Thakur remained seated, unperturbed. A few devotees went scurrying in to inquire about what had happened, why the man had become so agitated and then left in such a rage. I asked Thakur what happened. Smiling, Thakur replied, 'Don't worry he will come again.'

On 25 May 1971, the same man came back to Thakur, this time with his wife. Thakur was sitting in another room. The man and his wife kept waiting outside the room for Thakur's call. I could not contain my curiosity about the earlier incident, so took the opportunity to ask the man directly about what had caused his anger and why he had left the house so agitated.

He said, "That day when I entered the room where Thakur was alone, he wanted me to take a seat. Then he asked me, 'Do you know me?' I quickly and firmly replied, 'No.' He again asked me, 'Do you recognize my voice?' I replied back 'No, I can't remember."

Thakur said, 'You people have such a short memory. In 1957, in the month of May, you went to Kedarnath and Badrinath as tourists. Your wife and daughter accompanied you. The bus in which you were all traveling stopped at a roadside. A wandering mendicant (sadhu) entered the bus and handed over to your daughter 21 paise and to you 16 paise, (100 paise make one Indian rupee). He told your daughter this money would not remain with you and told her take special care to preserve it. I am that sadhu.'

The man continued, "When he reminded me of that day at Badrinath, I instantly recalled everything. I don't know why I suddenly became very excited and angry and left. When I went back home, I told the whole story to my wife. With tears in her eyes, she asked, 'How could you do that? Let us immediately go and have the saint's darshan, pay our respects, and ask for his apologies.' So, we both have come today to have his darshan and beg his forgiveness."

Here they were, exactly as Thakur had said. He was gradually proving to me that he is antaryamin, one who knows everything about the past and future, while being established in the eternal Present. I had no idea how any human could reach this state of omniscience. I thought, as many others do, that only God is omniscient and man is ignorant, with only limited knowledge. But here, again and again, Thakur was convincing me of realms of spiritual powers that were beyond my scientific rationality, which were utterly natural to him. The man was Sri Niranjan Pratap Mathur, a retired officer of the Hyderabad Mint, where coins were made. His daughter, Rani Kishori Mohini, was a practicing doctor.

• • •

Konika Bose came to meet Thakur. She came from a well-off family. After offering her obeisance she took a seat in a corner of the room, which was filled with other devotees from all over Hyderabad and Secunderabad. Thakur looked at her and burst into laughter like a child. Without being asked, he started talking about many episodes of Konika's early childhood days. She was in awe! She had not come to this holy man for spiritual company or to learn, but to test him, to see whether he was a fake. Yet, Thakur was not like the other so-called sadhus whom she had previously met. She could not deny his deep, authentic presence, so her apprehensions began to melt away. The thought occurred to her that it would be good to invite Thakur to her home in Hyderabad. Thakur responded immediately to her thought before she had even verbalized it, 'I visited your home yesterday, even before you invited me.' He then went on to describe every detail of Konika's home, including the furniture and curtains. Konika Bose began to realize that Thakur was doing all of this to prove that he knew perfectly well that the purpose of her visit was to test his genuineness. Feeling she should apologize; she fell at Thakur's feet. When she came with her husband and son one day to take Thakur to her home for a satsang, it was the first time that Thakur had physically visited that area.

• • •

Discernment is critical for any spiritual aspirant. In searching for a spiritual guide, it is good to test those who profess to represent the divine. There is no shortage of false teachers with less-than-pure agendas. We must be intellectually and spiritually honest about that. By testing, we make sure we do not put ourselves under the influence of anyone who is not worthy of our trust.

We all begin our journey in this world governed by the limited perceptions of the ego, seeing the self as separate. Our ego identification drives us into the world and worldliness. But it is also the ego that ultimately drives us to look beyond our self and selfish limitations, beyond the material. The spiritual journey cannot even begin without the ego. The ego creates the veils of ignorance. Ignorance then creates desires. Those desires inevitably create the miseries of life. It is those miseries that ignite the urge to free us from the fetters of all bondage. That is where the search for the enlightened teacher comes in.

We need the enlightened teacher, one who knows the vagaries of the mind and who has mastered them, because we cannot trust our own illusion-riddled mind to guide us beyond the conundrums and mechanisms of the ego as we move forward on the path of Light. We seek one with clear vision, one whose cataracts have been removed, one who has realized the Light beyond all darkness. The enlightened soul paves the way for salvation for others.

• • •

One more episode related in Dr. Banerjee's diary demonstrates how utterly Thakur's divine self is ever available to those who are in distress.

In 1972, Thakur's birth anniversary was celebrated in Durgapur, West Bengal. Another devotee whose surname was the same as mine, Banerjee, came to attend this celebration and seek blessings of the realized Master. After a couple of visits, he often referred during conversations to the fact that he had come from Varanasi and that he had the good fortune of having met many great saints and sages. On the day of his departure to return to Varanasi, as he touched Thakur's divine feet, he requested that Thakur visit his home in Varanasi. He promised to arrange everything if Thakur decided to visit, so that many people of that holy city could have darshan. Thakur said, 'I have visited your home and seen it. Isn't your bedroom on the south? And you have a small balcony towards the west of your bedroom.

Sometime back when you were very sick, I used to go to your home and stand on the balcony. From there, I looked at you on your bed. Do you remember the difficult conditions of your sickness when you were almost bedridden?'

Banerjee was awed! How could Thakur tell all about his house, about his illness? He had not discussed it with anyone else since he had come to Durgapur! He realized that coming to see Thakur was not accidental. It was caused. It was a call that brought him to Thakur's lotus feet. He was in tears of gratitude for the grace of Thakur that brought him through that very difficult physical ailment. At that time, he had no idea that Thakur was physically taking care of him and looking after him.

This, again, is the divine grace of the Guru at work. Guru takes care of the disciple not just from the time one is initiated. The Guru-disciple relationship goes far beyond that. As Thakur once told Sukumar, 'I have been looking after you since your very birth.' He said the same thing to many devotees over the years, including to Prabhat Ray when he said, 'Since childhood I saved you on many occasions from certain death. I have known you for many births.' This is the grace of Sadguru, the true Guru, the divine embodied in human form.

Dr. Banerjee's journal continues:

On 19 May 1971, Dr. D. Choudhury lovingly took Thakur to bless his home. Partha, his son, was studying engineering in Kanpur. Partha had come home to see his parents on summer vacation at the time. We were all sitting together with Thakur, when suddenly he looked at Partha and said, 'Partha, how is that fat friend of yours?' Partha replied, 'He is doing well.' Thakur continued, 'Don't mix much with those three students who live in the room to the south of yours. Don't make friends with them.'

Partha was a bit surprised, but thinking Thakur had visited his hostel, said, 'No, I don't mix with them much, but when did you come to our hostel? I have never seen you there!'

Thakur kept smiling meaningfully and started talking more about happenings in the hostel and what Partha did. He smiled and said, 'No, I have not physically gone to your hostel.' Partha's parents were sitting close to Thakur. They were moved to tears at hearing all about Partha's hostel life from Thakur. It showed them that Thakur constantly kept an eye on his disciples and on their children, too, as if he were the head of the family. Thakur had visited Partha in his subtle form and kept an eye on him to make sure he did not fall into the wrong company while living away from his parents. The divine grace of the Guru always takes care of the whole family, even when only one person of the family is given Guru Mantra.

• • •

On his visit to Bombay in 1971, the all-knowing Gurudev was sitting in a devotee's house, talking to the assembled devotees. Suddenly he urged Sri Chatterjee, who was a foreman in the Railways, to immediately leave and go back home. Thakur said, 'Go home! You need to be there right away. Don't delay anywhere on the way.' Chatterjee was a bit worried. He repeatedly asked Thakur why he was sending him home so anxiously.

Thakur did not reply. He only insisted that Chatterjee leave for home without wasting any more time.

Chatterjee's father was leaving his body. He was longing to see his son and inquired twice from those at his deathbed about when Chatterjee would come. Thakur could see the father was dying and longing to see his son before passing away, so he forcefully sent Chatterjee home. When Chatterjee reached there, his father was already dead. It was then that he learned how much his father had been looking for him before leaving this world.

Dr. Banerjee also narrates this episode from his own life:
In work life there are many occasions when one is totally frustrated and comes to a point where no options remain except to resign and walk out in search of something new. A similar situation arose in my life, too, as I was dejected with the state of affairs in the hospital where I worked. I made up my mind that I would leave the job. Of course, I consulted my wife and close friends about this decision and they all agreed. Thakur was in Calcutta at that time. A month later, Thakur came to Secunderabad. I went to the rail station with many other devotees to meet him, then brought him to my home. After he rested a while, he went to the washroom to freshen up. Standing at the washbasin, he suddenly placed his hand on my shoulder and said, 'No! No, you did not take the right decision. You can't resign or leave your job now.' My wife Anu and I were both surprised because we had never written to Thakur or talked with him about it. We had only discussed it at home. Until then, it was a closed secret.

This showed us that wherever Thakur is, he can hear our every word and is ready to set us right if we are making the wrong decision or nurturing wrong thoughts. Physically, he could be anywhere; but his subtle presence and omniscient self was always looking after each of us. Again and again he proved this, strengthening our faith in him, letting us know that there is nothing that was unknown to him. Physical distance or absence was no barrier for his all-knowing self to keep a vigilant eye on his devotees.

• • •

On another occasion when Thakur visited Bombay in the same year of 1971, a gentleman came to see him. The man was a manager of an established company. He and his family had been settled in Bombay for two generations. Seeing him, Thakur said, 'Baba, you will have to leave your job in the next month and you will have to leave Bombay. You will have to go to Calcutta. But don't worry, you will get a good job and also earn good money.'

The man could not believe Thakur's words. All was well with him in his job and he was well settled in Bombay. Very casually, he answered, 'Let us see what happens.' But as Thakur predicted, within a month he was in the middle of big row with the company's management and board of directors and was forced to resign. He moved to Calcutta in search of a new job opportunity. Very soon, he got one with good emoluments. Everything happened exactly as the all-knowing Thakur had predicted. The man became an ardent devotee of Thakur, following him with all his heart. He never had another doubt in his mind that there was anything that this simple man of God did not know.

Dr. Banerjee ends his journal with these words:

I could only share here a few of the innumerable happenings that brought to light how one who is totally surrendered to God manifests God's attributes of pure love, compassion and power to help and heal those in need of divine grace. I only hope that my account of this realized Master of mine will help many on the path of light to find the grace of the Sadguru. I am blessed that I came to take shelter under his divine umbrella and follow his instructions in the path of Self-Realization. Blessed are they who get to know true Mahapurushas, yogis, and saints of this exalted order and walk the path of light and love.

CHAPTER FIFTEEN

THE HOUSEHOLDER SAINTESS

Being with a living enlightened master is one of the greatest fortunes that one could have in life. With him or her, you begin to glimpse into realms beyond normal human comprehension. Such masters create an aura wherever they are. Drawn by an invisible force, spiritual seekers, as well as those who have already reached a high state of *sadhana,* come to be in their presence to see them, hear them, and to receive the grace necessary to take their soul to the next realm of spiritual realization.

I was a personal witness to one such episode of the meeting of two pure devotees of God. It was one of the most touching experiences of my life with the Master.

It was a summer afternoon, 11 May 1976, around 4 p.m. Thakur had just finished a short afternoon rest and was moving from his bedroom to the adjacent visitors' room in the 7A Cornfield Road apartment in Calcutta. Thakur's attention was suddenly drawn to the doorway. His eyes took on a different look as he rushed to the doors to welcome a newly arriving visitor. A woman in her eighties, with her small stature bent due to old age, had walked in with a middle-aged woman. Having lived with my Master, I had seen how lovingly he served those who came to him on many occasions. This time was even more of a sight to see. Like an alert servant, Thakur welcomed the woman into the room, embodying how God serves his devotees in the same way that the devotee serves the Lord or Master. He demonstrated to the devotees present how a true devotee of the Lord is adored by the saints.

In a hurry, he instructed me to spread a mat and offer it for the woman to take a seat. But he did not want to waste a second to serve the devotee of the Lord so before I could do his bidding, he went to the corner of the room himself, picked up a folded bedsheet and spread it on the floor. Then he got a mat and spread it over the sheet to make it softer. He helped her, holding her with his own hands, to take her seat, saying, "*Mother, why have you taken the pain to come up three floors? It must have been very painful for you! Oh! I am so happy to see you! Do you feel the same?*" The aura of pure love filled the room.

It was such a joy to witness this divine play of my Master. My only thought was how in the external world, love is more of a transaction, a matter of individual convenience. But in the world of the soul, it is an expression of pure self-giving and deep spiritual sharing. The extraordinary simplicity, the humility and purity of these two exalted souls meeting was beyond the material plane. Here was my Master teaching us, demonstrating what true service is, how to do *seva* (offering love to the divine through service). In the path of devotion and love, *seva* has a significant role to play. The journey of the soul is to rise above all false identification with the lower self, to identify the divine in all that is, and to serve it with love.

"Mother, do you want to say something?" The question came from Thakur with utmost humility. From the moment this old lady walked into the room, Thakur was looking at her and then back at me, as if he was hinting for me to be deeply observant and open to important lessons for my spiritual growth.

The training is to be a good disciple. That is a huge challenge. Discipleship is a discipline requiring our best efforts to be awake and available for the Guru's light and to how it dispels the darkness of our conditioned mind. Here was my Master, living the teachings of how one should serve with feelings of pure love and devotion to our one and only Lord.

The path of *sadhana* unfolds with each and every small effort to identify where the fangs of ego lie, where self-interest lies, where any motivation that is not in sync with selfless service to the Guru lies. Thakur was drawing my attention to the things that were happening in the moment. He was teaching me how you serve one who is a pure devotee of the divine. To him, the pure devotee and God are inseparable. Pure devotion indicates there has been a long *sadhana* of conscious self-consecration to the Beloved. *Sadhana* has transformed the ego into the higher energy of divine love. The heart of such a devotee is no longer the home of all the clutter seen in most people. The heart of the pure devotee is clutter free. It is a space of self-offering and surrender, filled with the music of divine union. Such devotees are dearest to God. In the *Bhagavad Gita,* Lord Krishna makes it clear that those who give their heart and soul to Him, who are in constant state of remembrance, are closest to His heart too.

Thakur's face was beaming. Wanting me to realize who she was, he said to me,

> *"Listen to her with deep attention. She will tell many of her stories. At a very advanced age, the doors to the enlightened world of supreme knowledge have opened for her. She has realized many things. She has received so much from the higher world of light. She is filled within. Age, of course, was a bit of an obstacle, but she is full of the light of the inner world."*

Ma (we will call her Sannyasini Ma) sat down a little away from Thakur. She took time to settle in after the physical exertion of coming up the stairs and from her inner excitement at seeing the one who to her was the physical embodiment of the Lord of her heart.

After a while, she started sharing her experience and encounters with Lord Krishna that had brought her here. *"I was sitting in contemplation of my Beloved Lord Krishna, lost in the ecstasy of His all-attractive form, when suddenly the Lord spoke out. 'Do you know who Bhajan is? He is Bhajan Mohan Banshidhari.' He said it again and again."* Her face lit up with remembrance of the Lord coming to her to reveal the secret of this great saint, who had been so close to her home and yet whom she had never met.

It is an indication of Thakur's state of attainment at the time to have Lord Krishna speak to his devotee about Thakur as inseparable from Himself. Bhajan Mohan Banshidhari is similar to the name of Krishna when He is called Banshidhari, the one holding the flute in His hand, playing the cosmic song to attract His devotees to become playmates in His eternal *lila*. Mohan is also the name of Lord Krishna, one who mesmerizes the mind and draws the devotee to Him. Calling our Master Bhajan Mohan Banshidhari, Lord Krishna signifies that Bhajan is the very embodiment of divine love, Lord Krishna Himself.

Thakur was listening to Sannyasini Ma with deep interest. When he heard these words, an impish smile, like that of a child who had been caught, flickered across his face. "*Who said these words, do you think?*" Thakur asked her. She did not reply at once, but meditated for a while and answered, "*It must be my indwelling Atman!*" (*Atman* being the inner Divine Self, or Soul.) Thakur looked very pleased with her answer.

Sannyasini Ma then tugged at one corner of her white saree where she had hidden some money and tried to offer it to Thakur as *pranami* (the customary offering made when visiting a saint). Thakur's voice changed when he said, "*Ma, are you not a beggar? How can a beggar give a money offering?*" Thakur realized that she had nothing of her own anymore. Being completely surrendered to Lord Krishna, her state was like a beggar who lives on what she receives as alms. She lives on what the Lord provides.

Sannyasini Ma continued insisting that he take the money as her respectful offering. She had come to have the *darshan* (glimpse) of a living saint and in keeping with the revered custom in the tradition of Hindu *dharma,* the law governing individual conduct, whenever one goes to have the *darshan* of a living saint or a deity in a temple, one does not go empty handed. Householders particularly are taught by the elders to always give money, flowers, or fruit. You offer whatever you have as *pranami,* an offering to the Guru or to God. The belief is that if you go to meet a saint empty handed, you come back empty handed. The underlying philosophy of the tradition is that when you give something, especially that to which you are most attached, you create an empty space within, which the Guru or God then fills.

This tradition is rooted in the fact that the entire universe runs on the law of reciprocation. If you are not ready to give, how can you receive? Those who are truly blessed have learned to give, to share. Sharing and giving broadens our heart. It is an expanded state of consciousness that leads to true emancipation of the spirit.

On Sannyas

When Thakur saw Sannyasini Ma years later, he said to her, *"You are a sannyasini,"* though she had not been formally inducted into the order of *sannyas* at the time. Hearing this from the mouth of a sage, she was a bit surprised and did not understand exactly what he meant. But Thakur saw the inner subtle body of the worn-out, older body of this pure devotee. He could see her aura had nothing to do with the physical body, its age or form. Her aura was glowing. Thakur knew that deep within, her heart was purged of all worldly desires and cravings which bind a soul to the world of fleeting changes. With the clear vision of his third eye, Thakur saw she had reached a very high state through the path of devotion and love, one usually attained through the most difficult yogic practices, even for yogis. Sannyasini Ma had achieved the inner state of *sannyas,* having given up all attachments to the phenomenal world. She was totally attached to the divine in all its infinite manifestations. Nothing can create any bondage in that state of freedom from all *karmic* illusions. This lady was beyond her eighties, and was physically fragile. Her true statue was her spiritual flowering, which Thakur could see. She looked at Thakur, puzzled, and Thakur reaffirmed, *"Ma, I am saying you are a sannyasini."*

Just a month later, Ma was sitting in her daily meditation when her mind drifted to the words of Thakur about *sannyas.* She immediately started meditating upon her own Guru and prayed, *"Gurudev, it is you who once promised me that you will give me sannyas. Do I not deserve it?"*

They say that faith moves mountains. Intellectual knowledge has its place in our lives, but it is faith, pure faith, based on determination and trust, that creates miracles that no amount of dry, undigested knowledge can bring about. That is what happened when Sannyasini Ma was praying with all her heart, earnestness, and yearning for the promise of her Gurudev to come to fruition.

Meditating at her home altar, she suddenly opened her eyes. As she sat there awestruck, her Guru's picture came to life and the great sage emerged from it. He offered her the ochre clothes of a *sannyasi* and initiated her into the most advanced yogic state of *sannyas.* No fire ritual or any of the other rituals formally connected with *sannyas* were performed. The subtle body of the Guru had materialized as the living fire of wisdom and divinity, fulfilling her wish and his promise. As soon as he gave the cloth and initiated her, he dematerialized and disappeared into the picture again.

Thakur could see the rarified heart of this devotee was totally offered to Krishna. There was no desire of an earthly nature left in her. That is the true state of *sannyas:* a state of natural renunciation of all worldly attractions and repulsions. His words came true. It was one Master foreshadowing her Guru's coming to fulfill his promise to her after she had reached that state of natural renunciation, pure love and devotion, a state of true egolessness.

Whenever I asked Thakur about the *sannyasins* that I had seen who were clad in saffron and had a lot of scriptural knowledge, but who did not have a deep feeling in their heart given to the Lord, his answer was always, "*Sannyas is a state. It has nothing to do with colored clothes or scriptural knowledge. You cannot take sannyas. It has to come; it has to happen. When it happens, you are beyond all dualistic perception of intelligence and are one with the all-enveloping consciousness.*"

Thakur drove that point home again and again. One day when I was sitting at his feet, a devotee asked, "*Why do you still wear white clothes of the brahmacharin* (celibate monk)? *Did you not take sannyas?*" Thakur's face lit up with a divine smile when he answered, "*This body says, 'in one who has attained inner sannyas, where is the need for the formal outer sannyas?'*" At times, Thakur would not use the word "I" and instead would say "this body." As always, Thakur was making it clear that *sannyas* is not something to be taken; it is something to BE.

• • •

Once, Thakur said to Sannyasini Ma, *"One only should pray for bhakti* (devotion) *prem* (pure love) *and jnana* (wisdom) *from the Mother Divine."*

She nodded her head in humble acceptance of this ultimate wisdom on the path of God vision and then responded, *"Though this body has grown old and is afflicted with age-related degeneration, deep inside I am ever filled with infinite joy of my spirit. I am by the Lord's grace, ever in pure bliss."* She stopped for a while, kept silent, and then asked, *"Don't you think it's time for me to leave the body? When do you think that will happen?"*

Thakur answered, *"You don't have to think about your death now. As long as the Lord keeps you here on Earth, know that there must be a purpose. When the time is up, He will call you to Him."*

"Will I know prior to leaving this body that the time has come?" she continued.

"Why, don't you know that?" Thakur quipped.

Sannyasini Ma began to reply in a state of trance, as if she was no longer in this world at all. Her facial expression, her voice, everything changed in an instant as she started talking from a different plane,

"Yes, the Lord has given me assurance from inside. One day when I was meditating, my beloved Lord Krishna appeared

before me. Without a word, he took me along. I could feel I was accompanying him. After a while he brought me to a place in another world which was so serene and peaceful. The Lord said, 'This is the place where you will come after the death of your body.' I told him that I am not interested in all this. Then in the next moment, I felt him taking me to a much higher astral plane, where he told me, 'This place is beyond the plane of knowledge.' Finally, he said, 'You and I are one and the same.'"

I personally witnessed this wonderful divine play of my great Master whom this living saint addressed as Bhajan Mohan Banshidhari. The woman was a simple householder in the eyes of the world. But she had reached the final state of *sannyas* living in a family life while ever united in constant communion with the Beloved of her heart. No one recognized her as a saint. No one guessed what state she had reached through the purity of her devotion and love. No one realized how she had converted her home and family life into her own Himalayan cave to become totally dispassionate about the transience of the world. Immersed in the eternal world, she and her Beloved Lord communed in love and bliss.

As the very embodiment of divine love, Thakur met and attended to every devotee exactly where they were. He would become engrossed with householders as they talked about the most mundane, material aspects of their lives, listening to all of their trifles with attention and care. The same Thakur, the same sage, met this devotee with the clear vision that allowed him to serve her advanced state—and even to remind her that she had already been assured by the Lord that she would be with Him in His eternal abode after she left her body.

Sannyasini Ma also shared with us that she had many visions of Thakur as Krishna. She knew that Thakur was the very epitome of Love divine. She had kept journals of those visions in a personal diary. Though I was very interested in seeing and reading her diary, she said she was not prepared to share it with anyone else, as they were very personal divine experiences.

The woman who accompanied Sannyasini Ma was also very devotional. She was in tears listening to the conversations between the two saints as they met and shared their experience. Before taking leave of Thakur she said, *"Tell me something that I can carry back home for my journey."* With a divine smile, Thakur said, *"I can't say anything new. The only thing that you need is to drown yourself in the repetition of Guru Mantra."*

When it was time for Sannyasini Ma to leave for her home, she bowed to Thakur and prayed for his continued grace.

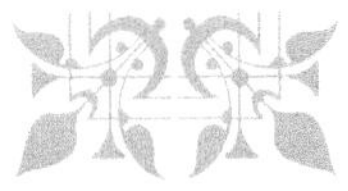

CHAPTER SIXTEEN

THE DIVINELY PLAYFUL MASTER

The Ego of a Good Cook

Pushpa Ma was one of the foremost of Thakur's disciples who left her home to join the ashram. Her husband had died long before then. She was middle-aged, very hard working, and outspoken. Looking after the ashram kitchen and its cleanliness, she cooked for the ashram residents, for Thakur, and the deities in the temple. Though she had a couple of assistants, she always cooked for the deities and Thakur by herself. She was deeply concerned about the sacredness of the food being offered to Gurudev and the deities at the temple.

She lived her life serving Thakur at the ashram. Though she had been initiated once, uniquely enough, she was initiated for the second time into *Gayatri Mahamantra* by Thakur. This was extremely uncommon in our tradition, since this initiation ritual is restricted to male Brahmins only. Pushpa

Ma was Brahmin by caste, but Thakur gave her the sacred thread to wear. We might possibly find a parallel for this in mythology, but it remains very rare. She lived in the ashram serving the Master until her last breath.

One day when Pushpa Ma was sitting in Thakur's room with other devotees, the Master suddenly said, *"Pushpa, these days you are not cooking well. It no longer tastes good. I can cook better than you."* Pushpa Ma was hurt. She thought that her cooking had been her most sacred form of worship and she had been doing it with all her might. To express her anger she said, *"OK, if you wish, you can cook."*

The next day, Thakur went to the kitchen and started cooking. He chose the same menu about which he commented to Pushpa Ma the day before. When the food was served, he himself was dissatisfied with the taste. It was most unusual, as Thakur's mere touch would always make any dish taste like nectar for all of us. We always longed for any food that Thakur would once in a while prepare. This time it was different.

Thakur was sitting with all the other brahmacharins to partake of the food. As he started to eat, he looked at Pushpa Ma and said, *"Pushpa, it does not taste good. Yesterday your food was better. You know, yesterday I said I could cook better than you with a touch of ego. Now God does not approve of it. He always chastises your ego because ego is never good for us. It destroys us."* Then he smiled at everyone present. The message was conveyed.

PUSHPA MA, AN ARDENT DEVOTEE OF THAKUR, WITH A CHILD

This is the subtle way the Master teaches. Inscrutable are his ways in bringing the message home, so that disciples and devotees can realize the obstacles along the path and take preventative measures to overcome them before they become deeply programmed in the subconscious. He himself was beyond the egoic mind. He was always anchored in his egoless state of purity. But he created this little play to exhibit that no one is spared when ego dominates.

Later, Pushpa Ma confessed that as she had been praised by the Master from time to time about her cooking skills, she had developed a subtle sense of pride and ego. Thakur enacted this play to open her eyes to her own follies. She learned her lesson and became more alert to the innate tendencies that the Guru tried to expose and transform.

The Master Eats Leftovers

In 1974, on the anniversary of his birth, Thakur again played a *lila* to convey that, to divine eyes, there is no discrimination. It took place at Jamalpur, a quiet town that primarily housed railway employees. Thakur had quite a few disciples and a good following there, so he would often visit. He said the town was sanctified by many saints in the past and that it was spiritually vibrant.

The bungalow in which Thakur stayed was well decorated. Devotees started pouring in from early morning. *Guru puja* and chanting of the divine name continued while Thakur sat on a couch, blessing everyone who came to have his *darshan*. At noon, the *prasad* was ready and was served to the close to three hundred assembled devotees.

Towards the end of the *prasad* distribution, when large numbers of devotees were having their blessed food, Thakur suddenly came out of his bedroom with a big smile on his face, greeting all the devotees. There were huge cheers seeing Thakur appear in person. Thakur said to them all, *"This is Puri Jagannath's prasad. I am sure you are all loving it."* So saying, he went to a devotee and stood before him. Lowering his head and opening his mouth, he gestured to the devotee to put the food from the devotee's own plate into his mouth. This was unheard of. The devotee was in shock. How could he put the food from which he had been eating into the mouth of the one whom he sees as God? But Thakur insisted, *"This is Mahaprasad* (holy food from Jagannath). *It is so delicious! Give it to me; give it to me!"* The devotee followed the wish of the Master and put his own food in Thakur's mouth, with tears in his eyes. Thakur then went to each of the devotees, lowered his head, opened his mouth, and took a morsel of the touched food from those who were eating *prasad*. The devotees assembled were all in ecstasy since, to them, Thakur was the very embodiment of Lord Jagannath of Puri. It no longer remained an event of *prasad* distribution. This was transformed into a great celebration of joy as each of them fed the Lord with their own hands, with food they had touched on their own plates.

Adding to the devotees' wonder was that Thakur had already taken his midday meal. How could he possibly take food from so many devotees? Toward the end, Thakur was in a state of *samadhi*. He had to be carried back to his room and laid down on his couch.

Thakur's body was no longer merely physical. Having transformed into living divinity, he was giving a simple lesson. Though initially one has to be careful about food, to avoid taking food that is left over, touched, or eaten by others in order to maintain the sanctity of one's own inner vibration, as one goes beyond the realm of *siddhi* (powers of soul), the *sadhak* (yogi) sees the extension of his own self in one and all. Then there is no more need for any restrictions. From the state of his enlightened consciousness, Thakur was showing he and the Lord are inseparable, one and the same in the intrinsic Buddha nature.

"The Betel Leaf Is My Earthly Anchor"

One day I asked my beloved Master a question about what had remained a puzzle for me regarding one of his habits which I did not see as good for his health. With a note of loving surrender, yet full of inquisitiveness I asked, *"Thakur why do you have this bad habit of chewing paan?"* (*Paan* is a preparation combining betel leaf with areca nut that is widely consumed in Southeast Asia, East Asia, and the Indian subcontinent. It is chewed for its stimulant and psychoactive effects). He smiled and kept silent. I was in a playful mood with him, which I often was when there was no one else in the room other than my brother monk, Satchidananda. I insisted that he had to reply to my question. (I had been given the impression from my elders that it is not good to chew *paan*, since it can lead to oral hygiene issues.) As he remained silent, looking away from me through the verandah of his room, I kept insisting that he reply, like a nagging child. Then he looked at me and said,

"When I reached that state of complete merger with the infinite reality, the Supreme Lord of the Universe, I was in the state of Nirvikalpa Samadhi for days. Then by divine will, when I descended to the earthly plane of consciousness, to my physical consciousness, I found it difficult to stay connected to this world. My consciousness would constantly soar high into that realm of pure bliss beyond all that is in the peripheral world of physical manifestation.

"But I had work to do! I felt the deepest call to help heal suffering humanity, to show the path of dharma, leading them out of the morass of the life of material bondage and pain, to the life that I now effortlessly experienced all the time. How could I see them suffer, while I saw all of them carrying the same potential of infinite happiness in the very core of their being?

"Yes, I needed an earthly anchor. In a mind where there is no earthly desire, the physical body has no attraction to be pulled to this mundane plane of consciousness. Then this paan came to me. Call it good habit or bad habit; it is my anchor to stay grounded. Otherwise, when I talk to you about the divine Lord, about that world of light, I am instantly transported to that world. I don't have to do any meditation, as you see many people doing. It is most natural to me, as simple as breathing. So, one part of me is eternally connected to the Supreme Reality beyond all definitions and the other part of me

> *is grounded through all these earthly things, my talking to the devotees and taking care of their tiny demands and problems. It keeps me grounded. So, don't take away my paan. It is my anchor!!"*

This is the advantage of being in the company of someone who abides in that world of infinite bliss and wisdom. I could never have imagined this simple *paan* had so much behind it. It had just always been one of the many rituals that I saw Thakur doing with keen interest, attention, and the keen artistry with which he did everything. I did not know that an enlightened Master of his state can never be touched by a habit such as betel leaf and nuts, which are harmful to an ordinary person. He was beyond right or wrong habits, having transcended his ego and mind to dwell in the realm of universal consciousness. He had divinized every cell of his body.

THAKUR PREPARING PAAN BETEL LEAF, HIS ANCHOR TO EARTHLY PLANE OF CONSCIOUSNESS

Music as Master's Medium of Teaching

Durgapur was one place in West Bengal where Thakur went many times to visit his disciples and devotees. A celebration was always held at each visit of Gurudev. On one such occasion of *Purnima* (full moon) it was decided to celebrate

Akhanda Hari Naam Sankirtan, a ritual of non-stop chanting of the Lord's Name from dawn to dusk. It is one of the rituals that have always been considered most sacred, as there is nothing more sacred than the name of the Lord Hari chanted together by devotees. If it continues uninterrupted, it heightens the holy vibrations, bringing all the more sanctity and grace to the participants. This is also called *Akhanda Nama Yajna*. (*Akhanda* signifying non-stop.)

Chaitanya Mahaprabhu, the great incarnation of Lord Krishna (1486-1534), brought this *Hari Naam* from the celestial planes to redeem humanity from all suffering and agonies. Bengal has been in the forefront of the wave of the *Bhakti* Movement that embraces *Hari Naam sankirtan*, the congregational chanting of the Holy Name, as its primary path for the mass upliftment of spiritual values and of life itself. It generates deep community bonds as it welcomes people from all faiths and religions within the community to join the chanting and be united in vibrations of divine love.

The great saints born in the eastern as well as other parts of India have been deeply inspired by Chaitanya's message of *bhakti* and redemption through *Hari Naam* chanting. They have continued this movement through the centuries, enshrining the *bhakti* path of devotion, love, service, and chanting of the divine names as the most flawless path to peace and harmony among all communities.

Thakur, being the gifted singer of devotional chants that he was, conveyed his message of spiritual practice and wisdom through his songs. Whatever he wanted to say to devotees about the path, he said it through his divine chants and songs. He chose music to teach his followers the timeless wisdom of the great mystics of the path of love and devotion. Most people, who were groping in the darkness, thirsting for a little happiness and peace, would fall under the spell of his mesmerizing voice and music. The words touched them deeply, opening the channels of higher life. He did not give lectures or speeches. His presence was the most powerful teaching of his divine message. He lived his teachings.

The word had spread in Durgapur that Thakur was coming and would be personally present, leading this great *sankirtan* from dawn to dusk. The *naama* (Holy Name) started in the morning, with people coming from far and wide to create a great wave of devotion. With the vibration of *Haribol* in the air, the assembled devotees joined in the chant, filling the air with ever-deeper intoxication. Later in the afternoon, the devotees assembled and set out for *nagar sankirtan*, singing in procession through the streets with pictures of Lord Krishna Mahprabhu and Thakur Bhajan Brahmachari, so that all the passersby could be blessed by the divine name. After going through all the main thoroughfares, they returned at dusk.

The full moon was in the sky and the place was vibrant with the fragrance of flowers and incense. The *naama* was at its peak. All the devotees were dancing with lifted hands, with cymbals and drums. Suddenly Thakur came down from his couch and joined the dancing, ecstatically singing *Haribol*. Then he dropped to the ground and began rolling from one end to the other in the dust of the feet of all the devotees, smearing the dust of their feet all over his body, in the ecstasy of divine love.

GURU PURNIMA GURU PUJA IN DURGAPUR

The assembled devotees had never seen anything like this before. They had heard that Chaitanya Mahaprabhu would do this to show that the dust of the feet of those who love his Lord is the same as the dust of the feet of the Lord Himself. In his divine intoxication, Thakur manifested the same *lila*, abandoned in his devotion to the Lord of his heart, showing that the dust of the feet of the true devotee is the most sacred thing on earth. It has transforming power in every atom if one goes beyond the egoic mind and totally surrenders to the Lord. His grace is the dust of the feet of the true devotee. As Thakur kept rolling, his face was streaming with rapturous tears and he went into trance. The devotees lifted him from the ground slowly and took him inside to his living room while his eyes were fixed on the large picture of Lord Krishna known as *Muralidhara*, the Lord of the flute.

Atma Puja-Worshiping the Self

In 1972, the devotees felt a deep desire to worship Mother Kali on the day of *Kali Puja* in the small apartment of Gurudev in 7A, Cornfield Road, Calcutta. The decision was made suddenly. They had little time to organize it in a bigger way. Their enthusiasm was so great, however, that in a couple of days everything necessary was in place. Thakur told his devotee Paritosh that he could find the idol of Mother Kali only in one particular place. Paritosh went to look for the idol of Mother and saw many idols for sale, but none matched his expectation. Then he remembered Thakur's directions to a by-lane in the area. Going there, he was awed to find the most attractive idol *(murthy)* of Mother Kali. It was exactly what he was looking for. He paid the price and took the idol to Thakur's apartment.

The word reached many devotees that *Kali Puja* was being celebrated at Thakur's apartment. A large number of devotees assembled. In the evening, they started singing *bhajans* while the priest began the worship of the divine Mother Kali. The smell of the flowers and incense and the presence of Thakur and Mother Kali transformed the small place. Everyone was in a state of intense devotion. Thakur sang a few *bhajans* to the Mother.

When the time for *Anjali* (a ritual flower offering to the deity) came, Thakur was asked to offer flowers at the feet of the Mother. Thakur came and stood before the living, vibrating idol of the Mother Divine and took the flowers in both his hands. As he started muttering some *mantras*, his body began losing its hold. In a state of *samadhi*, he offered all the flowers on his own head instead of at the feet of the Mother. The flowers fell from his head over his body. In total ecstasy of *bhav samadhi*, as his body began to fall, a few devotees rushed to hold him. They gradually took him to the couch and laid his body on the bed.

The assembled devotees were all in tears as they witnessed this touching divine play of their Master in the state of unity consciousness. When a *sadhak* reaches ultimate self-realization, he or she can only worship his or her own Self. In the deity, Thakur was experiencing himself, because within his Self, he experienced all the gods and goddesses. Thakur was already in a state of *sahaj samadhi* (continuously in a state of God Consciousness) after attaining the Brahman

Consciousness, but for the sake of the divine play and also to demonstrate how the Brahma Jnani worships the Lord; he played this divine *lila* on *Kali Puja.*

KALI PUJA AT CORNFIELD ROAD FLAT WHERE THAKUR OFFERED FLOWERS UPON HIS OWN HEAD

The devotees who were present to witness this exquisite play of the Master were supremely blessed, stirred to indescribably deep devotion and love for God and Guru. Showing us the pinnacle of devotion and total merger, Thakur was giving each of us a glimpse of that for ourselves. He was calling us to that Oneness as it naturally manifested in him. Enveloped in the mystery of it, seeing and experiencing all division between worshipper and worshipped melting into unity consciousness in front of us, we were forever called to that promise for our own souls.

Healing Power of a Saint's Words

Pradip Kumar Banerjee, a professor who was a man of simple nature, was going through turbulent and confusing times toward the end of 1982. Not knowing how to move forward, he came for *darshan* of Thakur. The following year, he was initiated along with his wife by Thakur at Dr. S.N. Chaudhury's home in Govindapur. This became the turning point of his life, as the worst of times were at his doorstep.

Pradip had always had a weak constitution. His health had been a constant problem. He often experienced acute pain in his stomach. In 1986, he consulted a physician from Rampurhat in the district of Birbhum in West Bengal. After some primary diagnostics, the doctor confirmed that Pradip had a serious case of ulcers. His condition further deteriorated when his mother passed away and he observed certain religious restrictions and rituals about food, further aggravating his ulcers. He started having frequent motions and urination and was passing blood. He experienced excruciating pain in the stomach and was throwing up what little he could eat.

The condition continued to worsen until he had to be brought to Calcutta to his elder sister's home at Belgharia. At NRS Hospital in Calcutta, the doctor confirmed that 85% of his duodenal was eaten away by ulcerous wounds and there was no recourse now other than surgery. Everything was set for surgery.

On second thought and the advice of a friend, Pradip was taken to a homeopathic doctor who lived in Titagarh, Dr. Sushil Chakraborty, who had a wide reputation for successfully treating many ulcer patients. Dr. Chakraborty agreed that it was a case requiring surgery but realized the patient's physical condition was so weak that he would not be able to withstand it. Dr. Chakraborty put Pradip on homeopathic medication to improve his health sufficiently to survive the surgery.

Pradip was emaciated. His weight had dropped down to only 35 kilograms (77 pounds). At this point, the demonstration of Guru's blessing came. Dr. S.N. Chaudhury, who Pradip respected as his elder brother, advised him to take refuge under Gurudev's lotus feet, as only Guru's grace could save him from his precarious state. As the *Guru Purnima* celebration was to take place at the ashram in Calcutta, he told Pradip that however difficult it might be, he should go to the Calcutta ashram and fall at Thakur's feet. Pradip and his wife Mala by now were convinced that there was no way to save his life but to seek Gurudev's divine intervention. So, they came to Calcutta the day before *Guru Purnima*.

MASTER IN MATRIBHAV HOLDING NARAYANA SHEELA, IN KALPATARU UTSAV, DURING THIS TIME THE WISHES OF THE DEVOTEES WERE AUTOMATICALLY FULFILLED.

At the ashram, hundreds of devotees and disciples were assembled, ready to celebrate with their blissful Gurudev. Pradip, however, had the most painful ulcer attack yet, with motions and vomiting. He had no power to even lift his body. Hearing the sounds of the ceremonies going on in the temple, he was consumed with negative feelings. He thought, surely he must be such a sinner to be in the ashram, with such festivities on such an auspicious day, and yet not even be able to have the *darshan* of Gurudev. So, he gathered what little strength he had and with the help of his wife, carried himself to Thakur's room. Thakur was sitting on his couch surrounded by many devotees and disciples. Pradip fell at Thakur's feet, crying profusely.

Thakur stroked his head lovingly and then chastised him saying, *"Go, live a life of carelessness. Did you not realize then how you were mistreating your own body? Did you not know what could happen to your health if you didn't take care of yourself?"* Then in the next moment, Thakur was full of compassion and love and said, *"Go, everything will be alright. You will be healed."*

This was not the first time Thakur's divine word became the cure itself. He had healed many patients suffering from untold misery and diseases that had been deemed unmanageable by medical science in just that way. This is the power of the Master whose compassion and word always carries the power of ultimate healing for the suffering children who have taken total refuge at his or her feet.

The word of Thakur created a divine vibration in Pradip's body and mind. A current passed through Pradip's body, assuring him of his recovery from the dreadful illness.

At this point, the bell for distribution of *bhog prasad* (blessed food) started ringing. Suddenly, for the first time in a long time, Pradip felt hunger again. He accompanied his wife and his two children to sit with other devotees and partake of the holy food. Sitting for the food, he began feeling unusually hungry. This was unimaginable for a patient who had had blood motions along with constant vomiting and who had been unable to move his body even a few minutes before. All of the food being offered was very oily and spicy, with different varieties of vegetables, sweets, and cream. They were almost like poison to anyone with a stomach as ulcerous as Pradip's. Despite that, he started eating without any fear, like a glutton, as if he had not eaten for days or months. The *prasad* tasted heavenly to his tongue. Never in his life had he tasted food like this!

In the afternoon, it was time to get back to Pradip's sister's home. He went with his wife Mala to Thakur's room to offer their obeisance to Thakur. As Mala offered her *pranam,* she said through a rush of tears, *"Thakur, give us permission to leave now. You are in the middle of me, my husband, and my two children. Remain with us, within us, always."* Thakur started laughing and responded, *"Don't worry! Go back home. There is nothing to worry about or to be afraid of. Your husband is alright now."* The words of Thakur and his love had healed all of them. With deepest gratitude, they left Thakur's room, praising the fortune of having this embodied divinity as the Guru of their lives.

After having such rich, spicy food, Pradip started feeling

much better. His constant colic pain had subsided since Thakur had uttered the word of his healing. That night, he again felt normal hunger and took normal food. There was no longer any uneasiness or pain. The next day, Pradip had a scheduled appointment with the doctor. When the doctor heard what happened the previous day, he was astounded. Examining Pradip, he said, "*You seem to be 90% better now.*" He suggested an endoscopy to confirm the improvement. Miracle of miracles, there was no trace of an ulcer. Pradip was healed for the rest of his life from this dreadful disease.

In later days, when Thakur went to Govindapur, the town where Pradip lived, he talked about this episode in his own way to his devotees and disciples. It was a winter morning and Thakur was visiting Dr. S.N. Chaudhury's home. There were quite a few devotees who had gathered to sit at the feet of the Master. Thakur was having tea. Suddenly, he spoke out,

"Do you know there is a sweet little girl who has two children? Once, her husband fell very sick. It was life threatening. He was almost dying. This little wife would sit at her altar in her home in front of my picture doing japa and cry and cry, saying, 'Thakur, have mercy upon our family. Please cure my husband. Without your grace he cannot survive. Only you can save him.'"

Thakur went on in his inimitable way of narrating the divine play (he always played with his devotees), and said, "*I thought, 'She is right. If her husband dies, then she will be left with her two children and her family would be in total disaster.' So, I prayed to the Mother to heal her husband and the Mother did that. Her husband returned from the jaws of death.*"

Pradip and Mala were sitting there, listening to the story being narrated by the Lord of their hearts and knew that it was none other than the story of their own family.

Inscrutable are the ways of the Master! No one can fathom the depth of his or her compassion. Their power to heal, to save suffering souls from great dangers and put them on the path to surrender and devotional love to Guru and God is infinite. All such miracles manifest only to bring the child to the path of ultimate liberation from untold misery and bondage.

KANAI LAL RAY ESCORTING THAKUR TO PUJA EVENT

Train Journey of a Disembodied Spirit

Once, something unusual happened at the bungalow of Kanai Lal Ray. It was a British Railway Quarter where Kanai, with his wife, sons and daughters had moved not long ago. It was said that during the British regime, a wicked man was buried at the far end of the back lawn of the house, and that was the reason that this bungalow had so far remained empty out of fear of it being haunted. One evening, after dinner, as the family was getting ready for rest, a strange sound coming from the Neem tree in the front yard brought the whole family and neighbors outside. The sound was a nasal long-drawn almost melancholic 'kiyoooooon-kiyoooooon'. Even as the strange call continued, nothing was seen even after flashing torchlights for a long time.

Everyone went back to their houses. The Ray family too came back and settled for sleep. But what happened next was too horrifying and supernatural to be fathomed by the common man's belief system. After all lights were out and everyone was in bed, a loud clatter of various sounds all happening together jarred the family's sanity. The eldest son Prabhat found that the steel almirah in his room was wide open and a pile of bedsheets were pulled out from inside and spread neatly on the floor in front of Thakur's altar. Not only bedsheets, but even carpets, rugs, and even Prabhat's meditation mat was spread out before Thakur's portrait which was in a corner of Prabhat's room. In the enclosed veranda where Kanai slept, the bicycle bell was wrenched off from the handle and flung violently across the room. In the bathroom, sounds of feet splashing in water, the iron bucket clanging against the floor were being heard. The bathroom was attached to the room where Prabhat's mother slept with her two daughters. Sitting up wide-eyed on their beds, they watched with horror as the bathroom door opened and shut on its own, marks of wet feet appeared on the floor and came towards their bed. A heavy old wooden cane that was kept in a corner lifted itself high up on the ceiling and loomed threateningly in a circle around their bed. At this point, they began to chant their *Guru Mantra* inwardly. After a few minutes of unbelievable mental torment, the cane dropped to the floor and all was still again. The family stayed up all night with lights on and meditating on their *Guru Mantra*. It was a test of their deep trust in the protective shield that the *Guru Mantra* offered that helped them pass the night.

The next day, Prabhat came up with a plan to restrict entrance of the spirit into the house. He plucked some Holy Basil leaves from the garden and wrote the words 'Jai Guru' on every leaf with sandalwood paste. Then he tied each leaf on the iron grills of the windows with cloth ropes made from his mother's old saree. This talisman was then sprinkled with Ganga water. The Holy Basil leaf, sandalwood paste, Ganga water and mother's saree are all considered sacred items. Due to their powers to ward of negative energy, these are worshipped as embodiments of Divinity. Prabhat believed that no spirit, however powerful it was, was powerful enough to transgress the powers of the talisman tied everywhere around the house.

At dusk, the strange call ensued from atop the Neem tree. To everyone's surprise, the same horrors as the day before unfolded exactly as the previous night. The talismans disappeared before their eyes in a matter of seconds. Not even a tiniest bit of the talisman had remained anywhere around the house.

The next day, Prabhat took the train to Calcutta to meet Thakur. That night, surprisingly, nothing happened. On the other hand, when Prabhat reached Thakur's place a day later, he found that Thakur was looking at him as if he had been impatiently awaiting his arrival. The moment Prabhat appeared at the entrance of Thakur's room, Thakur exclaimed, "*That scoundrel has come along with you! And is standing behind you.*" Prabhat could not understand who Thakur was talking about. Even as he stood there confused, Thakur continued, "*That is one wicked man. He had caused much sufferance. He did not deserve to reap the benefit of the talisman! He is so clever and powerful that he ate the whole of it to be relieved of his afterlife misery.*"

Prabhat now understood and asked, "*Why did he torment us? What harm had we done to him?*" Thakur explained, "*He was desperate to reach me. For that he needed a medium. He knew that it was you. He has not left your side for a moment since you left home. As a result of his bad karma, his spirit is undergoing tremendous sufferance. He is longing to take upon a physical birth again to alleviate his pain. But I do not want him to be born now for he needs this sufferance. He is already freed of much of his karma burden by eating the sacred talisman that you made. Yet, he must realize his mistakes before he may be granted a new body. You may go home to your family now.*"

Science and spirituality merge at the point of accepting there is no matter, it is all energy. In this story of paranormal, away from belief or disbelief, there are many things that our human brain or mind cannot perceive. The sages with their third eye, the eye that penetrates matter and the material cluster, can see that which is invisible to human eyes. The soul of the wicked man remained in the house for a long time and was longing to have a rebirth so that it could correct its path of life, which is possible in human birth. All the activities of this spirit may appear to be weird, but in the plane of energy and matter and its inter- convertibility it is all possible. A soul can manifest and unmanifest to human perception as grossed energy is matter and subtlest matter is energy. Thakur could see this soul's subtle energy and release it from its bondage and suffering while freeing his disciple's family from all the scary situations.

The Mysterious Door-Banging

If the saint wills, he may also keep lower spirits away from a certain place. Once, this very same Ray family began to experience banging at the front and back doors of their British bungalow. In the beginning it started with a light tapping on the back door. When the family opened the door there was nothing but darkness and silence. As days passed, the light tapping at midnight turned to repeated knocks, which in the following nights turned to prolonged banging and violent rattling of the wooden doors throughout the night. This continued for many days, and the family's strong faith and spiritual anchor in their Guru helped them survive the terrors. While they prayed to Thakur, they did not have a chance to go to Calcutta.

One day, suddenly Thakur arrived at their house. His visit was completely unannounced. The joy of the family knew no bounds on seeing that their beloved Master appear at their home. Why had he come all the way from Calcutta by an arduous overnight train journey suddenly, that too without any planning or telling anyone about it? The family forgot their worries and got busy in preparing for the Master's stay. They were so overjoyed that they did not mention anything about their nightly events to their Guru.

That night, for the first time in days, nothing happened. The next morning when Prabhat's mother got up at the crack of dawn, she found Thakur not in his room. Feeling restless, she began to look for him everywhere. She was crestfallen, thinking that Thakur might have left for Calcutta just as unpredictably as he had appeared. Soon her grief turned to joy when she saw Thakur walking around the entire circumference of the house covering the back and front lawns from the outside perimeter of the fence. As he entered the roadside iron gate to the bungalow, Thakur's face was alit with the light of the rising sun and his divine radiance was magnetic. Running up to him, she touched his feet in prostration. Smiling at her, he said, "*He won't disturb you at night anymore. No evil spirit has the power to cross the fence of your house.*" By walking around the house, the Holy One's footsteps had drawn a line that a spirit could not transgress. Beyond the supernatural in the above incident, what comes through as most significant is the love and care of a Guru for the devotee who is sheltered in him. If a true devotee is in danger, he rushes forth to remove the obstacles in his path.

PRABHAT RAY (LEFT) AND AARATI RAY (RIGHT) WITH MASTER IN FRONT OF BABA LOKENATH SHIVA TEMPLE AT THE ASHRAM

Guru always Reaches Out to the Disciple

Shobha Dutta, a resident of Chapra, a town in the eastern state of Bihar, lost her mother and was in a state of deep shock. When the news of this sudden death came to her, her husband, Gopal Krishna Dutta Chaudhury, a professor in the Chapra Rajendra College, was not at home. He was visiting Delhi in connection with a research grant. Hearing the news of the demise of her mother, Shobha took the next train to Calcutta with her son and reached her elder brother's home.

Here is her experience in her own words of the first night she spent at her brother's home:

> *"It was a full moon day. When I went to bed, I could not get to sleep, as my mind was tormented with memories of my beloved mother. The loss was unbearable for me. I was virtually tossing from one side to the other, trying to catch a little sleep and avoid the painful memories. But the more I tried, the more such memories of the past and the deeper my loss were becoming. I could not even close my eyes. I was looking through the open window seeing the night with the mystic light of the full moon. Suddenly I saw the face of a person very similar to Sri Ramakrishna Paramahansa surrounded by a mystic halo. He was smiling at me with much love. For a moment, I was in a state of awe, not able to believe my own eyes. When I jumped out of my bed to switch on the light to see the person more clearly, the image simply disappeared."*

The next morning, Shobha shared this unique experience with her brother and sister-in-law, but both of them were dismissive, saying that it was only a figment of her imagination. She did not push them on this, as her heart and mind were still full of the bliss of her vision, in the midst of all the pain of losing her mother.

Shobha's sister-in-law and her friends planned to visit a *sadhu* residing in Cornfield Road that very day, so she invited Shobha to accompany them if she wished. Shobha instantly said that she would be blessed to have the *darshan* of a *sadhu* and accompanied the group with her son. When they reached the flat, Thakur was sitting on his couch, busy talking to a group of devotees who had gathered there to have his *darshan* and share their problems with him.

Shobha was stunned. Thakur was the person she saw at the window of her bedroom the previous night! For a while, she could not believe her own eyes. How could there be such a similarity? How could such a vision become a physical reality? Thinking all of these thoughts and also about her mother with a heavy heart, she did not enter the room. She stood at the threshold of the door, filling her eyes with the presence of this holy man, soaking in his divine aura.

Thakur looked at her and she was transfixed. It felt like x-ray eyes penetrating to the core of her inner being, as if he saw everything about her in a single glance. At that moment, he waved his hand, gesturing for her to come inside and take a seat. Shobha went in and prostrated to him with all her devotion. When she lifted her head, Thakur asked, *"Have you come to see me before?"* She kept silent for a moment, hesitating about whether to disclose her experience. Then she told him about the blissful experience of seeing him at her window the previous night. Thakur was filled with joy. With a beaming smile, he said, "*You were my sister in my previous birth.*" Shoba felt a deep sense of inner bliss. She had totally forgotten the anguish and pain of losing her mother while in the presence of this saint, whom she was seeing for the first time in her life. To think that she had been his sister in their previous life was unimaginable. Thakur told her that he had so much to talk about with her and that she should come again soon with time at hand.

Several days later, Shobha went to see him. Thakur was so happy to receive her. They talked about many things. Then he said, "*Professor* (her husband) *is a very good soul, a very sincere devotee.*" He expressed a desire to visit Chapra, as he had often visited the nearby town of Patna before, but had never had a chance to go there. He said, "*When you go back to Chapra and meet your husband, tell him all about this meeting and also tell him that I want him to bring me to Chapra to your home.*"

Shobha went back home to Chapra and shared her joy at meeting such a great saint as Thakur while in Calcutta. Gopal Krishna was delighted to hear everything. He became instrumental in bringing Thakur to Chapra for the first time. In time, Chapra became yet another center where many thirsting souls were waiting for Thakur to come and lift them from all their suffering.

During Thakur's subsequent visit to Gopal Krishna's and Shobha's home, Gopal Krishna expressed his deep desire to be initiated in the path of divine love. Thakur replied, *"It is for this purpose I have come to your home on my own."* Gopal was very happy, but he could not bring himself to ask Thakur to initiate his wife Shobha, as he was uncertain about the protocol. Thakur told Gopal Krishna that he would initiate him on Ram Navami (the festival of the birth of Lord Ram), one of the most auspicious holy days. On the night before Ram Navami, Shobha could not sleep. Every time she opened her eyes, she saw Thakur's face smiling at her, again and again; then it disappeared.

The next morning, when she prepared Thakur's morning tea and went to serve him, Thakur playfully said, *"Do you want to say something to me?"* Shobha was just waiting for this opportunity, since she was longing to tell Thakur that she wanted initiation along with her husband. Thakur was all smiles and said readily, *"Yes, I will initiate both of you together."* She was ecstatic. It was as if God was saying, *"I accept you. You have nothing to worry about anymore."* A spontaneous, overwhelming thrill ran through her. She never knew that having a Guru could mean so much. She never knew that *deeksha* or *Guru Mantra* was such a divine gift, food for the soul which only the Guru can give. With the consent of the initiate, the Guru takes total responsibility for the child.

On the auspicious occasion of Ram Navami, Thakur initiated Gopal Krishna and Shobha together. Their journey had begun into the world of inner treasure, where Guru sits in his divine essence as the light dispelling all human-made fears and follies. Thakur later said to Shobha, *"You will realize later who I am."* Years later, Shobha confessed that at that time she had little understanding of spiritual truths. As she practiced the *japa mantra* given by Gurudev, she felt an ever-deepening connection to Thakur and the light within. Eventually, she realized the true significance of what Thakur had meant in saying, *"One day you will realize who I am."*

Shobha told other devotees of Thakur one of the simple miracles that would happen whenever Thakur visited her home in Chapra. During the day, Thakur would often visit her kitchen to see what she was cooking. By evening, many, many people would come uninvited to have his *darshan*. Thakur would ask her to serve them food. She would be afraid of not having enough food. How could she possibly feed all the people who showed up? Then, every time she served the devotees visiting for *satsang* with Thakur, she was in awe beyond imagining. However much she fed the devotees from her little stock of food, it never ran out. It always remained full, even after so many servings.

Thakur was inseparable from Ma Annapurna, the Divine Mother who feeds her children. He never said to cook more. He just went to the kitchen to cast his eyes on the food. That was enough to energize the food and infuse it with his divine powers so that it would feed any number of devotees, regardless of the amount initially cooked.

The powers of the great yogis defy all logic and reason. When the disciple is ready, the Guru appears and holds the hands of the devotee as they walk the path of light and love, toward the ultimate freedom from all bondage.

CHAPTER SEVENTEEN

MASTER TEACHES THROUGH DAY TO DAY INCIDENTS

They say true faith is blind. Those identifying with the analytical brain cannot accept anything on faith alone. They only trust what can be perceived or proven. To them, blind faith only leads to disaster. And it does in many instances. It can lead not only individuals, but many groups as well, into the pit of the narrow mind, which is a death trap. The evil of cults is known the world over. Each cult starts with the worship of their teacher or guru as if he is the only God. They despise others, their faiths and Masters. Looking at the history of religions, we see blind faith and blind following result in many massacres. It still happens, time and time again, in fundamentalism in every religion, in orthodoxy that has little to do with true religion or spirituality.

There are, however, many things in the world which cannot yet be explained in terms of analytical and experimental science. Many Himalayan Masters can perform acts which would put the scientific world in awe and leave it clueless. The Enlightened are beyond the limitations of everyday nature and human experience in the physical world. They have mastered every cell of the body and they have learned the magic of breath. They can cross the line between faith and reason, between what is possible and impossible, between life and death.

The Enlightened Masters have left the legacy of their extra-sensory (super-natural) experiences and mystical realizations for us as seekers to experiment and work with in order to fully and personally realize them for ourselves through our own experience. A certain level of faith in the instructions and teachings of the Master and masters, however, is necessary. It is akin to being a doctoral student. The student builds on the foundation of research done by those who came before him or her and carries it forward. Faith in the words of the Master thus becomes the foundation for spiritual flowering.

• • •

An ardent seeker, a disciple of Thakur asked him one day, *"What is dharma?"* Thakur replied, *"Dharma is that transforming practice which helps one to discover his or her own inner, infinite potential of divine energy and to manifest the divine in this human realm. That which is Truth is dharma."*

• • •

Samiran Dirghangi, another disciple of Thakur, brought out yet another facet of the religious life and Guru-disciple relationship. He asked Thakur, *"I have seen many people come to take shelter under your benign presence with immense enthusiasm to begin with, but after a while move away and leave you. Why do such things happen? Why do they come and why do they leave?"*

It is a pertinent question and Samiran Dirghangi was blunt enough to ask it directly. Thakur smiled and opened his heart to the assembled group, saying,

> *"Humans at times are very cunning. They think that no one is as intelligent as they are. When they hit roadblocks which they cannot resolve themselves, they are in such a mental and physical state that they become convinced they need divine intervention. They run to sadhus and saints who have healing powers and a big following. They go to gurus and take shelter. If they are in the dark tunnel, they stick to the guru. They work desperately to receive the guru's mercy. Once they are out of their turbulence, however, they are gripped once again by deep tendencies of greed, jealousy, and other dictates of their conditioned, egoic mind, which begin to foul the environment for themselves and for others."*

Thakur hits the nail on the head. This clearly brings to light why in most religious or spiritual organizations there have been and inevitably are such levels of power politics and such an unholy atmosphere, particularly in the inner circles of organizational hierarchy. This is the influence of *maya*, the illusive potency which clouds the mind and conspires from inside to be gripped by the influence of power, money, and control.

I have personally experienced this living in the ashram of my Beloved Master, when I was ordained as a monk. On one hand, the disciples demonstrated their *bhakti*, their devotion to the Guru. On the other, they were continually stirring the waters, muddying things up with conflict and confusion throughout the ashram. I saw all of that playing out again and again in the life of the ashram of my Gurudev. I came to believe that organized religion is often nothing but politics and ego-play that invariably lead to groups and power games.

Most people who come to the masters are worldly. Scratching the surface, they take anything of value they can, while keeping their ego intact. Over a period, the reality comes to the surface. Only a few are ready to fully embrace the world of inner awakening. And only a handful among those are alive enough to the seed of pure compassion to have the destiny of lifting others to their next stage of evolution.

Thakur was so soft, so kind, so forgiving and, above all, so loving and caring. At times I felt that he was overly compassionate and that was being taken as a weakness. I watched many people take advantage of his kindness and unconditional love. He always remained indifferent to that. He knew it was his *dharma* to love unconditionally and to forgive, and that it was the *dharma* of those who were trapped by their own mind to hurt others.

One day I told him *"Thakur, you are so kind; you love so much."* He replied, *"No, I don't love."* I was kind of taken back. I was young, fresh to the ashram as a renunciate monk. I said, *"If you do not love, then what do you do?"* With a smile on his face, Thakur taught me the greatest lesson of my life, one that would change the entire course of my thoughts and philosophy of life in later years. He simply said, *"Love cannot be done; Love happens."*

This was a revelation. Suddenly, I felt as if a curtain was lifted, that a cataract had been removed from my eyes. I could see the ways of the world of light more clearly. I realized that true realization shows us that there is no difference between nature and us. Everything in nature is flowing. Life is flowing. An enlightened Master does nothing but live in the flow of everything moving in its own time-space dimension. That is why there is no credit or discredit. No failure, no success. No gain and, of course, no loss either. He had revealed to me the basic flow of all existence, and the falseness of our human perception of "doer-ship."

• • •

God's infinite compassion for mankind manifests as the living teacher, the Guru, who is a living manifestation of the attributes of God. The Guru may look like any other human, but the Guru's vision is beyond the physical dimensions of time and space. The Guru's compassion, however, is intensely personal in responding to the heartfelt call of any devotee. As Thakur once said to me, echoing all the Great Masters, *"You know, whenever anyone calls me with a touch of their heart, I can hear it instantly."*

THE COMPASSIONATE MASTER!

On one such occasion, Thakur was scheduled to go to the Hyderabad ashram on the occasion of the installation ceremony of Radha-Krishna and also to attend the holy festival. Because all the devotees of Jamalpur knew that, they knew that Thakur would not be visiting Jamalpur in the near future. Nevertheless, he did come!

Back in the late 1950s, when Thakur (still called Bhajan at that time) lived in the temple ashram of Ma Anandamayee at Ranchi, he held a chanting session every evening with all those assembled there. Many people came to the ashram just for his enchanting *bhajans.* Among those who admired Bhajan were Ajoy Ghosh and his mother, Bikaskali devi. Bhajan addressed Bikaskali devi as 'Didi' (elder sister). Whenever Bhajan sang, Didi was beset with intense devotion. She came with Ajoy every evening and sat with other devotees. As Bhajan sang, the whole ashram would reverberate with ecstatic vibrations of love and devotion. Didi would be so touched by the melodies and the divinity in it all that she cried the entire time.

The time came when Ajoy was transferred and moved away from Ranchi. Of course, he kept track of Bhajan, who was like a brother to him. Ajoy knew when Bhajan became a much-worshipped Guru and that Bhajan had an ashram in Hyderabad. During his Ranchi days, Ajoy had glimpses of Bhajan's divine qualities, though both had been young then.

Years later, Ajoy came to Jamalpur as a personnel officer for the Railways. The Railways gave him a house across from Dr. S.K. Roy's bungalow. Ajoy was not married and his mother, Bikaskali devi, then old and failing, lived with him. When his mother's illness worsened, she was taken to the local Railway Hospital for a prolonged stay to receive special medical treatment.

One day at the hospital, Bikaskali devi suddenly started loudly proclaiming,

> *"Take me to my home! He is coming! After a long time, I will be able to see the apple of my eyes, my lost treasure. He told me in my dream that he is coming to see me. He is the Lord of suffering souls, my Bhajan! He always loved me so much and would pour his love out to me when he called me Didi."*

This continued for several days, growing in intensity. Seeing his mother's conviction about Bhajan coming to Jamalpur, Ajoy went to Dr. Roy to ask if Bhajan was coming. Dr. Roy replied that Thakur had already sent a message that he was not coming to Jamalpur.

Ajoy went back to his mother and tried to convince her that Bhajan was not coming anytime soon. His mother became so distraught that she literally began tearing at her own hair. Hospital authorities found it so difficult to manage her that they sent her back home. Once she was at home, she immediately calmed down and kept her eyes trained to see her loving Bhajan coming to her. She became the essence of attentive, patient, quiet waiting.

Then, wonder of wonders, Thakur arrived in Jamalpur on March 5th, 1986, within 4 days of her dream. He came to stay at Dr. Roy's bungalow just opposite Ajoy's home! When the devotee's heart cries to see the Beloved, he cannot remain away. His heart, too, cries for the devotee. This is the miracle of pure love, beyond all mortal limitations.

When Ajoy's mother heard that her Bhajan had come and was waiting in the house just opposite to hers, all of her strength returned. With her son's assistance, she ran to Dr.

Roy's home. The meeting was like the river flowing through all hurdles to meet the ocean. She cried out of ecstasy at her dream coming true. She was face to face with the one whom she had been calling to see from the core of her heart before leaving this world, if that was what the destiny of her illness was leading toward.

Bhajan welcomed his Didi and made her sit on a chair next to him. For the next few days, during the evening *satsangs*, Didi came to that chair next to Thakur. She sat like a statue, without a word, looking at Bhajan as he sang or talked to the assembled devotees. Throughout Thakur's visit to Jamalpur at Dr. Roy's bungalow, she came in the morning, and stayed the entire day without a word. Around 9 p.m., with the help of a couple of other devotees, Ajoy would take her home. Even then she would protest, *"Don't take me away from him; the separation is too painful."*

The day for Thakur to leave Jamalpur came on March 12th. Bikaskali devi was never the same again. She was healed. She became as calm inside as a *sannyasi,* totally dedicated to God. After that, Ajoy was transferred to Asanol, where both he and his mother lived peacefully. They had found the Beloved of their hearts coming to Jamalpur unscheduled, only to fulfill the deep desire of Bikaskali devi to see him and offer herself utterly to her Guru.

This is the glory of a true Master whose life is a living demonstration of God's love and compassion for suffering humanity. The Guru comes to this world only to bring God and divine grace into being as a physical manifestation of non-physical divinity.

Thakur's Cows

Thakur used to say that no ashram is complete without a comfortable shelter for cows where they are not 'animals' for a mercantile goal but members of the big ashram family where they would be loved, served and taken care for their whole life. The cow's needs and comforts are far superior in priority. He mentioned that cows are the soul and spirit of any ashram. *Goseva* or service to cows is as essential as serving the poor and the suffering. He considered cows as not mere animals but the Mother who nourishes us with her milk. Thakur said that to take care of the cows with as much love and respect as one would to one's own mother was imperative to attract harmony, prosperity and spiritual grace of the gods, goddesses, angels, ancestors and the universal Masters. Once, Thakur had also stated that if the cows are not taken care of well or loved, it is not a good sign for the progress of an individual soul or even the larger community in general.

The first cow that came to the ashram was an indigenous white cow from Bihar. The first time Thakur saw her, his connection with her was so deep that he was in divine ecstasy. He addressed her as "Mother". He said that she embodied the all-compassionate Divine Mother. Although her name was Gauri, Thakur used to call her not by her name but as "Ma". Anyone who saw Ma Gauri would be spellbound by her large black eyes filled with motherly love and innocence.

Thakur named the other cows that eventually came to stay at the ashram as Kali, Bhavani, Durga, Parvati—all different names of the one Cosmic Mother. When any cow was to arrive, Thakur taught everyone to welcome her not as an animal but as a tangible living form of the Divine Mother. He would himself stand on the road outside the ashram gate waiting eagerly for the cow to arrive. When she came, Thakur embraced her with tears, washed her feet, worshipped her, and welcomed her. The meeting between the cow and Master was so incredible that it seemed as though the two were reuniting with each after a long time.

Whenever Thakur got a chance, he would run towards the cow shed with child-like enthusiasm. Thakur's longing to meet the ashram cows was never one-sided but was always reciprocated. Whenever Thakur began walking on the path towards the shed, the cows would always seem to foresee his arrival and they began a joyous mooing. Once among the cows, Thakur embraced each one of them and talked to them in his unique language of love.

One day, a brown cow arrived. Thakur called her Mother Lakshmi (Lakshmi is the 'prosperity' aspect of the Divine Mother). Her demeanor was so soft and graceful that she grew to be everyone's favorite at the ashram. Little children would come every evening to cuddle and play with her. Her loving presence gave joy to everyone. In fact, ever since she arrived, true to her name, there was a surge in the well-being of the ashram from every aspect. Lakshmi once fell terribly ill. According to the medical team, her condition, a hoof disease, was incurable. Thakur said that though her days were numbered, yet every effort and medical care must be provided to ensure her comfortable and pain free departure. Despite Master's instruction, a few of the members of the ashram committee could not appreciate taking care of a cow who was not going to bring any income as she was sick and wanted to sell it off. Thakur felt shocked when he heard this proposal and he thundered, *"Hypocrites! How could you be so insensitive? So long as she was healthy and loving, you all showed her admiration. What do you do when your mother in her old age falls sick, do you send her out just because she is no longer of any use in your family, and is a burden? Laxmi will stay. Give her every care as you would to your own mother."*

Thakur strikes a strong note as to what should be our right attitude towards animals. Not only was he extremely loving and caring for every visitor who came to see him, he also kept everyone alert about the right attitude towards all other living beings. He once said to me, *"The more you are spiritually awakened, you will find that you are becoming overly sensitive to all other species of life and creations of nature. You will not be able to hurt even small insects. You will see your Beloved in every spark of life. That is the reason I always warn you to be very careful and not to harm or hurt anyone. It all comes back to you."*

Laxmi lived on for some time and she was given full care and treatment; children came and played with her even though she could not reciprocate as before due to her failing health, but she gave her company to them. As Thakur had said, she was Mother, she blessed the ashram and one day in the presence of the Master she left this world. Towards the end it was difficult for her to leave the ashram, and most of all Thakur's love. At the time she departed, her deep eyes had tears, and so did Thakur's. Thakur was in tears. He was most dispassionate yet most human.

Laali and Kaalu

Laali and Kaalu were two stray dogs who lived in Thakur's Mallikpur ashram. They roamed about freely in the ashram premises. Although they were Indian street dogs, they never went outside to the streets or visited other peoples' homes for food like the other local strays. 'Laali' meaning 'the red aura', was a female dog who had come in the ashram during the early days of ashram's foundation. Thakur had instructed everyone in the ashram, *"She (Laali) will remain here for as long as she wishes. I want everyone to make sure that she is well-loved, cared for and that no one disturbs her."* He also strictly instructed that she be served the regular prasad meals of the ashram along with all other devotees and ashram members. Often Thakur fed her from his own hands. Perceiving Thakur's special attention upon the dog, everyone treated her with respect and no one dared to send her away.

Once when Laali gave birth, Thakur instructed that the puppies be taken care of. When the puppies grew up they left one by one on their own accord. In the end there remained one particular pup that never left, just as her mother. His name was Kaalu, meaning 'the black one'. Kaalu was a beautiful black dog with white spots.

Every time Thakur returned to the ashram from some place, he would get down from his car with childish impatience only so that he could meet his two canine buddies sooner. Because of his illness his movements were much restricted, yet, as soon as he set his foot on the ashram premise, he began to call with joyful excitement—*"Kaalu! Laali! Where have you gone? Come! Come!"*— his eyes searching for them, in his child-like endearing way. Kaalu and Laali would come dashing from whichever corner of the compound they might have been, and wagging their tails vigorously, they would jump around Thakur often falling at his feet and licking them in sheer joy. While many devotees stood devoutly around the car waiting for his attention, to touch his feet, offer flowers and seek his blessings, Thakur's attention seemed to be singularly focused on his two canine devotees alone. They were the only ones who on every occasion of the Master's arrival enjoyed the foremost and unparalleled privilege to wash their Master's feet with the kiss of unconditional love.

Once, while Thakur was staying at his small apartment ashram in Jadavpur, Thakur's attendant monk noticed that Thakur grew increasingly restless during the afternoon meal. Such restlessness was quite common in those times when any of Thakur's close devotees was going through a physical suffering. At first, the monk did keep quiet, not wanting to intervene in Thakur's other-worldly consciousness. Soon Thakur was sweating profusely and was shifting restlessly while seated on his cot, as if he was experiencing some unaccountable physical as well as inner trauma. His eyes seemed to have drifted to some far-away place, as though he was taking upon his body and mind the sufferance of some other soul elsewhere. When Thakur's sufferance grew too painful to watch, the monk questioned Thakur. He was silent. After a while Thakur calmed down as if some intense sufferance was put to rest. His eyes, still forlorn, now had tears. With a soft and barely audible voice choked with pain of bereavement, Thakur broke his silence and said—*"Jaah! Kaalu ta choila gelo*." (Alas! My Kaalu is gone.) Thakur instructed a devotee to send word to Mallikpur ashram immediately that Kaalu be buried in the garden within the ashram premise and not taken anywhere outside.

Later, it was known from those who had witnessed Kaalu's death that at the precise hour when Thakur was suffering in his Jadavpur apartment, Kaalu had suffered a heart attack, and before any help could arrive, he had breathed his last. Kaalu's death happened at the instant when Thakur calmed down before announcing his beloved friend's departure from the mortal stage.

To the enlightened Master, all differences cease to exist. I have seen this happening to him when his closest disciples or devotees went through some serious life threats; Thakur took upon himself the pains and suffering, saving the devotee. But this episode only brings the reality that the enlightened state is beyond knowledge and only when one is identified with the rest of the universe, with every sentient being and feels their pain as his own, do we see the ultimate manifestation of the divine. Thakur demonstrated to us that true love transcends every difference created by human minds or society. His deepest love for animals only brings to light that Masters come to demonstrate to us about the most sublime philosophy of universal love and compassion.

Thakur was the very embodiment of love and compassion; we see him shedding tears of bereavement which is the very expression of pure love and is different from the bereavement that stems from worldly attachment that is rooted in physical identification rather than spiritual identification. It was a simple message to us all, that love knows no bounds and touches every creation of the all loving Creator, which is the essence of unity consciousness.

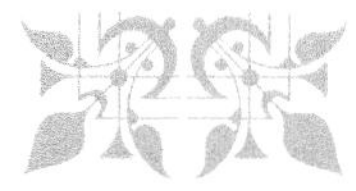

CHAPTER EIGHTEEN

ON WOMEN AND FEMININE DIVINE

To me, Thakur was more mother than father. Living with him for almost a decade, I experienced him as the feminine manifestation of pure love and forgiveness. He was male, but his way of dealing with all of us was like that of our mother, attending to every minor detail of our emotions, needs, and transgressions. Thakur was naturally supportive, taking us under his wing, always showing us the path forward.

During many annual festivities at the ashram, during *Guru puja* (ritual worship of the Gurudev), he dressed in a saree, wore golden jewelry given by his devotees and a big bindi on his forehead, just like a Mother. Even his physical movements were mother-like.

In the *Guru Gita* (hymns to the Guru), Adi Yogi and Adi Guru Lord Shiva reply to the divine consort Parvathi (Durga) when she implores him to reveal the path to salvation, "*Guru maddhe stitha mata matri moddhe sthito guru, gurur matanam namahstestu matri gurur namamyaham."* Simply translated, that means, *"In the Guru is the Mother Divine and in the Mother Divine is the Guru. I prostrate to Mother, the Guru, and to Guru, the Mother, as One with pure devotion."*

The spiritual literature on the path to self-realization in India's Vedic tradition is filled with the need for worship of Shakti, the feminine aspect of the Godhead. Awakening of the *Kundalini* (the latent Shakti energy coiled at the base of the spine), and merging in Shiva, the pure Self within is the whole point. Shakti worship is directly connected to Guru worship. Guru is not just a male or female person. Guru is the power, the light that dispels the darkness. That power or light is also being realized as Guru Shakti. Thus, Guru worship is part of Shakti worship in the Hindu tradition. Without the awakening of Guru Shakti through the grace of the Guru, pure wisdom, the awakening of *Kundalini,* does not happen.

Here, we have the privilege of hearing what our beloved Gurudev thought about feminine power and the role of women in the family and in creating a world that can sustain peace and harmony. Thakur had a broad vision to emphasize the role of man and woman and the harmony that we all look forward to for happiness and peace.

Thakur often visited Jamalpur, in Bihar, as he had a large following there. He often said that Jamalpur was one of the most spiritually vibrant areas, that in the past many saints and sages had lived there, and that their divine vibrations sanctified the quiet township. It was predominantly a town solely inhabited by Railway employees from the British period.

Once during his visit to Jamalpur, he was talking to a group of devotees who gathered in the home of the disciple where he was staying. Talking to the householders who had gathered, he smiled and commented, "*Men and women, male and female are complementary forces of one Cosmic existence. Together they keep the creative forces to sustain humanity and its evolutionary process.*"

Thakur was trying to impregnate the minds of the devotees with the need for more harmonious and loving relationships between men and women. He would always chastise the men when they hurt the feelings of their wives or other women. He told them that only by respecting women could any society thrive, not otherwise. He insisted that if we are interested in having a peaceful world, then respect for women and mothers must become a supreme priority.

Thakur's words are poignant and carry a deep message for the world. He emphasizes men and women as complementary forces of nature that need to mutually help each other move toward their own goals in life.

While women's efforts to attain gender equality are meant to create a more just society and are the only means to reach a sane humanity, Thakur was addressing the ancient ideology of Indian womanhood, which is founded on the spirit of purity and patience as an ideal embodiment of true motherhood.

Thakur made it noticeably clear that family chores should be shared between the spouses. In Indian families, women had always taken the brunt of handling all family chores, while husbands only worked to earn money to run the family. Thakur's vision was much ahead of the time. He saw that unless the responsibilities are shared between both spouses, family peace would be disturbed.

Once Thakur was visiting Kanai Roy at Jamalpur on the night before Shivaratri, the annual all-night ritual of worship of Lord Shiva. The women devotees sat with Gurudev and were immersed in laughter-filled conversations. Thakur always loved these lighthearted, informal get togethers where devotees talked about their everyday life and adventures. Bharati Roy, the young daughter of Kanai Roy, suddenly spoke to Thakur, *"It is our ardent wish that tomorrow, in Your presence as the Living Shiva, we would celebrate Shivaratri and stay awake the whole night singing and worshipping."*

Thakur instantly agreed, *"This is such a good proposition! I would be happy if you all fast tomorrow and worship Lord Shiva."* Thakur then looked at Samiran Dhirgangi's wife and said to her, *"I know that you cannot normally fast and you have small children to take care of but still try to fast tomorrow, as this will bring great blessings to your family."*

Samiran was sitting some distance away and overheard Thakur. He came to Thakur and said, *"Thakur, if she fasts tomorrow and comes to celebrate Shivaratri with all the others, who will look after the children at home? That would be such a hassle for me."*

Thakur's face turned stern. He frowned at Samiran and reprimanded him in an angry voice,

> *"Why? Do the children not belong to you? Why should your wife take care of them all the time? Is she here in your family to take on her head all the liability of house*

and children and the chores? You are all so selfish. You should have a little bit of feeling for your wife. Who are you to always stop her from having a bit of joy in life? Of course, she will be here worshipping Lord Shiva throughout the night! You go, take care of the children. And in the morning prepare some food for her so that she can break her fast with that food."

Thakur's heart always ached for oppressed women. He felt the physical and emotional burdens they carry, the pressures they are under.

Samiran also recalled that on another day Thakur had said to him,

"Always keep in mind women are the very embodiment of the universal Mother. Your wife is an active partner in all your happiness and agonies. Never despise or disrespect your wife. If out of your ill treatment she sheds a drop of a tear, all the peace and prosperity of your family will be torn apart, possibly forever. Women are the embodiment of the goddesses. They play different roles with a strong sense of sacrifice and love as wife, beloved, mother or sister."

• • •

We find similar messages coming from Thakur in later years. In 1991, on the anniversary of his birth, there were quite a few devotees who were sitting around Thakur's bed. Thakur was talking to them about the challenges of householders, particularly of the women and what they go through in the grind of household chores. He suddenly remembered his ardent disciple and devotee Manju Das and said, *"Dipali, why has Manju not come yet?"*

Dipali Ghosh was another very ardent devotee and disciple. She saw Thakur as her Gopal, the child Krishna, so she responded, *"Gopal, you should understand that Manju has to come only after completing all the household chores. How can she come so early? In addition to her chores, she has to come all the way from Behala, which is quite some distance from the ashram."*

"But the children are all grown up now!" Thakur quipped.

"Yes, they are grown up, Gopal, but so what? One has to take care of so many things of daily life. She has to pull all of it by herself," Dipali answered.

Thakur took a deep breath. Right then, Manju Das came in. She was almost panting for breath. Another devotee, Gauri, said, *"See Thakur, Manju is here."* With a big smile, being happy to have come to the presence of her beloved Master, Manju tried to explain the cause of her delay. *"How can I come, Thakur? Even at this age, see how I am being ground down in worldly chores. I had to prepare food for everyone and only then could I leave home and take a bus to your place."* She then lovingly prostrated to Thakur. Overwhelmed with frustration, she suddenly burst into tears and said, *"I cannot go on like this anymore."*

Thakur's eyes were moist. He was touched to see the pain of women and their daily suffering. Though Manju wanted to come much earlier, and even though it was the birth anniversary of her beloved Master, she did not have the freedom to leave home due to the daily routine that she had been handling for so many years. Feeling the acute pain of his devotee, Thakur said,

> *"Manju, take each chore of your daily grind more as a tool of your sadhana. You can rest assured that all of these sacrifices that you make for your family and children, if you can do them while repeating your japa mantra in a state of surrender to the Lord, gradually the all-compassionate Lord will diminish your work responsibility and give you more free time to contemplate on higher realities and realize God in this birth. Know that as you do this practice of japa and consecrate your work to the Divine, your Guru's grace will loosen the chains of the bondage of body-identification, uplift your mind to a state of equanimity, and finally free you from all ignorance to the world of Light."*

This powerful teaching is relevant to us all, not just to women. It bears deep contemplation. Who, functioning in today's demanding and chaotic world, does not feel at one point or another overly burdened by the complexities of our obligations? The power of *japa*, of surrendering our efforts and burdens to the divine as we attend to all that we feel we must, is inherently transformative. Holding ourselves in the field of divine energy, inner conflict and resistance begin to lose their grip. The mind calms. Peace takes root. Consciousness opens. We come into greater harmony with what is most needful. Clarity comes. If change is needed, a path appears leading wherever it is that we are meant to go. To whatever it is we are meant to do. To who we really are, how we are meant to be and to live.

• • •

Thakur always sought to initiate a husband and wife together. Of course, there were exceptions. Having the same guru, spouses can help each other and grow together in spiritual bliss. Otherwise, conflicting vibrations can develop that affect a couple and their spiritual progress. Thakur's message was that spouses need unity of purpose to fulfill the highest possibilities available in their relationship.

Marriage is much more than two bodies meeting at peripheral levels. Friction and flaws generate disharmony. In the journey through the materialistic planes as well as the inner world, there is a need to have a common understanding and harmonic vibrations. Then each can be a complementary force to the other. Ultimately, marriage is meant to help each other realize the ultimate goal of life, *moksha*, or *nirvana*, the freedom from all pain and suffering.

Thakur was surrounded by householders. Most came seeking relief from the physical, mental, and emotional challenges of their lives. He knew that pain and suffering are primarily self-created and self-inflicted. He often said,

> *"I have rarely seen families where mother-in-law, daughter-in-law, sister-in-law and all other members of the family live with the prime focus on harmony rather than control and conflict. When you are able to become noble*

householders and give up false notions and superstitions, then you will not face so much unpleasantness in your family life. Keep in mind that one of your biggest enemies is the practice of speaking ill of others, picking on others, and judging them. Be vigilant. Keep a safe distance from the instinctive urge to indulge in these harmful practices."

MASTER IN HIS CHILDLIKE PLAYFUL MOOD!

CHAPTER NINETEEN

TRUTH IS DHARMA, THE PATH

During his long *sadhana* in the Himalayas and in Vrindavan, Thakur had attained the highest state of *sahaj samadhi,* that state in which one's silent awareness is absorbed in the Self within while operating simultaneously with the full use of everyday human faculties. Thakur had mastered this. He was always utterly natural. I never saw him meditating or performing ritualistic worship of any kind. To be in his presence was to be in the presence of the living God. It was to witness the two selves, human and divine, flowing in natural manifestation, time and time again.

On one such occasion, a Sunday evening in 1979 in the ashram in south Calcutta, the Master was sitting on his couch. Behind his bed, the open balcony overlooked the big mango tree in blossom. The small room was filled with seekers from far and wide who had come to drink from the nectar of his teachings and love.

The seekers were all householders. Initially, they spoke among themselves of the family problems and issues that are common to the life of seekers. They were all searching for peace, for harmony and happiness. It was like a mirage that came but never stayed. What stayed were their day-to-day struggles and worries, problems and anxieties. Everyone was looking forward to hearing from Thakur about how they could move along the path and overcome the obstacles that their minds were constantly creating.

One devotee spoke up,

> *"Baba, we are all seekers of happiness and joy, but we face so many challenges in our family as well as in our work and businesses. At times we feel helpless and depressed. Would you please tell us something simple that we can do in order to overcome these difficulties?"*

Thakur, in his inimitable, almost melodious way, responded,

> *"The Truth is God. The Truth is Dharma, the Path. Be steadfast in your devotion to Truth. He who has single-pointed devotion and love for Truth has all that is needed in the path of divine unfoldment. He who has everything yet compromises the Truth can never advance in the path of Truth or attain true peace of mind."*

As usual, I was sitting at his feet, taking everything down in my journal. He spoke in his mother tongue, Bengali. I looked up to see if he would say more, but he stopped. For a while, he was lost in *samadhi.* His eyes were glazed, looking far away into some supra-physical realm of pure existence beyond this physical one.

Thakur motioned to me, as he often did, to explain in my simple way the wisdom that had flowed out of him. He was preparing me for the work that he had ordained for me in the years ahead. Sitting there in the ecstasy of his divine presence, it was his grace alone that made it possible for me to be an instrument of his work and to explain his words in more detail.

What was Thakur talking about when he said, *"Truth is God?"*

The truth that we know of in this world is relative. That which is true to me may not be true to you. That which is so tangibly appealing to me may make no sense at all to another. Truth is relative. This is our perception. We play with words and manipulate our thoughts and expressions. We steal the attention and care of others and fool ourselves by saying what is untrue. We always have a rationalization to justify it. We don't feel bad about it. It is a kind of norm in worldly life. When others gain advantages by saying something which may not be true, why should I deprive myself of opportunities by sticking to something which is only relatively true, relative to time and place and person?

All of that may be acceptable to those who are only out for the pleasures, acclaim, and success available in the world. After all, the everyday world is far more concerned that you get the job done. Why worry about the means? The world is far more concerned with the results. Who is bothered about the Truth or untruth in the short run in today's world?

Thakur, however, is pointing to a much deeper perspective. Thakur is talking to a group who had gathered at his ashram seeking the ultimate path to freedom from all fears and unhappiness. He is seeing each one of them in their personal divinity. He is seeing not just their pain and agonies, but more precisely the reasons why he or she is getting into the quagmire of pleasure and pain, birth and death. He is talking from another height of consciousness altogether, planting seeds of Truth that can blossom into the light of freedom with careful tending through time.

What Thakur is saying is that if you want to see God, the first step is to be steadfast. The path is to worship the Truth, to listen to the whisperings of your higher self in the cave of your awakened conscience. Thakur is talking about the language of the *Viveka,* the Guru within. God and Truth are one and the same. One who has known God has known the Truth.

Here the word Truth needs proper understanding. Truth is not external. Truth is that which is *Sanatana,* that which is changeless, eternal, beyond any modification, beyond anything that mind and intelligence can fathom. It is the ultimate, unmanifest essence of the whole cosmic process of creation, preservation, and annihilation. It is the root, the core from which all manifestations spring forth into myriad names and forms. It is that which is beyond all earthly definition that language can create.

Thakur is pointing beyond all that is relative. One must have eyes to see the hands of the divine. There are many occasions in our life when we are confronted with situations beyond our control. Yet, some unseen hands come to our rescue. Miracles happen, establishing in us a perception or faith that is beyond the peripheral. There is something, some power. Some force is continually in play which is beyond our ability to fathom, yet it leaves its footprints for us to follow. That power defies definition. It is a force that can't be seen, but it is felt. And it transcends our relative perception of worldly truths. Without understanding this higher force and how it plays out, we keep oscillating between the pleasures and pains that our worldly desires create. We get farther and farther from the Truth. Ultimately though, there is a turning. Relative truths gradually pave the way toward a higher perception, a higher philosophy of life anchored in the deepest reality of God. It emerges from the chaos created by untruth, by all that is fleeting and transient.

Thakur is speaking about the quality of character that a true seeker of peace must develop. Once we realize that there is a higher reality than what appears on the periphery, we set our eye on that. That higher reality, that transcendental reality, is the Truth that a seeker must seek and find. Hence, realization of God and realization of the Truth happen simultaneously. One who knows God unravels the mysteries of the universe, the intricate mechanism of duality, the play of opposites. Where all dualism merges, where all opposites converge, the Truth shines in its eternal glory. This can only be experienced by one who walks the path of divine love, holding the hands of one who is enlightened, of one who has reached the Truth of the divine. The Guru brings the Truth home. The Guru brings the disciple to the Truth of his or her own inner Self. Guru embodies the Truth eternal and points the way.

Thakur says, "*Truth is Dharma, the Path.*" In India, whenever we hear the word *dharma*, we think of religion, the different religions known to common man. But the *dharma* Thakur is speaking about to my heart is the order that governs the universes. It is that life force which is the very essence of all existence. "*Truth is Dharma,*" was Thakur's way of saying *dharma* is the eternal Order, driven by the force of Truth, the changeless, immutable power of the One Supreme Being.

In all spheres of life, whether the material or astral, Order governs. This Order is ordained by the Supreme Being. With form or without, the fact remains: *dharma* sustains the universal process. It is only when a seeker of Truth walks the path of *dharma,* honoring its universal laws, the universal principles that govern life in its totality, that one becomes whole and finds lasting peace and joy. That is the path of which Thakur is speaking. Anyone wanting to reach the ultimate intuitive wisdom of Oneness must follow the path of Truth, which governs the Order of all existence.

Here, Thakur summarizes the foundational spiritual understanding which is essential to move on the path to true awakening. Truth is God. Truth is *Dharma:* the very Order by which the seeker realizes the sought.

Then he moves on, "*He who has single-pointed devotion and love for Truth has all that is needed in the path to divine unfoldment.*"

Now Thakur brings our focus to the essential ingredient of our love, our devotion. The seed of divinity is embedded in each human soul, ready to germinate. Our love and devotion are critical. Until our heart joins the head, it is a dry journey. Heart is the center. Thakur is beautifully showing us the path that will eventually open the petals of the lotus of our heart center to see, feel, and be in the enchanting world of divine unfoldment. The truth is, until that unfoldment happens, restlessness and unhappiness envelop the mind despite the fact that life is moving forward with all its material comforts and conveniences. Discontentment cannot go until the mind is soaked in divine love and absorbed in the ecstasy of divine union.

Finally, he makes it clear that there is no short cut to Truth. There is no space for compromise. Truth has its own price and here it is: *"He who has everything yet compromises with Truth can never advance in the path of Truth or attain to peace of mind."*

Those who think they can realize God by performing daily rituals, by being religious with external observances and paraphernalia, or by acquiring extensive knowledge of the scriptures, are mistaken. There is no scope for shortcuts or compromise. Truth needs your total surrender to Truth. Truth and God are a totality that requires your totality. It may take any number of births, any number of years of austerities, but you can't have any reservations. You must give yourself totally to be total. Peace of mind is the expression of your mind purged of all false notions and concepts, freed from identification with the ever-changing, objective world to which the mind, in its impure state, clings. Peace arises from the mind that is pure and one with the Spirit.

Thakur told them all,

> *"There is no hurry in this path. Have patience. That is most important. Patience and devotion, these are your companions. Why should you worry? In this path, your Guru is always holding your hands, taking you along. You just have to love him and surrender to him and move on without any fear or doubts."*

When the bell rang, Thakur asked the devotees to go for *prasad* (blessed food; all food at the ashram is considered blessed). One by one, they all paid their respectful obeisance and left the room.

• • •

The next day, the group returned in the evening and took their seats at Thakur's feet. They had further follow-up questions about Truth and God. Again, at his request, I continued explaining in my own way, elaborating on what Thakur had said so precisely.

A devotee asked, *"How would I know which is the truth? How do I know my mind is not deceiving or manipulating me?"*

Thakur replied,

> *"Be quiet and ask your mind. It will give you an answer about the truth and any untruths. You will see that you will get a response from your inner mind.*

> *"Your mind will give you an answer that is a deeper Truth. Thieves steal, murderers commit murder, liars tell lies, but their conscience still gives them a knock. Most often you don't pay enough heed to the voice of your conscience. It is more convenient to walk the path of the mundane, material life, not paying attention to your inner voice."*

Thakur is addressing the typical behavioral pattern of human beings all over the world. Conscience does speak, but it whispers. Not many people have the intention or the attention to pay heed to the voice of the higher, deeper mind. The voice of Truth is the voice of conscience; it is an inner voice. I would call it the inner Guru, the One who guides from within!

Thakur reminds us to be silent. Truth reveals itself in the quiet space of our mind. When the mind is chattering away with random thoughts and concerns about our life in the world, the voice of Truth that is conscience simply becomes unavailable to us. The moment we quiet our mind and become more in-drawn, contemplative, or meditative, our inner mind will speak out. The quieter mind is closer to our inner Guru.

Thakur is also talking about the deeper mind here. The mind from which we all operate in our mundane, routine life is surface mind. It is primarily the unconscious or subconscious, programmed mind. Living on autopilot, we can hardly differentiate between the transient and permanent, between what is right and what is wrong. The *viveka-vani*, the whispers of conscience, of the deeper, higher mind, does come however. Ignoring them, we fall victim to living from the force of circumstance, habit, or the call of the lower mind.

Thakur offers us incredible reassurance, lovingly pointing out the path of inner transformation. We can rely on the voice of our conscience to become available when we seek the Truth, provided we calm ourselves and take the time to listen and meditate. In the space of stillness, our mind's dross and negative patterns have a chance to reboot. The mind can begin the process of reconditioning itself into a healthier pattern.

If we are to survive on this planet as a species, we need to learn the art of calming the mind. Reprogramming our subconscious mind is essential. It is key to transforming the restless and addictive unconscious living that deepens the cycles of pain, pleasure and human suffering. There is no other way to reclaim the inner reservoir of bliss that is our higher human destiny.

How can we ever taste the nectar of our inner mind unless we practice calming it down? Restlessness and distortion are inherent, the very nature of the unconscious mind. The calm, stilled mind gradually transforms into sane mind, one that can see through the myriad differences of manifestation to the One Truth that envelops all of existence.

Truth is not an abstraction here, just as love is not an abstraction. Neither can be scientifically analyzed or measured. Still, we know when a father or mother cuddles a baby or a lover hugs their beloved, there is an emotion, a chemistry, an energy at play which defies all definitions of science and technology.

Thakur points us toward God which, he says, is Truth. He is drawing our attention to the intangible reality that hides behind the veil of *maya*, the illusive and potent haze of the unconscious mind.

Thakur is so humble. He asks us to create a pause, to just stop all our addictive busyness and look within. He is telling us, "*You have no idea what you are missing in the humdrum of your daily life.*"

Truth is elusive, not because Truth or God is difficult, but because our human mind has become so removed from its core inner nature of purity and calmness. It has lost its memory of how to get back to its source.

Thakur knocks at our hearts and minds. He reminds us of the enlightened Masters of all faith traditions who have told us that we are not human beings going through spiritual experiences, but spiritual beings going through a human experience. If we forget the root purpose of our visit to Mother Earth, we will be an unhappy lot. Like the musk deer, we will be searching for the exotic fragrance in the forest, not knowing that the enchanting fragrance we seek is being emitted from our own navel.

What I see Thakur is telling us is that our lives are manipulated by our conditioned ego. It blocks the very path that we are meant to walk inhaling the fragrance of our true being. Human beings are scattered, our minds distracted in every direction possible. We are not sure what it is we are seeking or where we are heading. Thakur is trying to bring his children back home, for until we are home, our Divine Mother can never be happy.

Thakur continued his *kathamritam* (words of pure nectar).

> *"By being indifferent to the Truth, there is no escape. Truth is Truth. The verdict of the divine is infallible. He who treads the path of Truth enjoys a calm and peaceful mind. The path of Truth is straight and simple."*

Thakur makes it clear that there is no way you can attain that higher reality by being indifferent to Truth. Truth is the verdict of the divine. It is conclusive and inclusive. Those who tread the path of Truth are simple; they don't get into complex theories of life. A seeker of Truth has to pierce the veil of the fleeting nature of the physical, mundane world. Withdrawing his or her mind from all that glitters and distracts on the surface of life, as they move through its ups and downs, they come to see life is intrinsically very simple and straightforward. They come to understand the peripheral attractions of name, fame, money, and sensual pleasure are ego traps that complicate life; that the ego is insatiable and the root of all struggle and suffering.

Thakur emphatically draws our attention to a simple fact: *"He who treads the path of Truth enjoys a calm and peaceful mind."* To have a peaceful mind, we must practice calmness which, again, needs our steadfast devotion to Truth.

Thakur couldn't be clearer. The path of Truth *is the only sure path* to a calm and peaceful mind. Conversely, those who settle for the peripheral and the transient miss the simple happiness that comes from a truly peaceful mind and loving heart.

The devotees had been listening to Thakur and my explanations for some time when a devotee asked,

> *"But how can we have a mind which is calm when every time we try to calm our mind, it becomes more restless? What is the way out? At times, we truly feel this is not for us, that this is for saints like you who leave everything of this world and only love God. We can't do it. We want the honey of the sensual world and we also want the nectar of the spiritual world. It appears we are stuck".*

Appreciating the devotee's honesty and this predicament among devotees, Thakur acknowledged that it is true that it is not easy to lift the mind from all the attractions and distractions of the world to higher reality. Then he continued,

> *"In a child you will never see any sign of malice. That is the reason they always have such profound simplicity and purity. In the same manner, one who worships the Truth is a beggar of divine compassion and grace and is ever blessed with God vision. They envision the grace of the Sadguru (true Guru) in all circumstances and situations of life and maintain serene calmness of mind, ever in a state of divine bliss."*

Here, Thakur pinpoints the importance of devotion, love and our deep urge for divine grace. Those qualities alone attract the higher forces into our life. Having the innocence and simplicity of a child, having a child's purity of heart induces the response of divine grace, making sustained practice and attention toward the one goal of God realization possible. Our realization of Truth wholly depends on that purity of our mind and heart.

We need to be beggars of divine grace. We need to be humble in our day-to-day activities, to make sure that we accept the path to God as the path of surrender and devotion. One who is steadfast in his or her devotion and is conscious of the grace of the Guru eventually burns off bad *karma* (the chain of cause and effect) and evolves to a state of divine bliss. Steadfast practice and utmost faith in the gift of divine grace create the magic of divine revelation.

Thakur concludes his flow of wisdom on Truth and God with words that carry the power of a promise: *"Move forward with your heart and soul committed to Truth and sincere dedication. God will surely help you."*

What a beautiful assurance Thakur gives us! If our seeking is sincere, if our heart cries for God, then God's heart cries for us. But we must keep moving, with faith and dedication, until our soul's eternal journey to merge in the ocean of Love and Truth is complete.

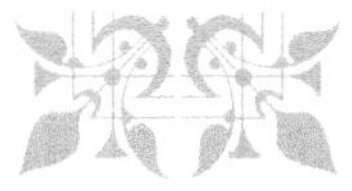

CHAPTER TWENTY

INSCRUTABLE ARE THE WAYS OF SADGURU

In 1971, Thakur had come to Durgapur. As always, he was staying with Narayan Bandopadhaya, who was popularly known to the devotees as 'Naruda'. Another devotee, Ashok Das, reminisces about what Naruda told him. One morning, Thakur suddenly asked Naruda to arrange for a car to go to the Durgapur Barrage (a tourist spot). Thakur looked a bit restless and left home in the car for the barrage. On the way, however, he told Naruda to take the car via Chinta's (Sacchidanandaa Das, a disciple of Thakur's) home. The moment the car approached Chinta's house, Thakur quickly got out of the car, went to the door, and started calling out to Chinta. Chinta was not feeling well, had not gone to work, and was lying on his bed, resting. Hearing Gurudev's voice, he got up and escorted Thakur to his bed. Thakur sat next to him on his bed, embraced him with much love and affection, and started stroking his head and body, while saying again and again, *"Don't worry. Nothing to fear. You will be all right."*

Neither Chinta nor his wife could understand what Thakur was talking about! Chinta only had a mild uneasiness and was just resting, thinking he would be fine the next day. Thakur moved around the home, sat for a while talking to his wife, and gave her some instructions regarding her daily worship then he told Naruda to take him back home, since he did not want to go to the Barrage any more.

The next day, Chinta suffered a severe stroke and was taken to the Hospital in an ambulance. As the doctors struggled to stabilize Chinta in the emergency room, his wife, who was an ardent disciple and loved Thakur with all her heart, was gripped with deep fear of losing her husband. She started praying and warning her Gurudev that if anything happened to her husband, she would never worship him again, since Thakur had come to her home on his own accord and promised that Chinta would be all right.

Right then, a miracle happened. Thakur appeared at the head of Chinta's hospital bed. In his divine form, full of radiant light, he smiled and blessed Chinta, with his hand in *abhya mudra* (a gesture of blessing). She was in tears. Realizing that Thakur had come to their home to bless Chinta, knowing well ahead of the impending danger, she was overwhelmed at how compassionate and loving he was to his devotees. And here he was again, when she was losing her nerve, in deep agony, complaining to her Guru! Appearing right then and there, he was proving to her that the Guru is always with the disciple and manifests whenever the disciple is in danger.

At the same moment Thakur was at Chinta's bedside, he was also at the Durgapur Rail Station, waiting to catch the Coal Field Express train back to Calcutta.

Within a few days, Chinta's condition improved and he returned home safely. No one in the family ever forgot those moments when Thakur came to their home all by himself, uninvited, to sit beside Chinta and hug him, caressing him like the most loving mother and repeating again and again, *"Don't fear! You will be all right."* At the time, no one could have guessed what was behind this *lila* of Thakur. Then within a day, the inevitable happened and it was only through his divine grace that Chinta was able to come home alive from the hospital.

I Have Known You for Births

Thakur would often say that he went to each place because there were souls who were connected to him from other births who were waiting, who needed him to bring them back to the path of spiritual *sadhana*. Once he told me that the Guru comes again and again to take the disciple through the next stages of soul evolution. The journey started with the Guru continues birth after birth, until one is free from the cycles of births and deaths. The disciple cannot see the past lives of the Guru, but the Guru, if highly enlightened, can identify his disciple birth after birth. The Guru-disciple relationship is a continual journey together. He also told me that the Guru is not totally free until all his disciples attain *mukti* or *moksha* (in Hinduism, total freedom; in Buddhism called *nirvana*).

The true teacher is one who has transcended the egoic mind to the realm of egoless universal self. The seed of compassion remains with these masters while the past and future are burned in the fire of self-illumination. That is the reason the Guru needs to have the responsibility of walking the disciple through the haze of egoic mind to the light of eternal Truth. It is a divine destiny that each exalted Master who is like living Buddha promises to come again and again to earth to guide the disciples to the ultimate state of self-realization. This is the supreme state of selflessness and divine love.

• • •

Nandagopal Chatterjee, a disciple of Thakur who lived in Patna, also had a house in Chapra, a small district town in the State of Bihar. It was his wish that Thakur visit his home there. Thakur readily agreed while visiting Patna. In his Chapra home, Thakur's presence was a great celebration for the town. As the word spread about a great saint visiting Nandagopal's home, people from far and wide poured into his small house, seeking the *darshan* of the great saint and the blessings of his nectarine wisdom and love.

The Principal of Rajendra College, Chapra, Professor Sushil Singh, never missed a chance to have the *darshan* of great saints and learn while sitting at the feet of the living Masters. When he heard about Thakur, he wasted no time. He rushed to Nandagopal's home and prostrated before this simple man of God. He was overwhelmed by the presence and aura of this self-realized Master and was deeply touched by his simplicity and divine love. He prayed to Thakur for the divine grace of initiating him with *Guru Mantra*. Thakur realized that Professor Singh had been waiting to be blessed by him. Sushil was initiated and gradually the purpose of visiting this small town started unfolding. More and more people fell at the feet of the Master, praying for his divine shelter and guidance through initiation.

Sushil talked about his newfound Guru and his infinite grace to most of the people he knew. He thought this was the richest gift that he could give anyone who is truly seeking peace and happiness. Kamaleshwar Prasad Singh, one of his close friends and relatives, who was holding a high position of authority in the government services, heard from Sushil about the visiting *sadhu*, his spiritual powers and deep wisdom. He had always trusted Sushil, who now spoke highly about his Guru. Kamaleshwar felt a deep call from within, as if the saint was calling him in subtle ways beyond his understanding. He felt he could not waste any time in going to meet Thakur and take his blessings.

In the words of Kamaleshwar, *"I loved Gurubaba the moment I saw him."* Thakur, too, was overjoyed to find his child for whom he had come to this small town of Chapra. He said, *"I have known you such a long time. I have known you for births. Do you remember me? Do you know who you are?"*

"Without your divine grace, how do you expect me to know myself or you, Gurudev?" Kamaleshwar submitted with humble devotion. Thakur blessed and initiated him.

A new life began for the man who had always been busy with his work and preoccupied with money. A part of him had always wanted to see beyond the haze of material possessions and the wealth that he had amassed. His inner soul whispered often about the Mother Divine and Her love for him, but there had been no one there to channel his energy towards that reality hidden behind the daily chores of authority and wealth. The moment he saw Thakur, he recognized him. He knew that this was the man who could take him to the other shore. He knew that his attachment to the material world was deep and only the divine grace of a great, enlightened Master could tear away the thick veil covering his eyes.

Once Kamaleshwar was initiated, his large family of brothers, sons and daughters, as well as their extended families, came under the umbrella of Thakur's divine grace and protection. One after the other they were all initiated. Thakur started visiting Chapra more often, and his grace widened, sheltering many more thirsting souls on the path of the Spirit.

In the seventies, I visited Kamaleshwar's house along with Thakur and witnessed how the whole house would be transformed into a huge temple. Large numbers of people were fed. *Satsangs*, *bhajans* and *kirtans* enchanted family, friends and others from every walk of life. It was always a great celebration.

Kamaleshwar had a big heart and never hesitated to donate generously for anything that Gurudev wanted to do. He funded the establishment of the ashram of Gurudev to the extent he could out of love and gratitude for his Master. Thakur loved this child of his and they always enjoyed each other's company.

MASTER IN ECSTASY AND SAMADHI WHILE SINGING BHAJANS AND KIRTAN

Kamaleshwar one day complained to Thakur, "*You are doing so much, giving grace to so many of your devotees and disciples, but here I am; I get nothing from you!*"

Thakur smiled and said, "*Grace (kripa) is always there my child, maybe you are not able to feel that.*"

"*Why don't I know this, feel it, when others can?*" Kamaleshwar persisted.

Thakur responded tenderly:

> "*When you sit to do your mantra japa, just think, where does your mind go? Just as you love your work, your family, your children, you think about them. The day you will deeply feel for your Guru and chant the Guru Mantra with love and devotion, that day you will feel your spiritual life is the most important thing of your life. You will feel the grace; you will feel the essence of your Guru.*
>
> "*When you are in distress, when you face unforeseen challenges in life, when your intelligence fails to solve some difficult situation in work or family, you turn to your Guru and start to pray. Otherwise, most often you don't even remember your Guru, his grace, his love or, above all, his infinite protection. Isn't it true that you can't even do the japa regularly at times?*
>
> "*I could show you a lot of miracles, but that would only divert your attention from the Truth and God. You would not get anything out of it. That would excite you, thrill you, temporarily give you some faith, but*

it would not last. What is important is your love for your Guru".

Then Thakur pointed to his own body and continued,

"The Guru is always longing to give you the real thing that will transform you forever. But first, you must cleanse your container. You must be able to hold the divine grace that the Guru is ready to pour. Cleaning the receptacle is your work. To pour grace is Guru's job. You must understand this fundamental and simple truth of Guru-disciple relationship and divine grace."

Thakur wanted to play a bit more with his child Kamaleshwar and said with a meaningful smile, "*Of course, if you want to have some toys from me, I will give them to you* (meaning Thakur was prepared to give him miracles of apparent grace)." But Kamaleshwar realized that he was blessed to have the Guru who had come to cut away the fetters of ignorance and illusion and take him to the world of light. He surrendered to the Master with folded hands saying, "*No, Gurubaba, I don't want any toys from you. I want the real thing. I want the darshan of the Divine Mother so that I am free forever.*"

Thakur blessed Kamaleshwar and through Kamaleshwar, his large family and his progeny as well. This is the true grace of the *Sadguru*! Kamaleshwar left this world, but all his family members remain ardent devotees of Gurudev and worship the Master with all love and devotion.

A Child's Experience of the Master

One day in Sri Rampur, a suburb of Calcutta, as many devotees sat at his feet, Thakur searched out a letter he had received from Subodh Dasgupta of Mahesh, Sri Rampur. Handing it over to Sri Mitra, he asked Sri Mitra to read the letter, which is shared below, to the assembled devotees.

> *"My brother's daughter, Shampa, aged nine years, started having experiences of my Gurudev Thakur Bhajan Baba when she was hardly five years old. She showed signs of deep spiritual longing and also compassion for the poor and needy when she was a small child. From the day she met my Gurudev, she would often narrate to me about her unique experience of directly seeing my Gurudev, though Thakur did not at that time visit my home. She could see Thakur standing before her, whether she was at school or at home. She also had dreams of Thakur which were such vivid experiences for her.*
>
> *"We were all absolutely amazed about how Thakur appeared before her. One morning at 5 a.m. when Shampa was getting ready to leave for her morning school, she went to bathroom to wash her face. Usually she takes very little time for this morning ritual, but that day she was in the bathroom much longer. When she did not come out of the bathroom, her aunt started knocking on the door and calling her. After a while she came out, but she did not look normal. She was in a daze. Her eyes were red, and she had hardly any control over herself.*

> *In a semi-trance, she walked out of the bathroom and sat on a couch nearby. After a while she came back to her normal self and started narrating her experience. 'Uncle, what a beautiful vision I saw just now. None of you can imagine how vivid and alive it was. I just quickly finished washing my hands and face, when suddenly the semi-dark bathroom was flooded with an extraordinary light. I thought at this early hour of the dawn, how could so much sunlight get into this bathroom? I soon realized it was not sunlight, but a dazzling aura, a divine effulgence. In the midst of that wonderful light I saw Gurudev (Thakur) smiling at me! I was awestruck and was afraid and wanted to shout in panic. Right then his smiling face, along with the light, disappeared.'"*

The letter also narrated another episode of Thakur's divine play with this child at school. Subodh Dasgupta wrote,

> *"One day at her school classroom, the teacher wanted her to do an arithmetic problem on the board. She was about to do it and the same thing happened. In the midst of an effulgent light, Thakur appeared with a playful smile on his face, as if he had come to play with her. Seeing the divine aura and the face of Gurudev, Shampa was once again transfixed. She could not move; she could not talk. She just stood still. The teacher thought that she had a problem, so she immediately caught hold of Shampa and helped her to go and take her seat. Shampa came back home that day and told us about her experience."*

Sri Mitra finished reading the letter. Silence and curiosity filled the room. Sri Mitra finally remarked,

> *"She is such a small girl, who does not understand anything, who does not do much practice, and is not even initiated by you. Why and how is she receiving the divine grace of seeing your divine form and aura? Why don't we get to have such divine visions?"*

Thakur replied,

> *"It all depends upon the soul, the spiritual state. These souls come to the world not to get attached to the worldly things of life but to lead a divine life. Even if they get married and live a householder's life, they live a life of pure devotion and surrender to the Master. The grace of God is perennial; it is always flowing. You also receive it all the time, but you can't perceive or feel it. That is the reason you miss it."*

This *lila* with the little girl continued until she was nine years old. Over that time, her parents started to be more and more concerned about their daughter. They thought that if she goes through this trance-like state on and off as Thakur appeared in her dreams or in a waking state, one day she would leave home and become a nun. They did not want that. So, one day Subodh Dasgupta came to Thakur with Shampa to express her parents' concern and explain the parents were losing their peace over these recurring episodes of divine experience.

Thakur heard the story. Looking at the little girl like his divine playmate, he smiled and said, *"OK, from today on, I will leave Buri alone and no longer disturb her."* *(Buri means old lady, which is what Thakur had called Shampa since she was five years old.)*

To the surprise of the whole family, Shampa (Thakur's Buri) never had any more dreams, visions, or *darshans* of Thakur. Peace returned to the parents, but not to the little girl, who felt she was suddenly deprived of her heavenly companion and inner bliss.

Inscrutable are the ways of the mystics and seers! Their domain is beyond human intelligence and rationality. Who can explain why the little girl, who never had any spiritual practice or even prayed to Thakur, had the Master come again and again in her dreams and visions, filling her with the bliss of the celestial world?

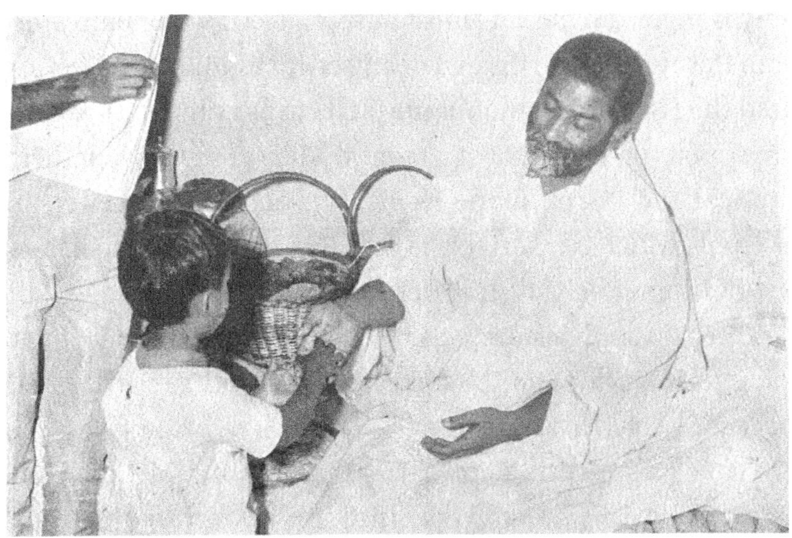

THE MASTER PLAYS WITH A CHILD

Visit to Kumbh Mela in Subtle Body

The topic of Kumbh Mela (the largest Hindu religious gathering in the world) came up when Thakur was sitting with his devotees and disciples one evening at his Cornfield Road residence in Calcutta. Peace and joy were in the air. Everyone had the privilege of enjoying the presence of the Master along with his loving words and occasional spells of meditation.

That year, the Kumbh Mela festival was being held at Haridwar, the gateway to the sacred Himalayan mountains. This remarkable Hindu festival takes place once in every twelve years, with the half Kumbh Mela being held every six years. That year was Purna Kumbh Mela, which took place after twelve years. Many disciples and devotees had planned to visit the Kumbh Mela at Haridwar, about five hours drive from Delhi. It is believed that those who take a dip in the Holy Ganges during this most auspicious time are delivered from the cycles of births and deaths. Great saints and ascetics from the Himalayan mountains and caves come to the festival, which runs for almost a month. They come both in their physical and astral, subtle forms. It is an amazing religious assembly which is inscribed on the UNESCO's Representative List of Intangible Cultural Heritage of Humanity.

One of the devotees asked Thakur, *"Baba, are you not going to Kumbh Mela?"* Thakur smiled and replied, *"Yes, indeed, I very much wish to go."*

After this meeting and talking on Kumbh Mela, we all forgot about this great event since it was over by that time and people had returned to their own places.

On a later occasion, a few devotees were sitting at the feet of the Master, when a letter was delivered to him from Hyderabad by post. Thakur, took the envelope, handed it over to a devotee, and said, *"Read it."*

The devotee followed Gurudev's instructions, opened the envelope, and started loudly reading the letter to Thakur. A devotee from Hyderabad had written as follows:

> *"Baba, I never could have dreamed that I would be able to see you at the Kumbh Mela. I saw you in the midst of many sadhus and mahatmas (great souls), all moving toward the holy confluence to have the sacred dip in the Ganges. You were so kind to identify me amid such a huge crowd of pilgrims, lovingly waving your hands to me and blessing me with a smile. I tried to keep my eyes trained on you, even though I was being tossed about in the middle of the crowd, but at some point, I could not see you anymore. After that I searched everywhere to meet you personally and take your blessings, but I could not see you anywhere! Where did you stay during your stay in Haridwar? How long did you stay? When did you return to Calcutta?"*

The assembled devotees were in shock. How could Thakur go to Kumbh Mela which had just concluded, when during the whole course of the time that the Kumbh Mela was celebrated in Haridwar, he was staying in Calcutta, never moving anywhere else?

It was evident that Thakur had gone to Kumbh Mela in his astral form, though he was in Calcutta at that time. He had created a divine play with this one witness and the letter, demonstrating that.

In fact, there were many cases when Thakur's body was at one place while he was also seen elsewhere in his physical body at exactly the same time. Those who were with him never had a clue about his simultaneous manifestation in physical form in another place.

Yogis and great sages like Thakur have that natural capacity to materialize and dematerialize their body at will, just as easily as we move from one room to another. Thakur once told me that one who realizes the ultimate reality, transcends the bounds and limitations of the material world, and that the attributes we associate with God are conferred by God upon him or her. When a moth is transformed into a butterfly, it no longer remains a moth. So, too, when a human is transformed into divinity, he or she is endowed with all the divine attributes. Of course, for us, when we see a human exhibiting superhuman manifestations, we are awed and clueless as to how they can do this.

• • •

Many Yogis in the Himalayan traditions live for hundreds of years. They do so by mastering the breath and every cell of their body through intense Hatha yoga and other advanced yogic practices. The arduous disciplines involved and the skills they develop are beyond the comprehension of ordinary human beings. There are countless awe-inspiring stories of the Yogis of India doing and undoing things beyond the most advanced knowledge and capacities of modern science or technology.

As I have said before, I never saw my Gurudev practicing any yoga, meditation or other spiritual ritual or discipline. He just lived an ordinary life, being available to people in distress and to seekers of divine light. Even when he talked about the most mundane aspects of a householder's life, we all listened to him with delight. It was not what he said. It was his presence that thrilled people, attracting them from far and wide. Once they were in his physical presence worries about their family and the world melted away. His presence was like the dawn that dispelled the gloom of night and all darkness.

I often heard inquisitive seekers who were first-timers say,

> *"Initially, when I came into his presence and saw him sitting on the couch chewing betel leaf and nuts, and joyfully talking all about worldly things in life, I was a bit taken aback. After all, my expectation of a saint was to see him talking about God and how to reach God or attain peace of mind. But he hardly talked about that. Instead, it was mostly mundane. Then after a while, I felt that even when he was talking about the mundane, he was referring to many things I myself had experienced. They were my sore areas, areas I didn't understand why it all happened. Now, in his presence even without asking any questions, he was addressing many of my unresolved questions. Above all, what transported me was his simple, utterly humble divine presence. In that room there was something we all cherished in life but hardly got anywhere else! I came to realize*

that what he had was what we had all been missing in life: Presence. We are frantically searching, without even knowing what we are searching for. We seem to be moving in every direction, not knowing where to find it. It turns out to be in the quiet, calm space of our inner Self that we begin to feel in his presence. In his presence we realize this rarity that he must have found what we all are missing. Now he is just there, without any restlessness, without the unending questions that plague us. He seems to have reached home, while we are all homeless wanderers. What was most amazing was that he never laid any claim to have reached home, or to be a realized Master. But his presence was so strong that it was evident. This was the deepest teaching I ever had. With no teaching, the student learned what he or she was looking for."

Answers in Silence

Another thing that I often heard from devotees and disciples was about his eyes, the way he simply looked at individuals and communicated without any verbal or physical communication at all. Aarati Ray shared her experience with me when she came to have Thakur's *darshan* at the ashram. She would sit at the corner of the room intently looking at the Master. Suddenly, he would look at her and a series of thoughts passed through her mind in direct and conclusive answer to any questions she had. She had just been silently sitting, looking at him. No words were spoken. He just looked at her and she felt as if he had spoken. The answers she was looking for had come from within.

Manju Ma, another close disciple of Thakur, also shared that her deepest experience of the Master had come from a mere glance. She, too, would be sitting in the middle of the crowd of devotees with queries about her journey with her Guru. She was always too shy to initiate a conversation. Suddenly, the Master would look directly into her eyes, and she could hear words as if he were speaking to her, resolving the doubts that kept her stuck, opening the floodgates to the path. She could virtually hear Thakur talking to her with much love and compassion the moment he cast his eyes on her.

Both Aarati Ray and Manju Ma felt this silent teaching was more powerful than even Thakur's spoken words. Though his words were wonderful in the moment while you are listening, later it all disappeared. The silent communication was different. Here, no words were spoken, no teaching done. There was no normal question and answer. It was a profound, deep level of teaching happening between the Master and the disciple. It is typical of the way great Masters transmit profound teachings through thought transfer. Though I mentioned these two devotees' names, many close disciples, myself included, had this profound experience of being taught in this intensely personal, intimate way.

"I Want a Separate Temple for Me"— The Grand Master Commands

I have mentioned many times while narrating Thakur's early life and *sadhana* about the great Himalayan Ascended Master of the eighteenth century, Baba Lokenath Brahmachari. Baba Lokenath appeared before Thakur in his materialized body many times during his *sadhana*. To Thakur, he was the living Shiva, the living God. When the thought of constructing temples for different deities in the ashram came up, Thakur initially planned to have Ma Kali, Gopal Krishna, and Radha-Krishna idols in the central shrine under one roof. Baba Lokenath would be in the same temple with other deities to be worshipped in the ashram under one roof. That was the plan.

One day, when I went to Thakur's bedroom after his afternoon rest, he was waiting for me. The moment I walked in, he said with a beaming smile, *"Do you know, Buira (the old man) came today, just a little while ago?"* (Thakur always called Baba Lokenath *"Buira" meaning the Old Master* when talking about him to me.)

I was thrilled. I knew every time Baba Lokenath came to Thakur it was not just a vision or the occasional dream. Baba materialized in his body. With huge excitement, I asked, *"What did he say?"* Thakur replied, *"He took me to the window and pointing to the temple under construction, he said, 'You have planned to put me inside that temple along with all other deities, but I am not going to sit there. I want a separate temple for me."* With wide-eyed wonder, I said, *"Oh Lord, then what did you tell him?"*

Gurudev continued, Buira said, *"Look at that jackfruit tree. That is where you need to construct a temple exclusively for me, that is where I want to sit and be in this ashram."*

"Was that all from him?" I asked.

"No," Thakur replied,

> *"When I asked him where can I find the money for such construction, since lots of funds have already been spent on construction of the ashram and the temple, with granite brought all the way from Rajasthan, Baba Lokenath stuck to his point and said, 'You don't have to worry about money or anything else. Just ask Shuddhaanandaa to do everything and he will do it.' So, saying, Baba Lokenath dematerialized his body into space."*

I was overwhelmed with tears of joy. I could not imagine that Baba Lokenath, who was considered the living Shiva by my own Master, would instruct my Master to delegate the whole task of constructing a new temple, which was not in the plan, all on me, an insignificant servant of my Master. I felt a surge of energy and a thrill inside, along with the deep conviction that I had to build the best temple for Baba Lokenath. I had to do nothing but to be an instrument. Baba would do all that he thinks right. The temple would come by his grace; he only needed a tiny instrument in the physical plane to translate his wish into action.

After a thorough search, I ended up at a huge granite temple that was under construction in Calcutta. I found the architect, Mr. Noni Bose, at his office on the tenth floor of a multistoried office complex and explained to him all about my Gurudev and Baba Lokenath. He was in awe! He promised me that he would help me with the project in every way he could. I asked him if he had any draft sketches of granite temples designed in the North Indian tradition. He didn't even think. He instantly opened one of the drawers of his desk and pulled out a few sketches of temples.

Excited that it was right at hand, I quickly flipped through the drawings. Deeply impressed with the beauty of one lovely temple, in my mind I selected it to become the temple of Shiva Lokenath. I asked Mr. Bose if I could take the draft sketches to show to my Gurudev and return with them as soon as he gave his opinion. Mr. Bose was kind and generous to a stranger like me. Having met me only once, he handed the whole stack of drawings to me in a big envelope. I expressed my gratitude and left his office.

All the way back on the bus, I was thinking of the grace that Baba Lokenath and my Gurudev had bestowed upon me. Before I could put forward any difficult effort, things were in my hand. A renowned architect firm had assured me of all its cooperation to create the best possible temple for Baba Lokenath. Dancing in with joy of my spirit, I came to my Gurudev at the ashram and started showing him the grand designs, praying that he would select one out of the many that were given as options.

To my surprise, Gurudev took no time to quickly pick the same sketch that I had chosen. I had not told him, so that he would not be biased. Now we are set to move ahead.

After this, there were a series of miracles, or should I say a stream of grace, that flowed from both my Master and the Grand Master, Baba Lokenath. We hired the best team of workers who brought special granite stone from the mines of North India.

The huge, all-granite temple to Baba Lokenath and Narmadeshwar Shiva Linga was completed in the late 1970s. Gurudev installed and consecrated the Narmadeshwar Shiva Linga as "Lokenath Shiva," along with an oil painting of Baba Lokenath painted by Mohammed Isha, a Muslim and the principal of Calcutta Art College.

Shiva Linga is a stone symbol of Lord Shiva, the Destroyer of the Hindu Trinity, which reminds us of the Omnipotent Lord, who is formless. The *Linga* (translated as "mark") is an egg or phallus shaped stone. The *Linga* symbol is an attempt to give form to the formless, referred to as Supreme Being or Brahman in Hindu religion. When a *Linga* is installed on a *Yoni* (translated as "womb"), it represents the union of Shiva and Shakti, the beginning of creation.

After the temple was dedicated and Shiva Lokenath was installed, Thakur would often come, stand looking at Baba Lokenath's portrait, silently communing with him. The temple's main shrine radiated with the divine presence of the Universal Mother Kali, whom Thakur named as "Bhavaharini Ma Kali", Gopal Krishna and Radha-Krishna. Baba Lokenath has his own, separate temple, which looks stunning and graceful.

BABA LOKENATH TEMPLE AT THAKUR'S ASHRAM

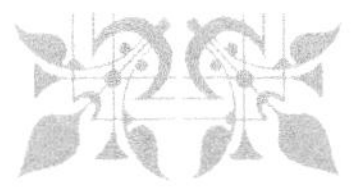

CHAPTER TWENTY-ONE

THE SCIENCE OF GURU MANTRA

The whole of the Vedic tradition of Hindu *dharma* is anchored in the basic doctrine of the Guru-disciple relationship. Truth is beyond all logic and rationality. With Truth being non-dual, in the absence of any "other", no knowledge is possible as we understand it in the physical world. We can only know an object, that which is separate from us. To be knowable presupposes the need for the knower. Only then is knowledge possible. All the physical knowledge that we find in the libraries of the world belongs to the world of knowledge that is knowable.

The science of spiritualty has always been shrouded in mystery. The seeker must penetrate beyond the veil of what is apparent and superficial in tangible manifestation. That is a most difficult and arduous process. It requires rigorous practice to rise above all normal modes of perception, as well as the deeply ingrained tendencies of the body-mind, in order to access the hidden realms of deeper reality that are beyond mind and intelligence. The rich literature of the Vedic or Upanishadic tradition only points the way. Mere knowledge of spiritual literature in any tradition, however, can never open the gates to the mystic world of subtle reality. From time immemorial, the Guru in Hindu tradition was always the embodiment of divinity and stood as symbol of Truth and pure devotion.

Guru literally means the dispeller of darkness. The Guru is one who comes into the life of a soul in desperate need to tear away the knots of ignorance and the darkness of self-forgetfulness. Guru is never a person. Guru is one who brings the light of the divine to full flame in the heart of the seeker. Once ignited from within, the disciple walks the path while the Guru monitors and provides critical guidance. When the disciple reaches the peak, both Guru and disciple merge into each other, for Truth is non-dual. Even the Guru-disciple is a concept rooted in dualism.

Without the external help of one who has mastered that journey, the path is indeed difficult to tread. That is because the mind, rooted as it is in ignorance and egotism, cannot free itself from its own misconceptions. Most often *sadhaks* (seekers) without proper guidance will fall into ditches, misled by the treacherous mind. Ego is very cunning. It will never give the impression that it is misleading us! But it does. The need for one who can help channel the power of ego into the path of Self-realization is immense.

India, with its culture of soul, has been the land of sages and saints, of savants of pure divinity. They came from every corner of this holy land, mostly in poor, illiterate families. Through the help of an adept, a great Master, they reached the stage where the Master and disciple mirrored the one Truth in each other. Thus, the legacy of the Master and his or her lineage continued.

The Vedic tradition affirms that the ultimate goal of the spiritual path is impossible to attain only through one's self and self-knowledge. Ultimate God-realization requires the grace and guidance of one who is enlightened, one who has successfully trodden that path, and reached home, one who knows the pitfalls and who has mastered egoic mind.

• • •

One evening, when Thakur was at his ashram and many devotees had gathered, we were treated to the following dialogue between him and a devotee:

> *Devotee: "Thakur, why do you initiate people with a mantra (deeksha) and who is eligible to receive this mantra?"*
>
> *Thakur: "Whoever is destined to receive mantra, he or she gets it from me. This formal initiation with Guru Mantra purifies your body and sanctifies your mind."*
>
> *Devotee: "But I have seen many who took initiation from you or other gurus who do all kinds of immoral acts and continue to glorify their false vanity and ego. In such cases, what is the use of this formality?"*

Thakur: "Those who do the mantra japa with a bit of sincerity would get the benefit and have purification of their body-mind. Those whom you see are not benefited and have not changed their behavioral patterns are the ones who are insincere and do not abide by the instruction of the Guru. This is pure transgression. They do suffer, but the Guru keeps on creating situations and circumstances so that the disciple comes to realize the true purpose of life and feels the responsibility to respect the Guru and Mantra."

Devotee: "Please let us know how we should move on this path of Guru-bhakti (devotion to one's Guru)."

Thakur: "Always abide by the instruction of your Guru. This is of prime importance in the life of a disciple who is formally initiated. Guru will never leave you or throw you away. He will always save you from all the dangers and pitfalls of life. He will always help you to regain your mental stability in distressing times. But keep in mind, I have seen that humankind does not want peace. They invite problems to their life and suffer. Until such time they realize that it is by walking the path of peace and happiness that one can attain to peace and happiness, they keep suffering. The Guru keeps on reminding them to tread the simple path of devotion, humility, continual remembrance and surrender.

"Guru may be showing the way, but if the disciple is not ready to listen to his words and even at times becomes

> *judgmental about the Guru as he tries to correct him or her, that only delays the whole process of inner transformation. As such, a disciple must realize that the Guru is never a human body or a person, but only comes to light the inner shrine of the disciple so that all the darkness of past births is dispelled and the disciple can see the light of God everywhere."*

The devotee here was sincere and humble in his desire to understand the responsibility of being a disciple, which is often thought of as more mundane. Thakur was showing the path of all disciples for all Masters who are the embodiment of the Universal Mother.

Most people today have a very common question about the genuineness of the guru and the guru's capacity to deliver what the student is asking for. Indeed, there are many instances where the priest or the guru, who is supposed to be the embodiment of divine qualities, takes advantage of the innocence and faith of devotees and exploits them. But isn't it also true that seekers are often more interested in a quick fix and easy spiritual gains? Are they ready to jump in with any cultish guru who has a big fanfare, one who uses gimmicks and interprets the scriptures to his or her own personal advantage? Too often people are more interested in techniques that relieve their immediate problems or that offer quick results awakening their *kundalini* or other latent spiritual powers. These people help grow the numbers of such priests and false prophets that readily take advantage of the seekers of overnight enlightenment.

In Hindu tradition it is said that one who seeks a Guru should see him during the day and during the night for a year before deciding whether he or she is the person who can take you across the ocean of life. A true seeker will invariably find odd vibrations in the presence of a false teacher. A true seeker will invariably start feeling a sense of quiet and inner peace and will have many long-unresolved questions answered in the mere presence of a true teacher. Thus seekers, too, have to assume responsibility to save the sacred path of spiritual illumination from unethical commercialization.

Thakur showed the simple path of *Japa Yoga* and devotional surrender. He was love personified. He gave initiation and continually guided his students towards a simple, humble life of pure surrender to higher providence. He taught the path of devotion and self-introspection so that old *karmas* are burned and no new ones are created.

Deceased Soul Receives Sacred Initiation

One day when Thakur was talking to a group of devotees, the conversation moved to the question about devotees who died before they were formally initiated with *Guru Mantra.*

Devotee: "How can those souls who are gone from this world find their liberation?"

Thakur: "When they take shelter in the Holy Name or the Guru Mantra, they even get the mantra after they are dead and gone. That paves the way for their liberation."

Devotee: "Did it ever happen in your life, Thakur, when someone who died came to you and you initiated such soul?"

Thakur: "Yes, it has happened."

> *While they were all still talking about this very interesting topic, a couple entered the sitting room at Cornfield Road, where Thakur was seated. It was in 1972. Thakur immediately said,*

> *"Look here comes Prodosh and Chitra Mukherjee. One such episode happened in their home, in their family. So you should listen to that story first-hand from them. Their mother and father were initiated together though the surviving father never knew that his deceased wife was also called for the initiation and was initiated."*

Eager to hear the story, everyone looked at Thakur, wide-eyed, expecting him to continue. Thakur said, *"Ask Prodosh. He will say."*

Prodosh began narrating the story,

> *"My mother died quite a few years back. My father was very successful in a company job and made enough money, but he was very atheistic in his attitude. My whole family was very indifferent to anything religious and to God. No one had any kind of faith. We hardly talked about God in those days. My uncle was the Chief Engineer in the Railway Board, which was a high profile, executive position. We are so blessed to have found Thakur, as he brought a life of faith and devotion into*

our life. In his own inimitable way, he had attracted us, one by one, to his divine shelter and initiated us. Now we all live a life of spiritual practice every day, seeing new meaning and purpose of life, which was totally missing in those days of that Godless, Guru-less life of ours.

"The most surprising thing was how my father was magically drawn to Thakur. On the very first day he met Thakur in the company of one of his friends, he felt a deep sense of peace and bliss that he had never ever experienced in his life, which had been focused only on work and family. But the person who brought my father to Thakur disappeared from Thakur's company soon after his instrumentation of bringing my father to him. It was as if it was his destiny to bring father to Thakur and then walk his own way!

"Anyway, Thakur instructed me that for my father's initiation I should spread out two mats, five kinds of fruits and a couple of towels. I was taken aback. I could not refrain from asking Thakur why I should buy things for two people, when it was only the deeksha (mantra) ceremony of my father? Thakur replied in a very casual note, 'It is because your mother will also be initiated along with your father. But don't let your father know about this now.'

"I have been a student of science all along. With my scientific bent of mind I could not understand how my

> *mother, who died long ago, could be initiated along with my living father. But I wanted to just follow the instruction of Thakur and, accordingly, bought two sets of the requisite items for the initiation and put them at Thakur's place at his Cornfield Road residence. Finally, the day of deeksha came and I reached Thakur's place with my father. The arrangement for the ceremony was made with two mats spread, one on each side. To Thakur's right sat my father and to Thakur's left there was an empty mat spread. I left the room as Thakur closed the doors for the secret ceremony."*

All this while, Chitra, Prodosh's wife was sitting quietly listening to the story. Suddenly she jumped into the conversation and said,

> *"Just a couple of days before father's initiation, I suddenly felt a deep longing to meet Thakur that was overwhelming. But I had just gone to meet Thakur at his Cornfield Road home the day before and had spent much time talking to him. Nevertheless, the pull was so strong that I could not resist. Though Thakur's house was quite a distance from where we stay, I left again and went to meet him. I saw Thakur and sat for a while, then wanted to take leave of him, when Thakur suddenly asked me, 'You came to see me yesterday. How come you came to see me again today?' So saying, he gave a meaningful smile as he looked at me. I said, 'I felt a deep pull from you, so I had to come.' I just sat for a while and then left for my home. The*

> *question kept coming into my mind, why did I come all the way to Thakur's place when I did not even stay at his place very long? I felt a deep satisfaction within a short while."*

When another devotee wanted Thakur to reveal the secret behind his smile to Chitra that day, Thakur opened up,

> *"OK, hear the story then. That day, as Chitra's late mother-in-law was supposed to be initiated, she came along with Chitra to my place. That day, when Chitra was so eager to come to me, it was because her mother-in-law wanted her to come, so that she could accompany her without her knowledge. Just behind Chitra, I saw a woman with downcast eyes and somber face standing there. When Chitra left, she asked me for deeksha. I told her, 'I will initiate you along with your husband. Now you can go back peacefully and come right on time the day when I initiate your husband.'"*

"Then what happened?" someone asked. By this time, all the assembled devotees were holding their breath to hear the next part of this mysterious story. This was something they had never even heard of or even dreamed to be possible.

Thakur said with a smile,

> *"Puranjan (Chitra's father-in-law) got his initiation. Then I told Chitra's mother-in-law, 'Once I initiate you, do touch your husband's feet and offer your respects before you leave.' She did accordingly. Puranjan suddenly spoke out in panic, 'Who is touching my feet?'*

I told him, 'Don't be afraid, it is your deceased wife. All these years she had a deep desire to be initiated along with you; today her wish has been fulfilled. Now she is free.'"

This episode, however unbelievable it may appear, was true and the message that Thakur wanted to share with us is that the path of higher evolution of the soul is not restricted to this mortal body and life span on earth. It continues after death. Chitra's mother-in-law was no more in her physical body, she was dead, but her soul lived on and waited for Thakur to take her to the next realm of the astral world. She knew that to Thakur, in body or in soul dimension, was one and the same. She also knew that to reach to her next height of spiritual realization, she needed to be initiated by a living Master. Hence, she prayed to the Master for his grace and the Master granted her wish. She was now happily on her way to her own astral plane where she could continue her earnest practice with *Guru Mantra* to evolve further in the sphere of the Spiritual Light.

A Disciple with an Eye for Occult Powers

Kalidas Chatterjee, a special officer in Railways, came in touch with Thakur in the early part of Thakur's manifestation of divine *lila* as Guru. In 1969, when he was posted in Hyderabad, his senior officers had already met the Master. They knew that Kalidas had a deep inclination towards spiritual knowledge. Though he met Thakur in Hyderabad, within a short time he was transferred to Jamalpur, in Bihar.

In later years, Jamalpur became a place for several visits of Thakur and many devotees and disciples found shelter under Thakur's presence there.

After being initiated by Thakur, Kalidas attended to his work in the railways but took up the path of spiritual practice very deeply. He practiced rituals that could awaken the latent powers for which he had a desire. After a few years of *sadhana*, he developed some *siddhis* (occult powers) and people of Jamalpur often talked about this disciple of Thakur, whom they thought had reached a high spiritual state. Kalidas would often go over to a hill called Kalipahar, which was considered to be a high-energy place, to do his practice for the whole night, sitting under the sky on the rocks.

One day, Kalidas was in his own home at his altar, deeply engrossed in meditation. He suddenly started feeling very sad. He was hit by uncontrolled emotion, feeling very low. Then, at next moment, he could see on his mental screen a close relative getting involved in an accident on the street of Calcutta near his ancestral home. He was shocked and could not continue with his chant and meditation, so he walked away from his altar and sat at the garden outside his house with a very sad state of mind, wondering what he should do.

Then he saw a small piece of paper floating in the air right in front of him, which landed on the ground. He was intrigued. He picked up the piece of paper and was awed to see that it was from his Guru, who had written it in his own hand. The small note read, *"Don't get distracted from your 'work' and feel sad. Keep doing your japa (repetition of Guru Mantra), everything is taken care of—Thakur."* Kalidas was deeply moved, realizing that, however far away he may be from his Guru's physical presence, Thakur always had an eye on him and was watching over every act of his spiritual practice. He immediately went back to his home altar and resumed his practice with even deeper faith and contemplation.

In later years, Kalidas once talked to Ramakrishna Shastri Mahashay, a Sanskrit scholar who was the main priest for the ritualistic worship of Thakur, as well as the deities installed at the ashram. He shared his experience, "*So many times Thakur just dropped out of thin air small pieces of notes written in his wonderful handwriting, instructing me to be steadfast on my path.*"

Kalidas reiterated,

> *"Thakur was always very particular about our 'work' meaning spiritual sadhana. He would remind me, time and again, to be drowned in doing japa or mantra sadhana. I realized that Thakur is always with us whenever we do sadhana, bestowing his divine grace."*

Though Kalidas believed in attaining *siddhis* or powers, Ramakrishna Shastri Mahashay would always insist that nothing is more powerful than surrendering to the will of the Guru, humbly and simply waiting for transforming grace to happen on its own terms, in its own time.

One day, Kalidas and Shastri Mahashay were sitting together, engrossed in spiritual discussions and exchanging their experiences about the Master. They were sitting in the temple of Ma Kali, at the residence of Shastri Mahashay. When Shastri Mahashay said that he needed to go worship the Mother, Kalidas expressed his desire to accompany him to her shrine and join in the rituals. He suddenly threw out a challenge to Shastri Mahashay, *"Today let us both meditate upon our Master. I assure you that I will get him to this temple, and we will see him right in front of us."*

So, saying, Kalidas closed his eyes and was immersed in meditation. After a while, Shastri Mahashay could feel someone was right behind them, walking around the temple. He clearly heard the sound of wooden sandals walking in the temple. Then in the next moment, when Kalidas opened his eyes, both saw it was none other than the Master. Thakur, with wooden sandals, was standing right beside the divine Mother Kali. Then in a blink of an eye, he disappeared. His wooden sandals were left behind, though, right inside the temple, with red hibiscus flowers strewn all around them. Kalidas was overjoyed. He told Shastri Mahashay, *"Look, did I not tell you that if I call my Guru he will appear before me?"* Shastri Mahashay agreed and called all his family members to see with their own eyes the wooden sandals of Guru and his divine grace of answering the call of his ardent devotee.

Every year on the auspicious occasion of the birth anniversary of the Master, one place was selected well in advance for the celebration. That year it was in Durgapur and Thakur went to Durgapur to attend the ceremonies. Kalidas said that he would celebrate the anniversary in Jamalpur itself to prove to all the devotees that Thakur would be as present to take the offering of love and devotion in Jamalpur as he would be in Durgapur, where he would be physically present. When

Thakur was told this, he agreed and asked the Jamalpur devotees and disciples to stay with Kalidas to celebrate the anniversary.

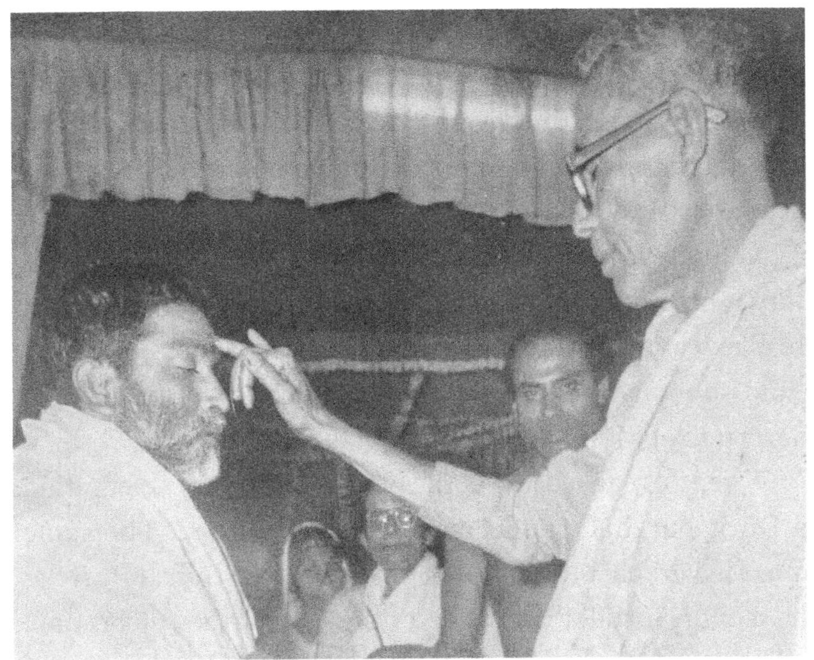

RAMKRISHNA SHASTRI MAHASHAY, AN ARDENT DEVOTEE AND A SCHOLAR IN SANSKRIT WORSHIPPING THE MASTER

Kalidas wanted to show all the assembled devotees the power of his yogic *siddhis* (miracles), so he sat before the altar and its beautiful picture of Gurudev and began worshipping with *mantras* and meditation. After a while, to the amazement of all assembled devotees, the picture of Thakur and his lotus feet started to be covered with number of fresh, blooming lotuses. More and more lotuses manifested out of thin air, filling the floor of the room around the already well decorated altar of Gurudev. The entire room was filled with the ecstatic fragrance of lotus flowers.

With everyone already in pure awe at seeing this miracle, the footprints of Mother Kali suddenly appeared prominently all over the altar space. Everyone could see them with their naked eyes, so they knew that both the Guru and the *Ishta* (cherished form of divinity) of the Mother Divine had graced the celebration with their subtle divine presence.

Prabhat Ray, an ardent disciple of Thakur and resident of Jamalpur, who was present during this miracle, left for Durgapur to inform the Master of this unique experience. He also wanted to know how all this could be possible. How could so many lotus flowers come from nowhere, and the footprints of Mother Kali could be left at the altar?

When he reached site of the birth anniversary celebration in Durgapur, his wonderment only intensified. The same lotus flowers that Kalidas had brought out of thin air were at the feet of Gurudev and all over the area of the celebration, only there were even more here than in Jamalpur!

When the festivities were over, Thakur had gone to his own room and retired to bed. Prabhat sat at the feet of the Master, lightly massaging his legs after the long day that Thakur had sitting in one place, accepting the devotional offerings, singing and giving his message.

Prabhat inquired about the miracle he had seen manifested by Kalidas. Thakur replied calmly,

> *"No one should perform this kind of exhibition of occult powers. If you want, I can show you innumerable*

> *miracles, but then what would be your gain? Whatever I say, will happen. If I say let this stainless container of betel leaf hang in thin air, you will see in no time this container would be in the air, hanging for as long as I want. But what will your friends tell you? They will only say your Guru is only a glorified magician. You can spend money and see all these kinds of miracles, but you can never receive the true blessings and grace of the Master that can transform you from within."*

Thakur continued with conviction in his voice, as if he was giving a message that he knew would one day find its place in a book to be read by millions across the world. He said,

> *"Keep it in mind, anything that has been there in this world, that existed somewhere, or is in existence, you can move from one place to the other, but that which was not there, cannot be shifted, moved, or brought into manifestation."*

Prabhat got the message. It was first-hand learning right at the feet of the Guru. He bowed at the feet of the Master with utter reverence and gratitude at being blessed with the embodiment of divinity as his own Guru on the path of the Spirit.

Kalidas had a deep attraction for such miracles. Thakur could smell that behind it all, Kalidas' subtle ego was at play, hindering the progress of his spiritual upliftment. Thakur gave him silent hints that he should give up this clinging to occult powers and their display, that they take the *sadhak* nowhere other than the pit of one's own downfall. Kalidas was blessed. As an ardent disciple of Thakur living the householder's life, he showed through his intense practice of yogic techniques that *siddhis* can be attained if that is the desire in the heart of the disciple. More importantly, he also demonstrated that this desire needs to be avoided, that nothing is superior to the miracle of true transformation of the inner self. As only a *Sadguru*'s patience and masterful guidance could elevate a sincere disciple to that highest state of inner transformation. Thakur led Kalidas' earthbound, ego-bound soul to become a true devotee surrendered to the Lord, living in deep communion with the universal spirit, manifesting pure love and bliss.

Grace or Power of Will?

I had just joined the ashram at Mallikpur. It was a new life. Of course I was excited and at the same time, I had lots of questions in my mind about the life that was to unfold in this new, completely unknown world of renunciation. With all of this going on, while I was free to act as I pleased, of course I was also trying to keep the root anchor of my spiritual goals foremost in mind. Being here in the ashram, everything was so wonderful; yet, initially there was also the energy of trying to understand the new space.

I had joined the ashram of my revered Master on 11 July 1976. When my Gurudev initiated me in the path of renunciation, he gave me the white clothes of a *Brahmacharin* (celibate monk) along with a new name, "Shuddhaanandaa". My head was shaved and my new life of a monk started as a full-timer, dedicated to God.

Many devotees had come to the ashram from different places in connection with Guru Purnima celebration the previous day, so quite a few of us were sitting on the floor of Thakur's bedroom where he was sitting chewing a betel leaf.

One of the devotees broke the silence with a question to Thakur on will power.

"Since nothing happens without the wish of the Lord, is it only when grace happens that true will power or aspiration to attain comes to a seeker or a devotee?" Assembled devotees were eager to hear what would flow from the Master in response.

> *Thakur: "If you don't assert your will power and your effort how will you perceive grace? As long as you have the 'I' that is your ego total surrender cannot happen. As a result, one cannot realize that everything is happening only by God's will or wish. The statement that everything is happening by divine will and dispensation is true, but only one in a high state of self-surrender can realize that since it requires a state of pure wisdom that is beyond intellectual understanding."*

> *Devotee: "But then we hear so much about the saying 'Everything happens by divine will.'"*

> *Thakur: "The divine is the source of all auspiciousness. It always wants all to seek to move toward the realization of that ultimate reality, ultimate truth. But humans, being subservient to their own ignorance and worldly tendencies, forget the truth and are deluded."*

Devotee: "What are these tendencies you are talking about? Are they our habits?"

Thakur: "Habit is nothing but your innate tendencies. Because of these habitual tendencies, you have the perception in your own individualistic way about good, bad, doubts and suspicions. Various states of your mind obstruct your efforts for genuine surrender. That is the reason you have to assert your will power. As long as you have ego, you have to assert your will power. Your will power and effort alone are not enough, though. You must have dedication and commitment. It takes both loving, dedicated effort and the assertion of will power to follow the instructions of your spiritual master without any sense of judgment or discrimination.

"If you try for a while with a little sincerity, you will find that your own flaws will become very clearly visible to you. You must work on them. You have to pray, 'May these flaws leave me by thy grace. Release me from the fetters of these instinctive tendencies of my lower mind, so that I can be truly free of my ego and realize that all that is is your grace, and all is your will in manifestation.' That is the reason I am saying, 'So long as you have ego, you are within the field of will power or effort on your part.' The day ego dissolves, divine grace dawns spontaneously."

Devotee: "There are many things which cannot be understood through logic and reasoning. Is it better to have blind faith and accept them?"

Thakur: "Why should you walk the path of blind faith? See your path! You are educated; how would you have blind faith? Where is that utter simplicity and innocence? You have to see the path and move. Be steadfast in your will power and efforts with dedicated commitment towards Truth, then you will surely experience divine Grace."

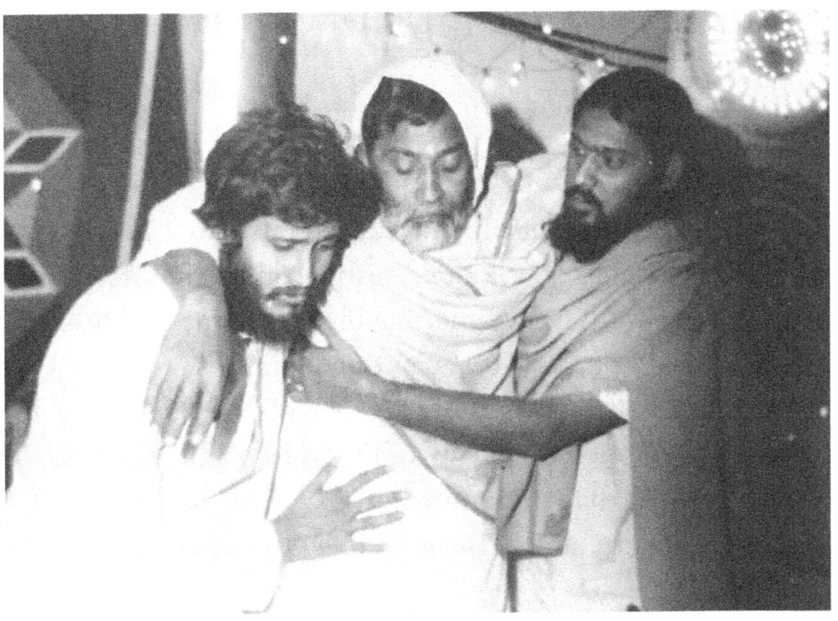

THAKUR CARRIED TO HIS ROOM BY SHUDDHAANANDAA (LEFT, THIS BOOK'S AUTHOR) AND SHIVANANDA (RIGHT) IN 1977.

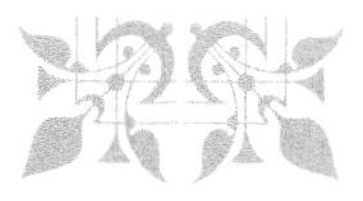

CHAPTER TWENTY-TWO

SIMPLICITY AND HUMILITY—THE ESSENCE OF SPIRITUAL LIFE

Dirghangi was with Thakur on the occasion of Guru Purnima Utsav at Prabhat Ray's house on 2 July 1985. He was lucky. Thakur was alone, resting during the afternoon when others were busy either having their *prasad* (blessed food) or talking to each other, sitting in groups.

Dirghangi was always a man of logic and did not get swayed by emotions, as many of his Guru brothers and sisters did. He also had the natural gift of writing with a flow of both reason and emotion. He opened the conversation saying,

> *"Thakur, many people pass judgmental comments about my writing about you. Have I really become self-centered by doing that?" Thakur's face lit up; his words flowed, "To know one's own self is the ultimate*

knowledge. He who does not know about his own self, how do you expect such a person to know others?"

Dirghangi was awed at how simply Thakur replied; yet the answer was so full of profound meaning.

He later reminisced,

"When we were with this great sage, we sat at his feet and there were moments his words flowed like the sacred water of the Mother Ganges. We were bathed inside out. But today, I repent that we have not taken instant notes of his priceless words of wisdom. We were just drunk with his presence, his smile, his divine radiance, and above all the profundity of his utterances. It just did not occur to us that the day would come when this great sage will no longer be among us, that his words could remain, not just for the few of us who came to him, but for the whole of humanity, as a beacon of light for seekers of Truth and peace."

Dirghangi loved to read and think all about the knowledge that he acquired through books. At times his mind was clogged with too many interpretations of the simple reality of life. It pulled him away from appreciating the source of direct knowledge that Thakur was.

One day on his own, Thakur said to him,

"Don't try to understand or fathom your Guru with the acquired knowledge from books. You won't be able to understand the true essence of Guru. Just give up all this constant chatter of your judgmental mind. In this field,

> *your intelligence can't take you far. Only faith can. Be in the presence of your Guru with an open heart, with an empty mind, and let faith talk to you. Surrender to your Master with unwavering faith and see what happens to you. Only faith can make the impossible possible. Know that faith, simplicity, and humility are the main qualities in the path of Dharma or Pure Essence. Simplicity is very important. From simple faith, true love for the Divine and love for all of existence as the veritable manifestation of the One Divine is born in the heart of a seeker."*

Dirghangi with his logical and rational mindset was not convinced that one could just leave things to God with a vague emotion like faith. He wanted to dig a little more, so he remarked, *"I am a family person, I have responsibility toward my wife, my children, toward my family; how can I just leave things to faith and sit quietly?"*

Gurudev replied, *"Every living being comes into this world and God takes total responsibility for every soul. We are mere puppets in the hands of the Divine."*

Thakur was not someone who could keep on explaining spiritual wisdom and giving discourses. He said time and again that he was a simple man. Once he told Dirghangi's wife, Swapna, *"After taking mantra initiation from me, isn't it true that at times you feel very overwhelmed?"*

"Yes, Thakur," replied Swapna, as she found it difficult to take care of her children and husband, juggling the many other aspects of daily life while also giving her mind to her practice of *mantra*.

To help her understand how she needed to trust her Guru more than her mind in its state of constant worries and tensions about the future and other uncertainties, Thakur continued:

> *"You have entered a new life (marriage and children). It is natural that you will have some problems to begin with. Did you not see when a child learns to walk, she falls many times? The child cries and sees if the mother is coming to lift her, but the mother hides and smiles, seeing all this. The mother knows that the day is not far when she will scale up the stairs effortlessly."*

Swapna was listening to the Master with utter devotion as he closed with, *"Don't you worry so much about your children and their future. Leave all your worries to me."*

Is God with Form or Formless?

On another day, a devotee asked the Master, *"Is God with form or formless?"* This has been a common question in the minds of most seekers on the path of God consciousness.

Thakur replied with a calm voice, but thundering with the Truth that is enshrined in the Vedic tradition:

> *"Ishwar is God without beginning and without end. He is there from eternity, beyond the frame of time, eternally at play with the process of creation and annihilation. That is the reason the path of dharma or Truth is the path of justice, the path of peace. Truth reveals, in its own mysterious ways, the untruths with which the whole of the cosmic play is happening.*

"You see God according to your own faith. You may call God formless or with form. Know that the formless aspect resonates to the nature of those who follow the path of Jnana (knowledge), while the divine in form speaks to those who follow the path Bhakti, which is devotion and love. Don't force a formless God on the ones who are treading the path of devotional surrender. In the path of Bhakti (devotion), if the devotee cannot relate to the form of God, if he cannot see or touch God, his feelings would be hurt. If you have your ego—and your egoic existence is true to you so long as the world of form exists for you—various forms of God also are truth to you. Do you know what the great mystic saint Karbir has said? 'Formless is my Father, and form is my Mother.'"

This is the way Thakur used to flow spontaneously, though he never had any formal training or study of the scriptures of Hindu faith. Dirghangi noted these words in his personal journal about the eternal promise of the Master to his followers.

"I come again and again to give the seed of the Divine Name to your ears. My heart pangs to see you all, to talk to you all. That is the reason when I hear words of your pains and agonies, I cry. When I hear about your happiness, my heart surges with joy unspeakable!"

The Master Gives Hint of His Passing Over

In 1990, Thakur was in Jamalpur at the late Dr. S.K. Roy's home. He was not in good health. Seeing Dirghangi coming, he asked his assistants to take him inside the bedroom from the garden where he was sitting in a reclining chair. As Thakur was assisted walking down to his bedroom, he lay down on the bed and Dirghangi started massaging Thakur's legs to make him feel better. After a long while, Thakur broke the silence and said, *"Do you know I won't be with you all for long?"* Dirghangi could not comprehend what Thakur meant. He did not understand that Thakur was giving a hint that his time to leave the mortal cage was coming soon. Still in his own thoughts, Dirghangi asked Thakur, *"Why did you go away from the householder's life and become a monastic Brahmachari? Or did you come prepared to give shelter to all of us wayward children of yours?"*

After a long time, Thakur spoke out,

> *"Seeing the way humans live in this world, my heart was filled with dismay. There are various types of men and women in this world. There are a few who would leave wife, children, and their happy family and go to the brothels to find joy with prostitutes. A few try to find joy in drinking wine day and night. And there are others who, in order to find peace, leave their home and go in search of spiritual powers, who worship the Mother Divine and wander in the forests and mountains.*

> *"Bliss is God. God is Bliss. To find pure bliss in life, man and woman leave everything and search everywhere, patiently bearing all the austerities and pains."*

Suddenly he changed his topic, his face turned extremely pain ridden. For a while he kept quiet, as if he was remembering something very unpleasant, and then asked, *"Have you seen famine? Have you seen war? Have you seen communal riots, mass murders, and genocide?"* Dirghangi replied, *"No, Thakur, I have not seen such things."*

Thakur continued,

> *"So, you have not seen any of these, but I have seen them. I have seen famine; I have seen millions dying of hunger; I have seen during famine a mother falling at the feet of a man begging for nothing but the starch that remains after straining boiled rice. Not even rice for the hungry, dying child! I have seen a mother crying bitterly, holding her dead, boney baby tightly to her chest who had died of hunger. I have seen communal riots in Calcutta between Hindus and Muslims where, in the name of God, religious people killed and butchered each other and spilled blood everywhere. I have seen brother kill his own brother for the sake of ancestral property rights, I have seen when undivided Bengal was divided into East Pakistan and West Bengal, how millions of people had to leave their homes, their hard-earned belongings, seeking for shelter as refugees."*

He could not continue anymore; overwhelmed with pain and emotion at those memories, he burst into tears. Dirghangi had never seen Thakur in such deep pain over human cruelty toward others.

Thakur continued,

> *"Then I cried out to the Divine Mother, I prayed to the Divine Mother. I could not remain indifferent to all this suffering of humanity everywhere. I fled from home many times, wandered in all the holy places, spent nights in the crematoriums where dead bodies were burned to ashes. I spent months in the Himalayas in the caves and at the banks of Mother Ganges, doing penance to find the way to end all human suffering. Finally, when I got the answer to all my questions, it was simple. The whole of creation is under the spell of maya, the law of impermanence and illusion. Only the Truth that is beyond impermanence is eternal and absolute."*

Dirghangi was sitting at the feet of the Master, spellbound. He could understand, though most of the things Thakur talked were beyond his comprehension. Thakur looked so different today, as if he was talking to his own self rather than to Dirghangi.

The Master continued,

> *"To sustain Truth, dharma, and human virtues, there is a dire need for the invocation and worship of Shakti, the Divine feminine. That is the reason I have installed*

the idol of Ma Bhavaharini (Mother Kali). I have been trying to make people realize that for the survival of humanity and the Earth, for the happiness and peace of all species, worship of Shakti and steadfastness to the Will of Mother Divine is the way to protect the divine principles and establish peace on earth. I have never, ever asked for my personal gratification at any level, for name, fame, money, or possessions. Nothing mattered to me; the only thing I have lived for is to see all of humanity be happy by being worshipful and meditative of the divine feminine. That is the reason I became a monk, a Brahmachari renunciate, abandoning all other earthly wants and needs: to be of service to all of humanity, to be of service to the mission of Mother Divine."

Other devotees were slowly coming in, gathering in the bigger, adjacent room for the evening *satsang* and *bhajans*. Dirghangi felt a deep sense of quiet dawning in his mind without any effort. He had never felt so close to Thakur and was overwhelmed with divine feelings. He waited for Thakur to resume speaking.

Thakur began with a low voice only audible to Dirghangi,

"Do you know why saints and sages give up the tranquility of the mountains and riverbanks? Why they come to live amid all kinds of people who continuously bring all their mundane worldly demands to them, expecting some miracle? It is because the seekers and devotees need to see amid their worldly life these women and

men of God who come with all their divine qualities, though living a simple humble life of a human being. They embody the attributes of God, like unconditional love, compassion, forgiveness, and make every effort to bring about a change in the lives of those people in order to help them realize the higher purpose and the light of God's grace. They bring divinity down to the level of perception of common human beings, making the glory of God and divinity visible. Otherwise, how could the common person realize all that they read in the scriptures could be a practical reality? They need to see to believe.

"Guru comes to exemplify what you all need to practice in order to find peace and happiness in life. Guru creates all the circumstances that are needed to push the devotee to the inner world from outside. Sitting in the core of your heart, he pulls you from inside to his eternal home, where there is abiding peace and silence.

"Once true faith in Guru dawns, once you grow total trust in God, then all the puzzles of your life will be solved instantly. You will be left with no more questions and riddles. One day, all the mysteries will become unveiled instantaneously. You will no longer judge good and bad. All prejudices will leave you for good. You will be flooded with an all-encompassing surge of the deepest feeling of pure, unconditional love and compassion for all living beings. Not just for humans. You yourself will become the personification of Love. That is the

height you can reach if you can surrender your false ego to your Guru and God and live the humble life as an instrument of his service and sadhana. His grace alone will transform you from human to an embodiment of pure divinity."

The time for the evening chanting had arrived. Thakur was led to the adjacent hall where devotees were waiting to drink the nectar of his divine presence and the bliss that he had come to share.

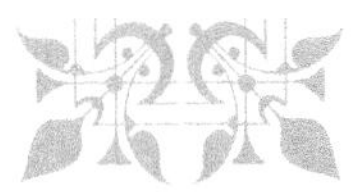

CHAPTER TWENTY-THREE

THE POWER OF FAITH

The Master was seated in his room at the ashram after his midday lunch and was in a relaxed mood. A few devotees were also seated around him. Thakur was speaking on different aspects of practical life with his usual child-like simplicity. I noticed Jharna Roy Choudhury, one of our Guru-sisters entering the room accompanied by another disciple, Subodh Roy Choudhury of Durgapur. The very sight of her was startling. She looked completely imbalanced. She cast a vacant look at Thakur. Within a blink of an eye, she lay prostrate at Master's feet, beside herself, with a profusion of tears rolling down her cheeks, wetting his feet. The entire atmosphere turned somber.

Still crying, Jharna prayed to Thakur,

"You are all merciful. Kindly save my daughter. No one else, nothing other than your holiness can save her life.

> *She has been in the hospital for the last few days. The doctors have given up all hope for her surviving. Now tell me, how can they snatch her away from me while I am at thy feet? Please save her life."*

A strange change instantly took place in Thakur. Stretching out his hands in blessings, he tenderly touched Jharna's head in her utter distress and said, "*What makes you cry, my daughter? Have faith in Him. Take His Holy Name, and your daughter will come round.*" In the next moment he turned towards us and indicated that her daughter was suffering from leukemia (blood cancer) and that any hope for her life was remote. But how can such painful truth be uttered before an affectionate mother? With much effort, he sent her back after letting a ray of hope into her distressed heart. Thakur spoke out in a compassionate voice, "*Now you try to understand how delicate and painful my position is. I can neither utter the truth, nor can I bear it.*"

Time went on. Thakur was not well himself, so he was taken back to his residence at 7 A, Cornfield Road. In the evening, a renowned physician attended him. Some of his devotees had already assembled there. Rama Bose (the girl's grandmother) entered the room hurriedly. She first went to the Mallikpur ashram, but after learning that Thakur was at Cornfield Road, she came rushing there. At the sight of Thakur, she could not utter a word, nor could she hold herself anymore. Her frail body trembled as she sobbed. Embracing Thakur's sandals tightly to her bosom, she lay prostrate. She was lost, in deepest prayer at the feet of Master.

The sight of the old lady laying on the floor, at the feet of Thakur, reminded me of certain temples where people lay before the deity, desperate to obtain the grace of the divine for the fulfillment of their wish. Most often, they are begging for the life of a near and dear one who is dying. But here, the deity was present in flesh and blood.

A gloomy silence prevailed in every corner of the room. The prayer of a devotee was not unknown to Thakur, who was Mercy Incarnate! Thakur somehow lifted the thin body of the old woman up and said, *"Get up, my mother. Why do you cry? Take His Holy Name. He is merciful. He must respond to your call."* The old lady helplessly yet firmly said, *"I don't know of any God, I know only you. I know that you are my only God. That is why I have come to you. I know nothing is impossible for you."*

Again, words of pity and consolation came from Thakur, *"Well, you pray, and she will come round."*

But the lady was not to be consoled so easily. She felt that Thakur was trying to cover the truth. In all eagerness, she said, *"No, don't give me those words of consolation. The doctors have given up all hopes for her life. Now I count upon your mercy only. You only can bring her back to life."*

"Ah! How could the doctors tell the parents that? Couldn't they refrain from telling that unpleasant truth?" Thakur remarked. He took a pause and continued in a soft voice saying, *"In these cases really nothing can be done. I had told your son-in-law all about that on the first day."*

"Don't say this Baba. With all my heart, I believe that nothing is impossible for you. I am confident that when you have

said, 'She will come round,' she must come round. Your words are infallible."

"Then pray to God," said Thakur.

"My prayers to God are hardly responded to, but they always reach you. I therefore pray to you only to cure her. I will not leave this place unless you give me your word," she said with resolute faith and firmness.

"Ma, you know I always pray that no child is taken away from the bosom of their mother. You also must pray." Suddenly as if to himself he quietly muttered, *"These children are as pure as flowers; it seems they come only to create agonies."*

The old lady was as tenacious as she could be. With tears she adamantly repeated her prayer, *"Baba, you will have to give me your word."*

Suddenly, Thakur looked as if in a state of trance, and spoke out to the lady,

> *"Do you have real faith in your Guru? Do you possess sincerity in the true sense of it? If so, now test your faith and sincerity. If your prayers come from the very core of your heart, He must respond to it. Pray to Guru, beg for the life of the child. Perform 1000 japa (chanting of Guru Mantra) every day for your grandchild. If your prayers are true, He must respond to it. Sincere and earnest prayers are always granted. It is already getting late. Go home now. Go and do as I say."*

On several occasions I had noticed many inscrutable ways of my Gurudev. This was not the only one, so my memory of this incident slowly faded. In the meantime, Thakur returned to the ashram at Mallikpur, but he had to come back to Cornfield Road on some work. One day, Jharna, the child's mother, entered the room accompanied by another lady. The sight made me realize that some miracle had occurred. This time, too, she sat at the feet of Gurudev and burst into tears, but these were tears of joy and gratitude. Smiling, Thakur said, *"Did you see how God listens to sincere prayers?"*

The following evening, the old lady came. Her face beamed with immense happiness. She said, *"Nothing in the world is impossible for you Baba. I know you are Lord Shiva in human form."*

Thakur did not say anything in reply. The spark of a divine smile flashed between his lips. He said in a soft voice, *"Your Guru did absolutely nothing, all was done by God Himself. You do not have unshakable faith in Him, yet He wishes you good all the time. He is All Merciful."*

CHAPTER TWENTY-FOUR

MAHASAMADHI—SUPREME UNION WITH THE BELOVED

Every spiritual Master who has lived in this world has left their footprints on the sands of time for generations to come. The great Masters beckon us to evolve to a state where suddenly the dormant seed of God will wake up and manifest the seedling of the deepest yearning to return back to where we came from. Generations will come to see these footprints of great Masters and walk the path to the sublime heights of spiritual glory of enlightened Mastery!

The legacy of India has always been the search not just for the external but the search inside one's own self to unravel the mystery of the world both in and out. The puzzle has always been the gross reality of this solid world outside and the instinctive drive to be attracted to the material stuff of life, thus distancing oneself from the inner core of true reality.

This distancing over births creates a karmic pattern of a gap between the inner and the outer. This is always the core problem of humanity. The larger the gap between the inner and the outer, more the pain and suffering. Spiritual Masters have always come down to this mundane world from their highest heights of spiritual bliss, where they remain in the world of eternal bliss in *samadhi*. They come to awaken the sleeping gods, the dormant seeds of divinity to flower in those who are longing for and seeking the Truth beyond the veil of the changing flux of the material cluster.

A time comes for these great Masters to give up their physical bodies as we give up our clothes, after they are done with their work with the men, women and children who become the torch bearers of their legacy, their teachings and their stories. Their passing enables the Guru-disciple succession to continue for the spiritual emancipation of yearning souls. To the enlightened Master, there is no birth and no death, for they have unraveled the secret of this universe. The secret is that birth and death are but mere concepts or notions of mind in illusion of its identification with the body and all that is manifest. They realize that the true reality is beyond change. The unchangeable, the immutable, the indestructible, the indivisible, One and only. Once the Yogi transcends beyond the duality of birth and death, fear and despair, joy and misery, they are of the world but beyond the world. Such Yogis and such Masters live only to show that ultimate reality is with each one of us, and that we all can attain to that state for it is our most natural state. We already are That.

Thakur too had given the hint to Dirghangi that his time to leave was coming near, and his failing health had been a sign of his intention being manifest. Though Thakur was not physically well, his tour to places of his divine *lila* continued and the coming of more and more of the thirsting seekers to this well of nectar of life only increased. Thakur, despite all the advice of the doctors and restrictions by his caretaker monks, relentlessly reached out to devotees who had been longing for his shelter and divine grace. But then, as the months passed in that fateful year, Thakur's longing to meet all the devotees and disciples started increasing proportionately. He would continually remind immediate assistants to send the word to his disciples, devotees and followers staying far and wide to immediately come to see him. It was as if he was longing to meet each one of them and give them something known only to him.

Accordingly, news was sent to all devotees and they started pouring into the ashram to see him and take his blessings. He spoke with all love and compassion and gave them words of advice to walk the path of spirit with more sincerity. It was as if he was seeing them all for the last time, such was the urgency and the depth of his feeling and his urge to give and give.

Throughout his life he always longed to visit Puri, the holy place of pilgrims, to have *darshan* of Lord Jagannath in the most ancient and famous temple in the eastern India. A few of the disciples and devotees planned for a visit to this holy centre on 12 November 1991, and Thakur, even with frail health, joyfully joined them and spent a few days in Puri.

We never saw Thakur doing any kind of yoga, meditation, or rituals of worship or prayers, yet, we saw him ever immersed in his own world of blissfulness. But on the 1 July 1992, Thakur manifested a divine play which none had ever seen. As he was under the medical care of Prof. Dr. G.C. Mukherjee of Calcutta, the attending team would take advice from him about the Master's health. The doctor advised that as his blood pressure fluctuated a lot, his medication too had to be monitored. Sachidananda, the attending monk, was told to take note of Thakur's blood pressure twice at night before giving the last dose of medicines. But that night Sachidananda tried to take the blood pressure and was totally amazed to see the Master sitting like a statue on the bed, almost stone like erect holding his head high lost in deep meditation. Sachidananda spent years taking care of Thakur, attending to his daily needs and staying close to him day and night. However, he never in the years since he joined the Ashram as monk in 1977 had seen Thakur sitting in meditation or doing any such practice.

He tried to move Thakur's body with all his strength, but he found that Thakur's body was like a stone, unmovable. He thought Thakur would come out of it soon, so he sat at his feet waiting for him to be available for his regular blood pressure check-up. But minutes rolled into one hour and then another hour. For more than two hours Thakur sat on his bed lost in his own meditative state and then slowly signs of movements could be seen in his body. Sachidananda helped him to lie on the bed once he returned to the earth plane.

But after this semi-*mahasamadhi* like state when his body came to life with all its pulsation, he started feeling a deep need to immediately see all his devotees. It was as if time was running out. He knew that the time to leave his mortal body had come now and it was time for him to leave the cage and fly to reunite with his eternal Beloved in the highest astral planes. On one side he was in ecstasy as he was about to finish his earthly divine play and return to his own Home and his Beloved. Then there was the other side where he was apparently so attached to his thousands of children all around the world who depended upon him and his love and protection, that there was so much eagerness to see them all, right away, before it was too late and before his time to part arrives. This is the uniqueness of great Himalayan Masters who come down from the Himalayan Mountains to the plains to become part of the mundane world leading worldly people to the path of life beyond the physical illusions. Those who stay back in the mountains deeply absorbed in *samadhi* for tens of years and at times for centuries are the ones who do not come to the plains but in a subtle way, continually send vibrations of light to inspire those who are aspiring to see the light.

Thus, we see two kinds of enlightened seers. One, who remain in the mountains or in places unknown to humanity and are deeply absorbed in meditation reaching a state that transcends time and space; of course, incomprehensible to common humanity. They may not be coming down to the plains to personally guide the seekers as teachers, or gurus, but they either guide the masters who are then sent to reach humanity or continuously monitor or subtly inspire and trigger the latent thirst for Self-realization from a distance, unseen by anyone.

The second category is the ones who after Self-realization, feel the deepest urge to bless Mother Earth and all its creatures as acts of pure compassion. As purest instruments of the divine, they are the ones who exactly play the role of common humans with hunger, thirst and attachment for those who look up to them as the ultimate support to realize their Self. This is on the surface. How could you expect one who has gone beyond ego and mind to have attachment? How can you expect them to be like a common human again, those of us who have learned to walk on both our legs, do we ever crawl on the ground with hands and legs like babies anymore?

That is what we saw in Thakur. At times we saw him crying, not able to tolerate the pain and suffering of his devotees. At times he looked so helpless seeking our help. At times he was like a child crying for small things. All of it only gave the dimension of his man and God in one. Hindu philosophy and Vedic tradition talk of this ultimate state of freedom as getting back to your childhood innocence, you become as innocent as a child, but fully aware and conscious of innate divinity unlike children.

Thakur's sudden urge to meet all his children was one such manifestation of attachment—beyond attachment. It is not that ruthless detachment. His attachment only paved the ways to light the path of many who were toddlers in the path of consciousness but were convinced that they were living with a living divinity, living God. This is so important for any seeker of spiritual truth, without seeing someone who has the attributes of God, how can one have faith in something that cannot be seen or touched? Thakur came to personify the God in man. It was so easy for us, who were close to this living divinity, to understand the nature of God. The unconditional love, the unlimited compassion, the divine forgiveness, the natural flowing timeless wisdom, the ease of being established in *sahaj samadhi*, pure non-doer witnessing Self. We were blessed day after day to play with him, to dance with him, to sing with him and at times be overwhelmed to see the depth of his forgiveness and love for humanity and animals alike. Yes, we lived with God. A natural man.

On 2 July 1992, as in previous years he was scheduled to visit Sukumar Bhattacharya's home on the auspicious occasion of Ratha Yatra, the Chariot ceremony of Lord Jagannath, but at the last moment had to cancel the visit due to his ill health. He stayed mostly at his small apartment at Debdutta on the Prince Anwar Shah Road, Calcutta. Not only those who were informed of Thakur's wish to see them came to see him but many more came from far and near and shared the same experience that they felt a deep call from Thakur, as if Thakur wanted to see them. So, they too lost no time to immediately respond to the call of their beloved Master and come to see him.

Whoever came, if the husband came, Thakur would instantly ask about his wife and vice-versa. He needed to see the spouses together. The depth of his urgency to see the other spouse was so much that he would say, "*Make sure you send your husband or wife tomorrow.*" With his body very weak, whenever the attending monk would try to stop any of the devotees or those who came to see him with the excuse of his failing health, he would call by name whoever came to the doors as if he could see from inside his bedroom those who were trying to convince the monk to allow them to see just him for once. They all promised that they would not make Thakur talk or give him any kind of physical pain. With love in his voice, he would call the monk and tell him to allow the ones who had come to see him; he would even mention their names without being told.

A few of the devotees who were spiritual sisters and brothers talked among themselves that Thakur always loved them, but the way he was melting in love for each one of them, and the way he shared the spiritual tips for their individual practice was something not only new but overwhelming. They could guess that there was something beyond this sudden change in Thakur, which gave them a feel that perhaps Thakur was willing to leave his body and all of them. These whispers only spread among devotees and disciples. But Thakur remained unattached to all this and only longed to meet one and all and mostly in one on one intimate meetings to give something very profound, something that can take them to their next level of spiritual journey and also their material issues of mundane householder's life.

To the spouses he lovingly advised to overlook the routine differences of opinions and not take the words spoken in anger by anyone personally. He said,

"In the picture of mine, I will be there in your home, I will see everything that you both do and the way you

> *nurture your children. Know that true love for your Guru must be shown to me by appreciating and loving each other and practicing all that I have shared with you together. You both must walk hand in hand toward God. That is purpose of marriage. By seeing your loving relationship and mutual support to stand against all odds of life, your children will learn how they too can stand firm with you and in the future create happy harmonious families."*

A close disciple felt deeply that maybe Thakur was trying to tear the bondage with his body and leave the world, so he said, *"Thakur, are you thinking of leaving us alone? Do you want to leave this world? How can we live without you? We are ordinary mortals and to us, your physical presence was always the pillar of our faith and happiness. With heavy heart we would come to you and just your one smile, one word, one touch, or sheer presence would unlock the inner fountain of joy in us. How do you think we would survive in this difficult world without you?"* The devotee was in tears and he fell at the feet of the Master begging him not to leave all of them alone, to have mercy.

Thakur looked away through the windows, to the distant sky, as the evening sun was about to set. The birds were all flying in groups to their nests after the day's play. He was lost in deep silence. Then suddenly he came back, as if he went far away, and just returned to his body.

"Do you think death is the end of your Guru?" Thakur said in a voice that thundered the Truth that Guru embodies.

> *"I am not the body that you all see and are used to thinking that this body is your Guru. Remember how many times I reminded you not to cling to this body, as it is impermanent. But your Guru is deathless. When I was in the Himalayas, in the deepest state of union, I realized the oneness of all existence. That I have become all That Is. In every atom I experienced my Self. How can I stay away from you all? Where can I go? In the whole of existence, I am. I was always there, I am always there, I shall always be."*

Thakur was talking but it was as if he was not talking to the devotee sitting at his feet. His eyes were not of this world, but transfixed, the words only flowed in their own pristine humility and universality. He was voicing the eternal Truths enshrined in the Vedic scriptures, in the Vedanta, which proclaims the immortality of the spirit within.

After saying these words, he fell into a deep silence. The disciple had no clue what the Master said, for they were so abstract and mystical that he could not fathom the depth of it. He only understood that Thakur was saying something to mean that he was beyond death.

For the next few days, devotees and followers poured into his small residence in Calcutta. His health only deteriorated day by day. Though his body suffered, yet he tirelessly showered his unconditional love and wisdom to prepare everyone's mind for the eventual final retreat.

6 July 1992, on the fateful day, Thakur developed breathing difficulty, and had an inflated stomach. Sukumar Bhattacharya

was with Thakur along with many of the close disciples and devotees getting ready to take Thakur to a nursing home by the advice of the consulting physician. Sukumar remembered Thakur's words told to him personally a long time back, that if you see that my stomach bulges, and inflates abnormally, then know that it is time for leaving this world and my play would be done. Sukumar was shocked to notice this and was struck with fear that this is his last journey. His heart cried in silence. Thakur could not eat anything other than a spoonful of rice and the attending monk put his clothes on to get him ready to go to the hospital. Thakur insisted that everyone present there must have some food before they accompany him to the hospital. No one could put any food in his or her mouth, but they could not disobey the wish of the Master, so they all had some food to satisfy him.

In the meantime, Thakur lay on the bed while the others were getting ready and the ambulance was expected any moment. His breathing became heavier and heavier. Though the body went through all its phases towards the final leap beyond, Thakur's face was beaming and was full of peace. Then suddenly the breathing stopped.

The ambulance arrived. The devotees quickly lifted his unconscious body and took him to the ambulance; in a few minutes they reached Bellevue Nursing Home. Thakur was immediately taken to the emergency where the attending doctor examined him and gave the noting, "patient brought dead".

This was unacceptable to the devotees; they convinced the doctors on duty that Thakur could go into a yogic state where no pulsation of life is detectable. This was possibly one such state, and that any moment he could return to his body. Accordingly, he was allotted a suite. It was afternoon around 4 pm and as his body was laid on the bed, the devotees were all around the bed sitting and meditating or chanting the *Guru Mantra* so that Thakur would come back. There was hushed silence in the hospital room. Everyone sat with a painful face, desperately trying to pray to the Master to return to his body. But around 7 pm the senior disciples decided that it was no longer right to keep his body on the bed, and it should be declared to all that Thakur has taken his *Mahasamadhi*.

It was heart-breaking news that spread through news media as well as through the word of mouth. The devotees felt orphaned. The ashram was flooded with devotees. But there were many devotees who were scattered all over the world, and they all prayed to the central committee in Calcutta to keep Thakur's body for a couple of days till they could take the next available flight and reach Calcutta to have their last glimpse of the One who was their life line.

On the 6 July 1992 when Thakur left his body, almost at the same time, I was away to America visiting South Bend, Indiana, during my annual tour of North America. I was asleep and I had a dream but it was not a dream. I almost felt a physical presence of Thakur just on the right side of my head; he came, he sat at the head side, and blessed me and then instantly disappeared without a word. I got up, and looked around expecting to see Thakur, as it was so real, but found no one there. Then in the morning I had a phone call from Calcutta that Thakur took his *Mahasamadhi*.

I felt as if he came to bless me and tell me that he is not the body that died, but he is the very presence that I always felt ever since I met him. I felt, I should focus more in abiding in his instructions to me, in putting more efforts to do japa and meditation, and work hard to spread the Word. It was that year in 1992, that I also got the invitation to address the Parliament of World Religions to be held in Chicago in 1993 commemorating the Centenary of the first Parliament of World Religions held in Chicago in 1893. I also got the invitation to do a keynote address for a similar event, World Vision 2000, to be held in Washington DC at the Capitol Center, where it was expected a record assembly of more than 10,000 Indian diaspora would meet to celebrate Swami Vivekananda's immortal speech at the Parliament of Religions in 1893. I could deeply feel that wherever I went and addressed a big gathering of an intellectual audience, it was the spirit of my Master which was working. It was not that I spoke; it was as if I was made to speak and I was that hollow bamboo with holes, called the flute, which my Master played in his own delight. Thakur had empowered me from inside in such a way that I never felt he was no more, but I felt as if he was with me more than ever. When the other followers, devotees and disciples mourned and missed him, I was an exception to experience a deeper connection and unity.

Thakur's body was kept for the next four days, from 6 July to 10 July 1992, and on the 10 July his body was to be buried in *Samadhi*, following his wish, in the very premises of Thakur's ashram. Most monks of the Hindu order are given this burial in *Samadhi* which becomes a vibrant and holy shrine for ages to come. Though over time the body dissolves into natural elements, the power of the remains of the divinized body under the earth starts to gather more and more miraculous energy to make the seekers feel strongly the divine presence of the ascended Master. In India there are many such *Samadhi sthal* or *Samadhi* shrines, dedicated to the great sages and saints who are more powerful in inspiring people from inside the erected memorial in the path of devotion and dedication to walk the path of true spirituality than when they were in the body. When these great masters were alive in the body they possibly could talk to a few, inspire a few who could come to them, but when they left the body their *Samadhi* became, over time, the power house of spiritual dynamo that triggered transformation and deeper faith in the compassion and grace of the sage.

On 10 July from early morning, people from far and wide started to throng the ashram in thousands, many *sadhus* and *sannyasins*, senior heads of different ashrams and religious foundations started to pour in. The responsibility fell upon them to organize the detailed protocol of putting the body to rest in a big pit that was dug on the southern side of existing granite temple dedicated to Himalayan Master Baba Lokenath.

Thakur's divine body and his face, even after four days, remained as soft as ever, as glowing as ever. He was made to sit on a wooden chair and then his whole body was smeared with fragrant sandalwood paste, then ritualistic *puja* or worship was done following the injunction of the Hindu scriptures while priests and monks chanted Sanskrit *mantras* filling the air with divine vibrations.

Then suddenly came heavy rains making the whole ceremony difficult to continue. It poured and poured until there was knee-deep water all over the ashram, and the pit was flooded. But a miracle happened. Before the pit was getting filled with water, submerging Thakur's body in rainwater, suddenly from inside the three walls of the pit water gushed out from three different openings. A senior disciple of Thakur, Prabhat Ray, remembered that long-ago Thakur had told him that he would take *Jal-samadhi* with Ganga, Yamuna and Saraswati (three most sacred rivers in India) creating a holy confluence in the *Samadhi*. *Jal* means water; many great yogis by their wish at death were put in wooden box and allowed to sink in the flowing rivers like the sacred Ganges. This is called *Jal-samadhi*. When the ritual of Thakur's *Samadhi* started it was a clear sky, but eventually it poured and flooded and miraculously created the holy confluence of three most sacred rivers of India which drowned Thakur's body in water. His words came true even in a place of dry land with no rivers or water.

The monks and priests continued during the rains and completed the ceremony and then Thakur's *Samadhi* was filled with earth. Subsequently, the place was covered with granite and a temple was erected, round in shape covered on the top with a dome, but open all around, for seekers to come and sit and meditate around the *Samadhi* of Thakur. The sacred *Samadhi* of Thakur is vibrant with intense spiritual vibrations. There are beautiful gardens all around and trees and natural breeze, with music of the singing birds. It is a true abode of peace. One can feel Thakur without much effort to meditate. It is serene and sacred.

Sages never die. True teachers never cease to inspire and instill the faith that initiates the journey to the world of peace. It takes a long time for the whole of nature to produce one totally enlightened Master. One who comes with the seed of compassion to awaken the seed-god in millions over a period of time.

To me, he was pure love. He is pure love. Did he not tell us, that he is no longer bound by the frame of his physical body, that he is boundless, that he has realized his being as '*Beginning-less and endless. Beyond time and beyond space*'. That whoever, wherever, irrespective of their beliefs and traditions, wish to feel him and be helped in the path of Truth will find peace in life. For he was not a person but a Presence, he was not a saint from any particular country or faith, but Love that is universal.

He followed the path of love and surrender, service and self-giving. Most unassuming, as he was like a divine child, always eager to go through the most intense pain to heal the pain and suffering of his devotees. He came to teach us that the path of Truth is not difficult. That God can be seen and talked to. That reality is not as complicated as it appears or made to appear for most. That God is the very essence of our being. That we all are born to first realize God as the only reality and then live a life of true celebration. That none of us can find peace through the vain search in the external world of transience and continual change. That Guru is not a body but a Presence that is in each one of us, pushing from outside through different circumstantial happenings, and pulling from inside for us to come within, to meditate, to pray, to be centered, to realize the Oneness of all existence.

His timeless teachings are available for all of us. His deathless Presence is seeking every human soul on earth to spiritually inspire, uplift and finally unite with the universal Self that is inseparable from the Self within.

He would go into ecstasy while singing...*"Mira (the great mystic saint) says, without love none can attain the Blissful Beloved."* Thakur still sings in the silence of our hearts, the mystic melody of divine romance, the simplest path of love and love and love.

THAKUR'S SAMADHI MANDIR AT MALLIKPUR

ABOUT THE AUTHOR

SHUDDHAANANDAA BRAHMACHARI (BODHI)

The author was born on 10 May 1949 in Calcutta, India. He left his job as a lecturer of Economics at a college in Andhra Pradesh at the young age of 26 to join his Guru's ashram in Calcutta and embrace the life of a monastic at the feet of his beloved Master. Back in college, he was the most loved teacher who turned even the most notorious illiterate rogues of students into college toppers through the power of his love. Often during class, he would unconsciously start giving discourses of Vedanta, even as the students listened to him spell bound.

At his Guru's ashram, he found himself in a situation which was like crocodile infested water. Naive, innocent, and simple-hearted, his sensitive soul with transparent emotions found itself amidst nasty double-faced ashram politics. The only solace for his tender and spiritual heart was to serve his Guru and spend every drop of his blood for the ashram by building it brick by brick, from start to finish. He silently faced continuous humiliation from the committee members for he was the apple of the Master's eyes, much to everyone's envy. His blatant honesty and strict adherence to conscientious values earned him many insecure acquaintances who feared his presence but slandered him behind his back. He found that his Master was a Mother whose heart was a vast banyan tree that never refused shelter to any of her children be it a scorpion beneath her roots or a cuckoo bird on her branches.

After serving his Master for twelve years, the Master secretly instructed him to leave the ashram and join the ashram of the universe where there were no walls to bind him and the sky was the limit to expand his deepest spiritual potentials— *"You must leave the shelter of this banyan tree. If you forever remain under its shade, you will remain a creeper plant clinging to my body like all others. You are born to become a banyan tree to offer shelter to thousands of lives underneath."* By this time, his Master was not the external physical presence for him but was a non-separate entity of his own existence.

On the dawn of 28 February 1982, when the clock struck 4, he left his Guru's ashram forever, completely emaciated physically and mentally.

He went to the remote peak of Bageshwar in the Himalayas from where, in a state of meditation, he flowed, and the masterpiece *The Incredible Life of a Himalayan Yogi, Baba Lokenath Brahmachari* was created. Coming down to the plains therefrom, he began his journey as a harbinger of love and peace in the remote villages of Sundarbans, helping thousands of poverty stricken villagers to lead a self-reliant life of dignity and quenching the thirsts of many spiritual seekers around the world. Labelled as a Guru-renouncer by his own Guru brothers and sisters whom he had loved dearly, he only grew and grew as a tall, big and unmovable banyan tree, its deep roots nourished by the invisible waters of his Guru's eternal imprint over his soul.

After 38 years of him leaving his Guru's ashram, he wrote this ode to his beloved Master who had not left him even for a moment ever since he had left his physical shade on that fateful dawn of 1982.

This is the first ever biography of the Master written for a global audience. On the day its first edition was published, he said, as tears of love for his Guru flowed from his eyes,

"Oh Master, I have no words of gratitude, for you have willed this unworthy child of yours to offer this very first lotus flower of its kind at your divine Lotus Feet.

You may not have allowed me to serve your physical presence for long but have blessed my heart to serve your Spirit forever."

Biography

Shuddhaanandaa Brahmachari (Bodhi) is a globally acclaimed motivational and inspirational speaker, author, spiritual teacher, social advocate and peacemaker. Founder of Stress Management Academy, his Simple Art of Managing Stress and Course in Mindfulness Programs are known worldwide, inspiring corporate leadership, students and spiritual seekers alike.

He is recognized as a visionary social advocate for his development of groundbreaking programs that serve thousands of poverty-stricken individuals in slums of Kolkata, India and remote villages of West Bengal. He founded Lokenath Divine Life Mission in 1985.

His self-authored books include: "Your Mind Your Best Friend", "Cleaning the Mirror of Mind", "Little Book of Meditation", "The Heart of Meditation Practice", "Finding the Light of Your Positive Mind", "Quintessence of Sai Satcharitra : A Biography of the Incredible Sai Baba of Shirdi, and the classic, "The Incredible Life of a Himalayan Yogi: The Times, Teachings and Life of Living Shiva Baba Lokenath Brahmachari".

He was awarded the Man of Peace Award by the World Organization for Peace in 2012 in Mexico. He has spoken at the Parliament of World Religions, United Nations Global Youth

Conference and International Conference of Spiritualizing Leadership. He received a Lifetime Achievement Award from the S.T.A.R foundation at the House of Lords in the United Kingdom on July 21, 2015 for his invaluable and outstanding contribution to society.

www.courseinmindfulness.com
www.babalokenath.org
https://www.facebook.com/bodhishuddhaanandaa/
https://www.facebook.com/BabaLokenath108/
YouTube Channel: Bodhi Shuddhaanandaa